# Nazi Crimes and Their Punishment, 1943–1950

## A Short History with Documents

# Nazi Crimes and Their Punishment, 1943–1950

## *A Short History with Documents*

Michael S. Bryant

Hackett Publishing Company, Inc.
Indianapolis/Cambridge

23 22 21 20                    1 2 3 4 5 6 7

For further information, please address
        Hackett Publishing Company, Inc.
        P.O. Box 44937
        Indianapolis, Indiana 46244-0937

        www.hackettpublishing.com

Cover design by Rick Todhunter
Interior design by Laura Clark
Composition by Aptara, Inc.

Library of Congress Control Number: 2019952439

ISBN-13: 978-1-62466-862-3 (cloth)
ISBN-13: 978-1-62466-861-6 (pbk.)

The paper used in this publication meets the minimum requirements of
American National Standard for Information Sciences—Permanence of
Paper for Printed Library Materials, ANSI Z39.48–1984.

∞

For Reed and Patty

# CONTENTS

*Acknowledgments*                                                          *ix*

*List of Illustrations*                                                     *x*

*Chronology of Nazi Crimes and Trials, 1919–1957*                         *xii*

Historical Essay                                                            1

Brief Historiographical Essay                                             85

**Documents**                                                             **89**

**Section 1: Enabling Laws: The Legal Foundations**
**of Postwar Courts Trying Nazi Crimes**                                 **89**

1.1  The British Royal Warrant of June 18, 1945                           89

1.2  Joint Chiefs of Staff Directive 1023/10, July 15, 1945              94

1.3  London Charter of August 8, 1945                                    98

1.4  Control Council Law No. 10, December 20, 1945                      104

1.5  Decree of 31 August 1944 concerning the
     punishment of Fascist-Hitlerite criminals guilty of
     murder and ill-treatment of civilian population and
     of prisoners of war, and the punishment of traitors
     to the Polish Nation                                               107

1.6  Reich Penal Code, sec. 211 (murder), RStGB, as
     revised on September 4, 1941                                       109

**Section 2: The Nuremberg War Crimes Trials: Selected**
**Trial Documents**                                                    **111**

2.1  The Verdict of the International Military Tribunal:
     Crimes against Peace and Conspiracy,
     September 30, 1946                                                  111

2.2  The Verdict of the International Military Tribunal:
     The Criminal Organizations Charge,
     September 30, 1946                                                  118

2.3  The American Military Tribunals at Nuremberg:
     The Judgment in the Doctors Trial, August 20, 1947                 123

2.4   The American Military Tribunals at Nuremberg:
      The Judgment in the Justice Case,
      December 3–4, 1947                                          132

**Section 3: Trials by Army Courts: The Belsen and
Dachau Trials**                                                  **147**

3.1   Trial of Josef Kramer and 44 Others (The Belsen
      Trial), September 17–November 17, 1945                     147

3.2   *U.S. v. Martin Weiss et al.* (The Dachau "Parent"
      Case), November 15–December 13, 1945                       154

**Section 4: Trials by Polish Courts**                           **174**

4.1   Trial of Amon Göth by the Supreme National
      Tribunal, August 27–September 5, 1946                      174

4.2   Verdict of the Circuit Court of Lublin in the case of
      Wilhelm Reinartz, May 14, 1948                             182

**Section 5: Trials by Soviet Courts: The Kharkov Trial,
December 15–18, 1943**                                           **186**

**Section 6: Trials by German Courts**                           **191**

6.1   Euthanasia trials: The trial of Hilde Wernicke and
      Helene Wieczorek                                           191

6.2   Euthanasia trials: The Hadamar Trial                       197

6.3   Euthanasia trials: The trial of Drs. Karl Todt and
      Adolf Thiel                                                200

6.4   Reich Night of Broken Glass trials: Verdict of
      the Regional Court of Freiburg i.B. in the Case of
      Reinhard Boos et al., July 29, 1947                        202

6.5   Trials of Political Murders: Verdict of the Regional
      Court of Karlsruhe regarding the Murder of Ludwig
      Marum, June 4, 1948                                        207

*Select Bibliography*                                            215
*Index*                                                          224

# ACKNOWLEDGMENTS

While the cover of this book bears only my name, several important people and organizations have contributed mightily to it. I would like to thank Hackett Publishing Company and its knowledgeable, patient, and unfailingly courteous staff for the care they have given both book and author, in particular senior editor Rick Todhunter and project editor Laura Clark. Laura's capable hand was on the tiller as the manuscript advanced through the various stages of copyediting. Rick originally recruited me to write the book and has been nothing less than a reliable and friendly source of coaching and encouragement from day one. I would also like to thank my former research assistant, Shane Vyscocil, for helping locate several of the readings used in the book. Shane demonstrated not only his talents for excavating obscure documents from cyber cartularies but an uncanny curatorial instinct in finding period photos for the historical essay. He was enormously helpful in researching the copyright status of the readings and images that appear in this book. His successor, Connor Henderson, assisted in preparing the index.

I would like to express my deep gratitude to Axel Fischer of the Memorium for the Nuremberg Trials in Nuremberg, Germany. Axel and the memorium generously furnished us with many of the images gracing the text; nearly all the Nuremberg trial photos stem from them. In providing us with no-cost images, Axel and the memorium have set the bar for good-natured collegiality. In addition, Axel's taste in the German pinot noire (*Spätburgunder*) is, like his abundant bonhomie, without any discernible limit.

Finally, a note of thanks is due to my employer, Bryant University, which nurtured the compilation of this book through intramural grants. The university's support was indispensable to obtaining the more expensive materials for the book, that is, the trial transcripts of the US Dachau trial.

# LIST OF ILLUSTRATIONS

Figure 1. Wax figures of Adolf Hitler and Winston Churchill    2

Figure 2. How prisoners were punished on the Dachau
whipping block    6

Figure 3. The Auschwitz main camp morgue (Auschwitz I)    12

Figure 4. Crematorium I, Auschwitz main camp    13

Figure 5. The Palace of Justice in Nuremberg    17

Figure 6. Hermann Göring on the witness stand    26

Figure 7. Robert Jackson    28

Figure 8. Roman Andrejewitsch Rudenko    33

Figure 9. Hans Frank    35

Figure 10. Alfred Jodl    37

Figure 11. High-level Nazi leaders in Camp Ashcan,
August 1945    38

Figure 12. Defendants at the International Military
Tribunal trial in Nuremberg    43

Figure 13. Allied judges presiding over the trial of the
major war criminals at Nuremberg    44

Figure 14. Allied forces outside the Nuremberg Palace
of Justice    45

Figure 15. Defendants in the Doctors Case
(*U.S. v. Karl Brandt et al.*)    47

Figure 16. Otto Ohlendorff                                           48

Figure 17. Oswald Rothaug                                            49

Figure 18. Map of Allied occupation zones in Germany                 50

Figure 19. Martin Gottfried Weiss in the Dachau trial                54

Figure 20. Defendants in the Dachau war crimes trial                 55

Figure 21. Dina Pronicheva, a Jewish survivor of the Babi
    Yar massacre                                                     63

Figure 22. The gallows on which Rudolf Höß was hanged                65

Figure 23. Josef Bühler is brought in handcuffs to the airport       68

# CHRONOLOGY OF NAZI CRIMES AND TRIALS, 1919–1957

## 1919
January 5: Anton Drexler founds the German Workers Party (DAP)
June 28: the Allies and Germany sign the Treaty of Versailles

## 1920
February 24: Adolf Hitler renames the DAP the NSDAP (National Socialist German Workers Party)
February: nucleus of the SA (*Sturmabteilung*, or "stormtroopers") emerges
May: the Allies entrust prosecution of WWI German war criminals to the Reich Supreme Court

## 1921
July 29: Hitler becomes the party chairman of the NSDAP

## 1923
November 8–9: Hitler launches a failed coup to overthrow the Weimar government (the "Beer Hall Putsch")

## 1924
April 1: Hitler is convicted of treason; sentenced to a five-year prison term
December 20: Hitler is released from Landsberg Prison

## 1925
Volume 1 of Hitler's *Mein Kampf* is published

## 1926
Volume 2 of *Mein Kampf* is published

## 1928
Hitler composes his *Second Book* (*Zweites Buch*)
August 27: The Kellogg-Briand Pact is signed in Paris

**1932**
April: the SA is banned
June–July: ban on the SA is lifted in Germany; eighty-six political homicides
  ensue

**1933**
January 30: Hitler is named chancellor of Germany
March 22: the Nazis open the concentration camp at Dachau
March 23: the Enabling Act passes

**1934**
March 29: Socialist Party leader Ludwig Marum is murdered in his cell
June 30–July 2: Hitler purges Ernst Röhm and the SA ("Night of Long
  Knives")

**1938**
"Special action squads" (*Einsatzgruppen*) are formed for invasions of Austria
  and Czechoslovakia
November 9–10: *Reichskristallnacht* ("Night of Broken Glass") pogrom;
  destruction of the Lörrach synagogue

**1939**
September 1: Germany invades Poland
October 1941: euthanasia program (code-named "T-4") begins
December 15: Polish government announces support for judicial prosecution
  of Nazi war criminals

**1940**
Spring: Germany extends "general pacification" program to Polish political,
  religious, and cultural elites
February: the Germans create the Auschwitz concentration camp (Auschwitz I)
March 30: Polish president Władysłav Raczkiewicz declares Nazi perpetrators
  criminally liable for war crimes

**1941**
March: Heinrich Himmler orders expansion of Auschwitz
April 28: Heydrich-Wagner agreement concerning deployment of
  *Einsatzgruppen* units in army rear areas
May: High Command of the Armed Forces (OKH) immunizes German
  troops from prosecution for crimes on enemy civilians
June 6: High Command of the Wehrmacht (OKW) issues the "commissar
  order"

June 22: Germany invades the USSR
June–July: *Einsatzgruppen* shootings in Kaunas, Lithuania and Brest, Belorussia
July 31: Himmler orders SS mounted battalions near the Pripet Marshes to
　　shoot all Jewish men and "drive the female Jews into the swamps"
August 26–29: *Einsatzgruppen* shooting of 23,600 Jews in Kamenets Podolsky,
　　Ukraine
September 16: gassings of 900 Soviet POWs in Auschwitz I using Zyklon B
December 7: Japan attacks Pearl Harbor; United States declares war on Japan
December 8: Chelmno death camp begins operations
December 11: Germany declares war against the United States

## 1942

January 20: the Wannsee Conference is held in a suburb of Berlin
February: the first Jews are gassed at Auschwitz (the "Schmelt Jews")
February/March: Auschwitz II-Birkenau is established as the extermination
　　center of the camp
March 20: the first gassings in Auschwitz II-Birkenau take place at the "little
　　red house"
March/May/July: the Nazis begin gassing Jews with carbon monoxide at the
　　extermination camps Belzec, Sobibor, and Treblinka
June: British Foreign Secretary Anthony Eden argues against criminal trials of
　　top Nazis
June 2: Leo Katzenberger is executed by guillotine
July 4: the first gassings in the "little white house" are carried out at Auschwitz
　　II-Birkenau
September/October: Great Britain and the United States demand a war
　　crimes proviso be included in any armistice with Germany
September/October: Nazis begin gassings with carbon monoxide at the
　　Majdanek camp
October: Soviet Foreign Minister Vyacheslav Molotov publicly declares the
　　USSR's intent to prosecute German leaders after the war
October: Churchill and Roosevelt warn the German government of unspecified
　　future punishment for war crimes
November 2: the State Extraordinary Commission for the Determination
　　and Investigation of Nazi and their Collaborators' Atrocities (ChGK) is
　　created by the USSR

## 1943

Mid-July: trial of eleven Soviet citizens accused of collaboration is held in
　　Krasnodar, USSR
October 20: the Allies establish the UN War Crimes Commission
November 1: the Moscow Declaration is signed

November 28–December 1: Churchill, Roosevelt, and Stalin meet in Tehran
December 15–18: trial by military tribunal of three Germans and one Soviet
    citizen in Kharkov, USSR

## 1944

March 24: German forces shoot 335 people at the Ardeatine caves in Rome
May/June: British officials create lists of top-level German leaders to be
    summarily executed
May 15: 440,000 Hungarian Jews are transported to Auschwitz-Birkenau
August 25: German forces are driven from France
August 31: the Polish Committee of National Liberation issues the Decree of
    August 31, 1944
September 5: Henry Morgenthau proposes his plan to "pastoralize" Germany
September 12–16: Roosevelt and Churchill meet in Quebec
October 9–19: Stalin tells Churchill in Moscow there can be no execution of
    Nazi war criminals without trial
November 20: William Chanler proposes to Henry Stimson that the Nazis
    could be prosecuted for waging aggressive warfare
November 27–December 3: the first Polish Majdanek trial is held in Lublin

## 1945

January 3: President Roosevelt refers to charging the Nazis with illegal warfare
January 22: Secretary Stimson, Secretary of State Edward Stettinius Jr., and
    Attorney General Francis Biddle send Roosevelt a memorandum outlining
    the future prosecution of Nazi war criminals
January 27: Soviet troops liberate Auschwitz
February 4–11: Yalta Conference
March: the Main Commission for the Investigation of German Crimes in
    Poland is formed within the Polish Ministry of Justice
April 12: Roosevelt dies; succeeded by Harry Truman
April 28: Benito Mussolini is executed by Italian partisans
April 30: Adolf Hitler commits suicide
May 1: Joseph Goebbels commits suicide
May 2: President Truman appoints Supreme Court Justice Robert Jackson the
    head of the US prosecution team
May 8: Germany surrenders unconditionally
June 14: issuance of the Royal Warrant
June 19: the Combined Chiefs of Staff authorize prosecution of German war
    crimes in military courts
June 26–August 2: the US trial team meets with their British, French, and
    Soviet counterparts in London
July 8: the US Joint Chiefs issue JCS 1023/10

July 17–August 2: Potsdam conference
August 8: the London Charter is published
September 17–November 17: the British hold the Belsen Trial in Lüneburg, Germany
October: Marshal Philippe Pétain is convicted and sentenced to life imprisonment
October: René Bousquet is convicted of "national indignity" and sentenced to a five-year prison term
October: seven former staff members are tried in Wiesbaden for the murder of Eastern European workers at the Hadamar psychiatric hospital
October 6: the International Military Tribunal (IMT) issues its indictment
October 15: Pierre Laval is convicted of collaboration and executed
October 18: the IMT indictment is filed in Berlin
November 15–December 13: the US Army prosecutes the Dachau parent case (*U.S. v. Martin Weiss et al.*)
November 20: the trial of twenty-two major war criminals before the IMT begins in Nuremberg
December 20: the Allied Control Council issues Control Council Law No. 10
December 1945–February 1946: trials of Nazi war criminals are held in Bryansk, Kiev, Leningrad, Minsk, Riga, Smolensk, and Velikiye Luki

**1946**
March 2: the French establish the Tribunal général in Rastatt
January 22: the Poles create the Supreme National Tribunal (NTN)
March 1–8: trial of Bruno Tesch, Karl Weinbacher, and Dr. Joachim Drösihn in Hamburg (the "Zyklon B case")
March 25: Hilde Wernicke and Helene Wieczorek are convicted by a Berlin regional court
June 22 –July 7: NTN trial of Arthur Greiser
July 29–August 2: trial of General Nikolaus von Falkenhorst by a British military court
August 27–September 5: NTN trial of Amon Göth
September 30–October 1: trial of major war criminals before the IMT ends in Nuremberg; the judges announce sentences
October 15–16: Hermann Göring commits suicide; death sentences of major war criminals are carried out the following day
October 18: Office of Military Government-US (OMGUS) issues Military Government Ordinance No. 7
October 17: Robert Jackson resigns as the head of the US trial program; succeeded by his deputy, Brigadier General Telford Taylor
December 5–February 3, 1947: seven trials are held under the Royal Warrant related to crimes committed at the Ravensbrück concentration camp

December 9–August 20, 1947: the "doctors case" (*U.S. v. Karl Brandt et al.*) is tried by the NMT

December 17, 1946–February 24, 1947: NTN trials of Ludwig Fischer, Ludwig Leist, Josef Meisinger, and Max Daume

December–January 1947: Hessian euthanasia trials by Frankfurt regional court

## 1947

January 2–April 14: NMT trial of Field Marshal Erhard Milch

February 17–May 6: trial of Luftwaffe Field Marshal General Albert Kesselring by a British military court

March 5–December 4: the "justice case" (*U.S. v. Karl Altstoetter et al.*) occurs before the NMT

March 11–29, 1947: NTN trial of Rudolf Höß

March 8: Ludwig Fischer is executed in Warsaw

February–March: trial of Hadamar psychiatric hospital medical staff by a Frankfurt regional court

April 8–November 3: NMT trial of Oswald Pohl (*U.S. v. Oswald Pohl et al.*)

April 19–December 22: NMT trial of Friedrich Flick (*U.S. v. Friedrich Flick et al.*)

May 27–28: US forces execute forty-eight staff members of the Mauthausen camp

June 23: the Poles hang Hans Biebow in Łódź

July 8–February 19, 1948: NMT trial of the "hostages case" (*U.S. v. Wilhelm List et al.*)

August 27–July 30 1948: NMT trial of the I.G. Farben case (*U.S. v. Carl Krauch et al.*)

September 29–April 10, 1948: NMT trial of the "*Einsatzgruppen* case" (*U.S. v. Otto Ohlendorff et al.*)

October 20–March 10: NMT trial of the "RuSHA case" (*U.S. v. Ulrich Greifelt et al.*)

May 14: Circuit Court of Lublin retries Majdanek guard Wilhelm Reinartz

November 24–December 16: NTN trial of forty-one Auschwitz staff members, led by Arthur Liebehenschel

December 8–July 31, 1948: NMT trial of Alfried Krupp (*U.S. v. Alfried Krupp von Bohlen und Halbach et al.*)

December 30–October 28, 1948: NMT trial of the "High Command case" (*United States v. Wilhelm von Leeb et al.*)

December: the US Army trial program concludes

## 1948

January 6–July 13: NMT trial of the "Ministries case" (*U.S. v. Ernst von Weizsäcker et al.*)

January: the Poles hang Heinrich Josten
January: the Poles hang Maximilian Grabner
April, 5–29: NTN trial of Albert Forster
June 17–July 5: NTN trial of Josef Bühler
August 8: the Poles hang Josef Bühler

**1949**
August 23–December 19: the British Army tries General Erich von Manstein
    in Hamburg
November: the War Crimes Modification Board is created

**1950**
The United States begins release of Dachau trial prisoners on recommendation
    of the War Crimes Modification Board
The USSR releases 14,202 suspected war criminals into East German custody
April 26–June 29: the East Germans convict 3,324 defendants of war crimes
December 15: The Poles hang Ernst Boepple

**1951**
The United States continues to release Dachau trial prisoners
August: German courts are no longer able to charge Nazi defendants with
    crimes against humanity under Control Council Law No. 10

**1952**
February 28: the Poles hang Albert Forster
October: the British release Albert Kesselring from prison

**1953**
July 23: the British release General Nikolaus von Falkenhorst from prison
May 7: the British parole Field Marshal General Erich von Manstein
August 31: the Americans establish the Interim Mixed Parole and Clemency
    Board

**1955**
May: the Mixed Parole and Clemency Board succeeds the Interim Mixed
    Parole and Clemency Board

**1957**
December: the United States releases the last defendant convicted and
    imprisoned by military court at Dachau

# HISTORICAL ESSAY

## The Nazis as a Criminal Government

At Madame Tussaud's waxwork museum in London, the effigy of Adolf Hitler has glowered at the viewing public since 1933. At some point, the wax figure had to be moved behind glass because visitors routinely vandalized it, pelting the baleful Führer with eggs or spitting on him. In 2002 the figure was moved again, this time into the museum's Great Hall. Hitler's appearance alongside revered world leaders like Winston Churchill drew impassioned criticism from members of the public. "I believe such a statue is offensive to all minorities who Hitler tried to exterminate, including Jews," an Israeli visitor commented to the *Daily Mail* after visiting the museum in 2011.[1] It had been sixty-six years since Hitler committed suicide in his Berlin bunker, yet for many people he remained the quintessential archetype of evil.

This reputation is well earned. The passage of time has not softened the blunt-force trauma that Nazi crimes have dealt to the human conscience. Nearly all of the atrocities were committed during World War II (1939–1945), although some of them, like the "Night of Broken Glass" pogrom in November 1938, occurred before the war's outbreak. The truth, however, is that the Nazis revealed their criminal nature long before then. From its very birth as a political movement, the Nazi Party was, as the judges at Nuremberg accurately described it, a "criminal organization" and not as some may think a group that devolved into criminality under the pressures of waging a multifront war. By 1922 the SA (*Sturmabteilung*, or "stormtroopers"), deployed initially as "bouncers" at Nazi Party rallies in Munich beerhalls, were using rubber truncheons, brass knuckles, handguns, and bombs to attack their opponents. In September of that year, hand grenades manufactured by a Nazi watchmaker from

---

1. DailyMail.com, August 11, 2011, http://www.dailymail.co.uk/news/article-2028015/Madame-Tussauds-Hitler-row-refuses-stop-customers-doing-Nazi-salute.html (accessed 31 August 2018).

Figure 1. The wax figure of Adolf Hitler on display with Winston
Churchill in Madame Tussaud's museum in London.

Munich were tossed at the Mannheim stock exchange.[2] Hitler's tragi-
comic effort to overthrow by force the Weimar government in November
1923 not only was an act of high treason but involved numerous subsidiary crimes that are often unmentioned because unnoticed. These
included the shooting deaths of four policemen, the robbery of 14,605
billion paper marks (ca. 28,000 gold marks), vandalization of an anti-
Nazi newspaper, the *Munich Post*, and the seizure of Social Democratic
members of the Munich city council as hostages.[3]

The galling failure of the putsch, as many historians have written over
the years, led Hitler to pursue a "legal" path to power after his release from
prison. Hitler's outward commitment to legality masked the violent criminality of his party. When a federal ban on the SA imposed in April 1932
was lifted in June 1932, a wave of political killings rippled across Germany.
The second half of June alone witnessed seventeen political murders, a figure that swelled to eighty-six homicides (primarily involving Nazis and

2. Ian Kershaw, *Hitler 1889–1936: Hubris* (New York/London: W. W. Norton, 1998),
656n35.

3. Kershaw, *Hitler*, 217.

Communists) in July. In the Upper Silesian town of Potempa on August 10, five SA thugs displayed the sociopathy of the Nazi movement by kicking to death an unemployed Communist worker as his horrified mother and brother looked on. Only weeks before Hitler's breakthrough to the chancellorship, the *Munich Post* reported that an intraparty enforcement squad of the Nazi party had murdered a teenage SA recruit named Herbert Hentsch for a supposed infraction of party rules.[4]

With the levers of state power increasingly in their hands, Hitler and the Nazis intensified their criminal actions. Prussian minister of the interior Hermann Göring ordered the police to work with SA, SS, and Stahlhelm units to subdue "organizations hostile to the state"; in so doing, they should make "ruthless use of firearms," if necessary. Göring warned that police officers failing to employ maximum deadly force would be disciplined. There followed a spree of physical attacks by SA, SS, and Stahlhelm police augmentees on Socialists and Communists, who were beaten, grievously wounded, and sometimes murdered with impunity. With passage of the Enabling Act (March 1933), tens of thousands of them would fill jury-rigged SA detention centers. Some five to six hundred political "enemies" of the Nazis were murdered at this time, while others were severely beaten before and after their interrogations with iron bars and rubber clubs. According to Rudolf Diels, a Gestapo chief, in his postwar testimony concerning SA prisons in Berlin, the victims suffered "smashed teeth and broken bones. . . . As we entered, these living skeletons with festering wounds lay in rows on the rotting straw."[5]

The crimes Hitler and his followers perpetrated as they consolidated their power, transforming Germany from a republic into a totalitarian dictatorship, are so well known that they scarcely merit repeating. We pause here long enough to observe the ignoble means and motives that informed many of these acts. Too often it is assumed that Hitler's wickedness was impelled by political considerations. This was sometimes, perhaps often, the case, but not always. Several of the people killed during Hitler's first mass murder, the so-called Night of the Long Knives (June 1934), were targeted for reasons of personal score settling (e.g., Kurt von Schleicher, Gregor Strasser, Gustav Ritter von Kahr).

---

4. Kershaw, *Hitler*, 368–69, 381; Joachim Fest, *The Face of the Third Reich: Portraits of the Nazi Leadership* (New York: Da Capo Press, 1999), 157; Ron Rosenbaum, *Explaining Hitler: The Search for the Origins of His Evil* (New York: MacMillan, 1998), 52.

5. Kershaw, *Hitler*, 455, 501.

Von Kahr is especially noteworthy because of the atrocious style of his execution: he was, according to one report, abducted and taken to a swamp, where he was hacked to death with an ax.

By the late 1930s, as Hitler girded Germany for war, his henchmen resorted to extortion and sexual blackmail to cow opponents of German rearmament. The targets were the Minister of Defense Werner von Blomberg and commander in chief of the German army, Werner von Fritsch. Threatening to expose Blomberg's marriage to a former prostitute, Herman Göring engineered Blomberg's resignation in January 1938. Threats of public opprobrium were also successful against von Fritsch, whom the SS accused of homosexuality. Although the allegations were flimsy, von Fritsch nonetheless feared scandal and personal disgrace and resigned in February 1938. In a squalid epilogue to the affair, it became clear that the Nazis had suborned perjury when their main witness against von Fritsch, a serial blackmailer of homosexuals in the Berlin demimonde named Otto Schmidt, recanted his claims against the general. For such tergiversation, Schmidt was later murdered in the Sachsenhausen concentration camp.[6]

Cop killing, treason, terroristic bombing, armed robbery, vandalism, kidnapping and hostage taking, subornation of perjury, extortion, blackmail, and extreme forms of homicide like kicking the victim to death or killing him with an ax may not be associated with Nazi wrongdoing in the public's mind today; however, all of these acts were Hitler's stock-in-trade well before September 1939. They were a modest augury of the macabre and mind-bending crimes of the war years.

# Nazi Crimes during World War II

Always a quasicriminal organization run by ruthless leaders, the Nazi regime careened into nearly unimaginable barbarism under the stresses and pressures of the war. While the Nazis did not embark on systematic plans of genocide until 1941, exterminatory overtones are detectable in Hitler's thinking well before the outbreak of the Final Solution. As early as *Mein Kampf* (1925/27), Hitler's autobiography and primer on Nazi philosophy and policy, he made clear that when it came to power the

---

6. Rosenbaum, *Explaining Hitler*, 50; Ian Kershaw, *Hitler 1936–1945: Nemesis* (New York: Norton, 2000): 54–56.

racial state would conquer new territory that would then be "German-ized." He wrote:

> In pan-German circles you could [in the late nineteenth cen-tury] hear the view that Austrian Germans with the assis-tance of the government could undertake a *Germanization* of Austrian Slavs—a view oblivious to the fact that *German-ization* of *territory* can only be accomplished, and never of a *population*. This word [i.e., Germanization] was generally understand as the outwardly compulsory adoption of the German language. However, it is a scarcely conceivable fallacy to believe that a Negro or Chinese might become a German because he learns German and is ready to speak the German language in the future, or even to vote for a German political party. Our bourgeois national world will never understand that such a Germanization is in reality a de-Germanization.[7]

A paragraph later, Hitler set forth his rationale: "Because the population, or, better, the race, does not reside in the language but in the blood, Ger-manization can only succeed through a process of transforming the blood of the subjugated people." As the editors of the recent edition of *Mein Kampf* comment in their footnote on this passage, Hitler's denial that non-German inhabitants of conquered lands could be Germanized left only three alterna-tives: "expulsion, enslavement, or extermination."[8] In short Hitler had tele-graphed by the 1920s, and in writing, the wanton criminal impulses that would achieve their acme only when the war was in full throttle.

Hitler developed these thoughts further in his so-called second book (published in 1928), in which he argued that Germany's historical des-tiny was to expand eastward to colonize "living space" (Lebensraum) for an expanding German population. Read in light of the previous quota-tion from *Mein Kampf*, German seizure of land in the east, which could occur only through war, would necessarily involve Germanizing the newly acquired territory. How this would be achieved Hitler did not at that time reveal, but the three alternatives mentioned above—expulsion,

---

7. C. Hartmann, T. Vordermayer, O. Plöckinger, and Roman Töppel, eds., *Hitler, Mein Kampf: Eine kritische Edition* (Munich-Berlin, Germany: Institut für Zeitgeschichte, 2016), 2:997 (transl. by the author; emphasis in the original).

8. Hartmann et al., *Hitler*, 996n12.

enslavement, or extermination—are implicit in his thinking. If we linger for a moment at this point, the reader might glimpse the outline of the charges the Allies would pursue against the Nazis in their postwar trials: crimes against peace (for waging aggressive warfare), war crimes (such as enslaving civilians under Nazi rule), and crimes against humanity (genocide and other acts of mass killing). We can discern in Hitler's writings of the 1920s the major points of the Nuremberg indictment in 1945.

What existed only as sketchy implications and insinuations in the 1920s acquired a malignant solidity after September 1939. Tens of thousands of soldiers and civilians from the countries Germany had defeated were sent back to the Reich as forced laborers. Between 1939 and 1945, prisoners from dozens of countries flooded into the concentration camp

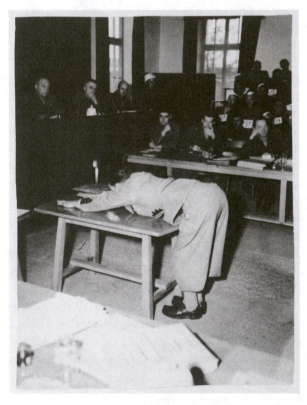

Figure 2. A prosecution witness demonstrates how prisoners were punished on the Dachau whipping block. United States Holocaust Memorial Museum, courtesy of Vincent Paul Donaghue.

of Dachau near Munich. Many of them were forced into a slave labor program administered by an SS office, the WVHA (SS Economic Administrative Main Office), under the command of a future Nuremberg defendant, Oswald Pohl. Over time Dachau and other concentration camps became not only centers of brutality and murder but important production facilities. By the end of the war, the Germans had built 980 concentration camps and as many as thirty thousand slave labor camps scattered across the face of the European continent. While only a small number of these were death camps, all of them subjected their prisoners to inhuman mistreatment. Among the legion of examples was the use of camp prisoners as guinea pigs in coercive medical experiments, in the course of which dozens of prisoners were tortured, murdered, maimed, and dismembered. Camps like Dachau, Mauthausen, Buchenwald, and Belsen became objects of Allied prosecution after the war, and the medical crimes performed there were often at the forefront of the indictments.

In their conduct of the war, German forces demonstrated a level of brutality unmatched in modern warfare. The Nazis' plan for Poland was to decapitate its leadership, thereby rendering a headless Poland unable to resist the enslavement of its citizens. To implement this plan, the Germans formed "special action squads" (*Einsatzgruppen*) comprising members of Nazi security organizations like the Security Service (SD), Security Police (Sipo), and the Protective Staff (SS). These squads were then deployed in Poland and the Czech lands to liquidate anyone considered hostile to the new German order. By late 1939 the German army and the *Einsatzgruppen* had executed fifty thousand Polish nationals. In the spring of 1940 the Germans extended their "general pacification" program to Polish political, religious, and cultural elites. Roman Catholic priests were specifically targeted as standard bearers of Polish national identity. Thousands of clergy were arrested and sent to concentration camps, where some 2,600 priests and 263 nuns would perish.

The *Einsatzgruppen* eventually carried their devil's work into the USSR, when the Germans invaded in June 1941. Military preparations for "Operation Barbarossa," as it was code-named, began in the summer of 1940; by December the plan had assumed definite form. It consisted of a three-pronged attack led by Army Group Center, whose final goal, the conquest of Moscow, would be reached by way of Minsk and Smolensk. In the meantime, Army Group South would move toward Kiev as Army Group North attacked Leningrad. Hitler's intent was to knock the Red Army out of the war with a single thunderous stroke of focused military strength, enabling the Germans to capture the USSR's agricultural and industrial sites. In the months preceding the campaign, Hitler described the looming invasion to his top military commanders as a "war of extermination" requiring all army members to "overcome their scruples." The law of war would be suspended throughout the conflict.[9]

A directive issued by the High Command of the Armed Forces (OKH) in May 1941 reduced Hitler's menacing words to writing. The directive effectively immunized German troops from prosecution for crimes committed on enemy civilians. Only when soldiers committed acts that endangered military discipline would they be subject to court-martial. Further, the directive ordered that partisans and saboteurs be summarily executed. In early June top secret guidelines enlarging the May directive were issued to German commanders. These guidelines, called the "commissar order" in the postwar trials of Nazi crimes, warned German troops that, if captured by the Red Army, they could expect "a hateful, cruel and inhumane treatment . . . by the *political commissars of all kinds* as the actual pillars of resistance."[10] [Emphasis in the original] Accusing the Soviet commissars of "barbarous Asiatic combat methods," the decree ordered that they be "immediately shot" upon capture. German commanders relayed the commissar order to their troops shortly before the invasion of the USSR. In the seventy-odd years since the end of World War II, historians have proven that most of the German divisions in the east carried out the order's terms. One German historian documented eight hundred executions conducted in accordance with it, while another showed that 80 percent of the Army Corps (army and tank groups) and one-half of all divisions obeyed it. During the period when it was operative ( June 1941–May 1942), at least 3,430 commissars were executed under its terms.[11]

---

9. Michael Bryant, *A World History of War Crimes: From Antiquity to the Present* (London: Bloomsbury, 2016), 161.

10. The original Commissar Order is reproduced in Hamburger Institut für Sozialforschung, ed., *Verbrechen der Wehrmacht: Dimensionen des Vernichtungskrieges 1941–1944* (Hamburg: Hamburger Edition, 2002), 52.

11. Christian Streit, *Keine Kameraden: Die Wehrmacht und die sowjetischen Kriegsgefangenen 1941–1945* (Stuttgart, Germany: J. H. Dietz, 1991), 83–89, 100–105; Detlef Siebert, "Die Durchführung des Kommissarbefehlsin den Frontverbänden des Heeres: Eine Quantifizierende Auswertung der Forschung," unpublished manuscript (2000), 13; Felix Römer, *Der Kommissarbefehl: Wehrmacht und NS-Verbrechen an der Ostfront 1941/42* (Paderborn: Ferdinand Schöningh, 2008), 13–15.

The two orders discussed above were catalysts to war crimes after the German army invaded the USSR on June 22, 1941. A third directive in late April 1941 would unleash mass shootings of Eastern European Jewish civilians. The directive encapsulated an agreement between the head of the Reich Security Main Office (RSHA), Reinhard Heydrich, and Quartermaster of the Army Eduard Wagner about the insertion of *Einsatzgruppen* units into the army rear areas. There they would liquidate alleged security threats. Supplementary orders spelled out the identities of the victims: "Bolshevik instigators, franc-tireurs [i.e., guerrillas], saboteurs, Jews. . . ."[12] The three directives together—the May 1941 directive, the commissar order, and the directive of April 1941—placed the entire military and civilian population of the Soviet Union in the Nazis' crosshairs. Over the next four years, the Germans would capture 5,700,000 Red Army soldiers. Of those, 3,300,000 died in German captivity, yielding a mortality rate of almost 58 percent. Thousands died during forced marches winding over hundreds of miles; others perished from exposure as they were shipped hundreds of miles in open freight cars in frigid winter temperatures. To death by exposure the Germans added death by starvation due to inadequate or nonexistent nutrition. On the field of battle, surrendering Red Army soldiers were frequently shot on the spot. At the end of June, one German regiment announced it would no longer give quarter to Soviet soldiers.[13]

For most of us today, the essence of Nazi criminality in Eastern Europe is not war crimes committed on Soviet troops but the deliberate extermination of European Jews. The so-called Final Solution—the Nazi program to kill every Jew within reach of the Germans by firing squads and poison gas—grew out of the *Einsatzgruppen's* mass shooting operations on Soviet soil as envisioned in the Heydrich-Wagner agreement of April 1941. Officially tasked with scotching alleged threats from saboteurs, Jews, and Communists, the *Einsatzgruppen* in practice conflated all of these groups into a single existential menace personified by the Jews. Waves of *Einsatzgruppen* shootings of Jews washed over every region invaded by the German army: in Bialystok, Poland (2,000 Jews shot on June 27, 1941, and another 1,000 between July 8 and 11), Brest, Belorussia (4,000–6,000 killed, mid-July 1941), and Kaunas, Lithuania

---

12. The original guidelines are reproduced in Hamburger Institut für Sozialforschung, ed., *Verbrechen der Wehrmacht*, 54.

13. Bryant, *World History*, 163–64.

(7,800 killed in a combination of firing squads and locally conducted pogroms, early July 1941), to mention only a few.

By late July the *Einsatzgruppen's* deadly harvest numbered sixty-three thousand victims; 90 percent of them were Jewish. The distinction between military-aged Jewish men on the one hand and Jewish women and children on the other was at this time erased. A momentous Rubicon was being crossed: until late July 1941, the Germans had focused on shooting Jewish men, perhaps because they could be identified more plausibly with saboteurs and guerrilla fighters. (This was for a time the case even though native auxiliaries in the Baltic states were murdering their entire Jewish populations in pogrom-style attacks.) On July 31, 1941, however, SS chief Heinrich Himmler ordered his SS mounted battalions near the Pripet Marshes to shoot all the Jewish men and "drive the female Jews into the swamps." Thereafter, and swelling to a crescendo in August and September, the *Einsatzgruppen's* shooting operations increasingly involved entire Jewish population centers. In the Ukrainian city of Kamenets Podolsky between August 26 and 29, they massacred 23,600 Jewish men, women, and children. Similar episodes of indiscriminate mass murder prove the German killers now understood that no Jews in German-occupied Soviet territory would be allowed to live.[14]

Mass shooting proved to be psychologically unbearable for many of the *Einsatzgruppen* troops. Largely for this reason, the Nazis decided to relocate the killing process to camps surrounded by barbwire in remote areas with access to railway lines. As they revised their killing methods, they drew on their earlier experiences in mass murder. Between September 1939 and August 1941, the Nazis had murdered the mentally disabled within the German Reich in gas chambers camouflaged as showers. In the fall of 1941, Nazi technicians associated with the SS combined the idea of mass killing in such facilities with the institution of the concentration camp to form a new phenomenon in world history: the death camp. In the USSR during the summer of 1941, the *Einsatzgruppen* had come to the Jews, automatic rifles in hand. With the opening of the death camps, the Jews would now be transported in trucks and boxcars to the camps for killing in gas chambers resembling bathing facilities.

---

14. Chistopher R. Browning and Jürgen Matthäus, *The Origins of the Final Solution: The Evolution of Nazi Jewish Policy, September 1939–March 1942* (Lincoln, NE/Yad Vashem, Jerusalem: University of Nebraska Press, 2004), 223, 238–51, 261, 276, 312–13.

Chelmno in the Wartheland (the western part of Poland annexed to Germany) was the first of six Nazi death camps. After several experimental gassings in which scores of local Jews were murdered, Chelmno began operations on December 8 with the mandate to kill the Jews of the Łódź ghetto and other parts of the Wartheland. Over the next four years, Chelmno killed 147,000 Jews and 5,000 Roma in "gas vans" originally designed to kill the disabled. In the General Government (the rump Polish state never incorporated into Germany), a separate program called "Operation Reinhard" was launched around the same time. Under the command of the SS police leader for the Lublin district, Odilo Globocnik, the program's goal was the liquidation of the 2,284,000 Jews residing in the General Government's five districts (Radom, Warsaw, Lublin, Kraków, and Galicia). It consisted of three camps, Belzec, Sobibor, and Treblinka, which were sited near rail lines and large populations of Polish Jews. These camps would use carbon monoxide produced by diesel engines to gas Jews in airtight compartments disguised as shower rooms. By the end of their existence, the Operation Reinhard camps had claimed 1.8 million Jewish lives.[15]

Of all the Nazi death camps, the most infamous was Auschwitz-Birkenau in Upper Silesia. Originally a Polish military base called Zasole, the camp was seized by the Germans and in February 1940 converted into a concentration camp to "reeducate" Poles who resisted the occupation. Himmler appointed Rudolf Höß, a Waffen SS member with administrative experience at the Sachsenhausen concentration camp just north of Berlin, as the first commandant of Auschwitz. When analyzing Auschwitz's role in the history of Nazi genocide, it is important to recall that Auschwitz did not begin as a death camp. Rather, like its models and predecessors, Auschwitz started as a detention center for the Nazis' opponents, real and imagined. By September 1940 the camp had acquired a second purpose: the production of war matériel through forced labor. Toward this end, Höß received orders to expand the prisoner compound to accommodate a fresh infusion of permanent slave laborers.

The SS converted one of the buildings into a prison within a prison called "Block 11," where condemned inmates were shot in an adjacent courtyard (the "black wall"). The corpses were then hauled to the camp morgue for cremation. Block 11 was also the venue for a sham court, the "Gestapo Summary Court," which held bogus trials of Poles accused

---

15. Bryant, *World History*, 166.

Figure 3. The morgue of the Auschwitz main camp (Auschwitz I),
site of crematorium I and the first gas chamber installed in the
main camp. Photograph by Michael Bryant.

of resistance. Under the supervision of the Gestapo chief from nearby
Kattowicz, Rudolf Mildner, the court interrogated its defendants, who
after their inevitable conviction were executed at the black wall. The
condemned were never registered as prisoners in the camp but simply
brought there for prosecution, conviction, and execution. Eventually the
SS transferred their executions from Block 11 to the camp mortuary, a
structure in which they had ready access to the camp crematorium for
incineration of the bodies.[16] Another threshold had been reached and
crossed: the Nazis found they could bring unregistered outsiders into the
camp and "disappear" them into the chimneys of the camp crematorium.

In March 1941 the Nazis added a third function to Auschwitz. In
addition to being a reservoir for slave labor and a place for killing the
Third Reich's enemies, Auschwitz would become the locus of a synthetic
rubber and gasoline plant administered by IG Farben, a German chemical conglomerate that coveted the proximity of the Auschwitz camp to
large coalfields. The agreement between Farben and the SS stipulated
that the latter would supply slave labor for construction of the plant—as
many as one thousand prisoners up front and a further three thousand

---

16. Robert Jan van Pelt and Deborah Dwork, *Auschwitz 1270 to the Present* (New York:
W. W. Norton, 1996), 130, 166–68, 176–80.

Figure 4. Crematorium I, Auschwitz main camp. Photo by
Michael Bryant.

in 1942. SS and Farben overseers worked the prisoners at a frenetic pace
that often led to exhaustion and premature death. One of the American
judges at the postwar trial of IG Farben executives wrote in his concur-
ring opinion that Farben's zeal for rapid completion of the plant "resulted
in thousands of inmates being selected for extermination by the SS when
they were rendered unfit for work."[17] At first, the plan was for the SS
to make available Soviet POWs (prisoners of war) as slave laborers for
Farben projects in the camp. When this labor pool failed to materialize,
the SS turned to Jewish workers as a substitute. The plan to lease Jewish
workers to IG Farben at Auschwitz reflected the policy that Reinhard
Heydrich would announce to the Reich's leading government officials at
Wannsee, a suburb of Berlin, in January 1942. Heydrich informed his
audience that the eleven million Jews in German-occupied Europe would
be "evacuated to the east." Once there they would be separated by gender
and assigned to hard labor. Many would perish through attrition; the
survivors would be liquidated.[18]

In the months following the Wannsee conference, the Nazis commenced the gassing by carbon monoxide of Jews at Belzec (March 1942),
Sobibor (May 1942), and Treblinka (July 1942). A gas chamber was

17. Bryant, *World History*, 168.

18. Bryant, *World History*, 167–68.

installed in the Majdanek concentration camp in March 1942, which began gassing operations in September–October of that year. The installation of a death camp at Auschwitz should be seen within this context of a specific policy to exterminate Europe's Jewish population using poison gas. Shortly after the Wannsee conference, an SS officer responsible for harnessing Jewish forced labor for road construction and armaments production in the provincial government of Upper Silesia, Albrecht Schmelt, sent four hundred elderly Jews considered unfit for labor from Beuthen to Auschwitz. His decision may have been prompted by knowledge of the Gestapo Summary Court and its practice of executing unregistered prisoners in the main camp's morgue.

If the SS could routinely dispose of unregistered prisoners at Auschwitz, why couldn't they relieve Schmelt of his unproductive Jewish workers? In the camp morgue Rudolf Höß's deputy commandant, Karl Fritzsch, had installed the camp's first gas chamber in mid-September 1941, with a gassing capacity of nine hundred persons. Unlike Chelmno and the Operation Reinhard camps that were already under construction in October, the Auschwitz gas chamber used a supertoxic pesticide, Zyklon B, rather than carbon monoxide as a killing agent. On September 16, nine hundred Soviet POWs were herded into the morgue and gassed with Zyklon B. Upon arrival in Auschwitz in February 1942, the four hundred Schmelt Jews suffered the same fate in this gas chamber. Their deaths marked the first mass killing of Jews by poison gas at the Auschwitz camp.[19]

The gassing of the Schmelt Jews proved disruptive for the SS. It was one thing to execute Poles "convicted" of subversion (no matter how spurious such convictions may have been); it was far more problematic to gas hundreds of elderly Jews in the very midst of the camp's daily life. An SS noncommissioned officer, Pery Broad, said after the war that the SS felt the need to drown out the screams of the dying Jews by running a loud truck engine during the gassing. An alternative was needed, and an alternative was found: the new plan was to build an extermination site near the Auschwitz satellite camp of Birkenau. Constructed as an adjunct to the main camp, Birkenau (also called "Auschwitz II") was at its origin intended as a slave labor camp serving the German war effort. In March 1941, Himmler had lured IG Farben into choosing Auschwitz as the site for its synthetic rubber/gasoline plant with the promise of a vast slave

---

19. Bryant, *World History*, 168; Van Pelt and Dwork, *Auschwitz*, 293.

labor supply to be housed at Birkenau. By February 1942, the original plan of installing an enlarged crematorium with multiple incinerators in the main camp was scrapped and the equipment redirected to Auschwitz II. It was installed in the northwest corner of the satellite camp beside a vacant peasant cottage, the "little red house." SS technicians converted the cottage into two gas chambers known as "Bunker 1." The SS inaugurated genocide at Birkenau with its first gassing on March 20, 1942—a second transport of Schmelt Jews deemed "unfit for work."[20]

As the Final Solution shifted into high gear, Bunker 1 proved inadequate to the gassing demanded of it. Not only did it have to handle transports of Upper Silesian Jews; it also gassed sick concentration camp inmates as part of a Nazi killing program code-named "Operation 14f13" (the numerals corresponding to its file number), a program designed to relieve overcrowding and epidemic disease in the concentration camps by murdering ill prisoners. Accordingly, in June 1942 the SS converted a second cottage (the "little white house") into a gas chamber, called "Bunker 2," which came online on July 4 to gas 683 Slovakian Jews deemed unfit for work. The July 4 gassing was notable, too, because it subjected the arriving Slovakian Jews to a "selection" to cull the "unfit." The victims so chosen were given towels and soap and sent to Bunker 2 on the assumption that they were taking a shower. All of them were killed, their corpses buried in a nearby field. Over the next several months the SS installed Crematoria III, IV, and V in Birkenau. (Crematorium I was in the main camp.) Crematoria I, II, and III were not originally designed as gas chambers, whereas IV and V were foreseen from the start as killing sites equipped with gas chambers, a morgue, and a furnace for cremating bodies. Historian Robert Jan van Pelt speculates that Himmler may have been inspired by the vertically integrated killing technology at the Treblinka death camp, advising Höß in July 1942 to emulate its example in building self-contained gassing/cremation sites in Birkenau. If van Pelt is right, then Crematoria IV and V, erected next to the little white house and little red house, respectively, were the fulfillment of Himmler's counsel.[21]

As Germany slid toward defeat in 1943, the myriad identities of Auschwitz as industrial production site, munitions factory, and beachhead for ethnic German resettlement evaporated, and the camp became more

---

20. Van Pelt and Dwork, *Auschwitz*, 302–3.

21. Van Pelt and Dwork, *Auschwitz*, 304–6, 321.

completely what it was tending to become in the previous year: a pitiless death camp devoted to the obliteration of human life. While many victim groups were murdered at Auschwitz, the Jews were the primary targets. The fatalities boggle the imagination: between March 1942 and November 1944, with the German army being routed on all fronts and staggering homeward toward the Reich, the Nazis accelerated their gassing of European Jews, killing more than one million at Auschwitz alone (on average, 32,000–34,000 per month). In 1944 the SS murdered one-third of all the victims killed at Auschwitz, primarily Jews from the Kraków ghetto, Salonika, and Hungary.[22]

## International Reactions to Nazi Crimes

One of the ironies of any historical event, including those recounted in this book, is that things could have turned out differently. If the views of certain powerful and influential persons had won out, the Nuremberg war crimes trial—arguably, the most recognized, blockbuster international trial in world history—would not have happened. Before the late spring–early summer of 1945, British Prime Minister Winston Churchill did not support trying top Nazi war criminals. His view was that, once the war was over, Nazi Party leaders, high-ranking members of the German army, and ministerial chiefs should be shot within six hours of their positive identification. In November 1943 Churchill lobbied the British War Cabinet to designate German leaders "world outlaws" who would be afforded a show trial to verify their identity, after which they would be "shot to death . . . without reference to higher authority." The senior advisor on legal affairs to the British government, the lord chancellor, Lord Simon, agreed with Churchill, arguing that Nazi perpetrators could be treated like "outlaws" in medieval Britain. During the Middle Ages, persons who failed to appear before the English Grand Jury to answer charges of grave crimes might be declared outlaws, meaning they could be legally killed by anyone encountering them. In the fourteenth century, King Edward III repealed this right of summary execution, vesting it narrowly in the authority of the local sheriff. On Lord Simon's analogy, the United Nations (i.e., the countries united in the struggle against the Axis

---

22. Van Pelt and Dwork, *Auschwitz*, 327–43.

Figure 5. The Palace of Justice in Nuremberg, in which the International Military Tribunal trial was held. Photo by Dierenbach.

powers) were like the English Grand Jury and Allied senior military officers were like the medieval sheriff. In short, Allied military officials would ensure the immediate execution of high-ranking Nazi outlaws upon capture. Under no circumstances, Lord Simon held, should top German war criminals be given a real trial.[23]

The views of Churchill and Lord Simon were shared by British Foreign Secretary Anthony Eden. When the topic of how captured German war criminals should be treated arose at a cabinet meeting in June 1942, Eden argued against criminal trials, warning that the fiasco of efforts to hold the kaiser legally accountable after World War I needed at all costs to be avoided. In any event, Eden declared, "The guilt of such persons is so black that they fall outside and go beyond the scope of any judicial process."[24] Rather than a judicial procedure, Eden advised the Allies to treat the Nazi elite the way Napoleon had been dealt with in 1815—with a political act. He had no objections to prosecuting minor figures for recognized offenses against the law of war; the trial of Adolf Hitler, however, was an entirely different matter because it would necessitate novel criminal charges that would prove controversial. Better a quick execution

---

23. Richard Overy, *Interrogations: The Nazi Elite in Allied Hands, 1945* (New York: Viking, 2001), 6–7.

24. Overy, *Interrogations*, 7.

of the malefactors by firing squad than a lengthy and incendiary legal proceeding.[25]

Other political notables in Great Britain agreed with the hard-nosed approach of Churchill, Lord Simon, and Eden. The head of the British Labour Party, Clement Attlee, raised the prospect with the War Cabinet of executing German businessmen implicated in Hitler's crimes as a deterrent to future would-be perpetrators. In March 1945 the Archbishop of York, second only to the Archbishop of Canterbury as the head of the Anglican Church, publicly announced his agreement with Churchill that the major Nazi war criminals should be "done to death." The dominant opinion within the British public in the spring of 1945 leaned toward summary execution as the best means for dealing with Nazi leaders after the war.[26]

If not for Britain's Allies, the USSR and the United States, the British may well have shot the major war criminals without trial. According to British historian Richard Overy, the Soviets were the decisive force in swaying both the British and the Americans to seek a legal solution to the Nazi war criminal problem. Overy's position stands at odds with the views of (mainly) American commentators—not all of them historians—who typically credit their own countrymen with persuading the British and the Soviets of the wisdom of an international trial. US historian Francine Hirsch refers to this view as the "triumphalist account," noting that "it dominates the literature" of the Nuremberg trials.[27] Richard Overy, like Hirsch, is openly critical of it. He points out that Stalin told Churchill during his visit to Moscow in October 1944 that trials rather than summary execution should be the Allied policy. Churchill related his conversation with Stalin in a letter to Franklin Roosevelt (FDR), quoting Stalin's words to the American president: "There must be no executions without trial; otherwise the world would say we were afraid to try them. . . . If there were no trials there must be no death sentences."[28]

---

25. Overy notes that the term "political act" was for British policymakers "a scarcely veiled euphemism for summary execution."

26. Overy, *Interrogations*, 8.

27. Francine Hirsch, "The Soviets at Nuremberg: International Law, Propaganda, and the Making of the Postwar Order," *The American Historical Review* 113/3 (2008): 701fn1.

28. Quoted in Hirsch, "The Soviets at Nuremberg," 8.

Stalin may have been harking back to the recommendation of Soviet Foreign Minister Vyacheslav Molotov given to the Allies in October 1942. At that time, Molotov had exhorted the British and Americans to join with the Soviets in publicly declaring their intent to prosecute German leaders criminally after the war. We should have no illusions about the quality of justice the Soviets envisaged. They did not have in mind a fair trial based on Western standards of due process; instead, the Soviets wanted to stage show trials of Nazi defendants similar to Stalin's prosecution of "counter-revolutionary filth" in the 1930s. Only after a high-profile public denunciation of the accused would they be convicted and executed.[29]

Churchill's own perception of Stalin's attitude toward trials may have been addled by the Soviet premier's half-serious, half-ironic proposal at the Teheran conference in late November 1943. At a postdinner meeting in the Soviet embassy, as Churchill relates the story in his history of the war, Stalin turned to the question of how the Allies should deal with the Germans when the war was over:

> The German General Staff, [Stalin] said, must be liquidated. The whole force of Hitler's mighty armies depended upon about fifty thousand officers and technicians. If these were rounded up and shot at the end of the war, German military strength would be extirpated. On this I thought it right to say: "The British Parliament and public will never tolerate mass executions." . . . Stalin however, perhaps only in mischief pursued the subject. "Fifty thousand," he said, "must be shot." I was deeply angered. "I would rather," I said, "be taken out in the garden here and now and be shot myself than sully my own and my country's honour by such infamy."[30]

Stalin and Molotov were later able to mollify Churchill by assuring him that Stalin had only been joking. In his memoir, however, Churchill could not shake the suspicion that Stalin had briefly bared his "serious intent," only to backpedal when Churchill expressed revulsion at the idea.

---

29. Hirsch, "The Soviets at Nuremberg," 8–9. On the linkages between the Nuremberg war crimes trial and the show trials of the 1930s in the minds of Soviet officials, see Hirsch, "Soviets at Nuremberg," 710ff.

30. Winston S. Churchill, *The Second World War*, vol. 5: *Closing the Ring* (New York: Bantam Books, 1962), 319–20.

Whatever Stalin's true thoughts in Teheran, in 1944 the USSR insisted on a trial of Nazi war criminals, prodding the United States gradually to abandon Churchill's proposal for summary execution of Nazi leaders. This fact is too often ignored, glossed over, or inadequately contextualized in the secondary literature. Even the US chief of counsel for war crimes at the Nuremberg "successor" trials, General Telford Taylor, tended to minimize the Soviet contribution to the ultimate decision to hold a trial. In his 1992 memoir, Taylor wrote that "in 1945 the United States . . . took the lead in planning and establishing an international tribunal and in expanding international penal law beyond the traditional limits of the laws of war." The US shift toward a public trial of accused Nazis, Taylor said, occurred in 1944 when American officials "made a 180-degree turn from its 1919 war crimes policies [opposing the trial of the Kaiser]."[31]

Taylor's statements here, while largely true, tend to downplay or overlook altogether the influence of the USSR on these decisions. They also minimize the degree to which the United States, like the British, clung to the idea of summary execution until nearly the end of 1944. Within the US government, the main advocate of execution without trial was the secretary of the treasury, Henry Morgenthau, who presented a memorandum to Roosevelt in September 1944 outlining his recommendations for dealing with Nazi leaders after the war. In addition to deindustrializing Germany to prevent it from initiating future wars (a plan called "pastoralization"), Morgenthau urged the Allies to divide Nazi war criminals into two tiers. The lower of the tiers (tier 2) could be tried for violations of the law of war in military commissions, or sent back under the terms of the Moscow agreement to be prosecuted by the countries in which their crimes had been committed. (See below for discussion of the Moscow agreement.)

The higher tier (tier 1) would be reserved for the "archcriminals," the leading policymakers within the Nazi state. Morgenthau did not spell out who precisely these archcriminals were, yet lists of top-level German leaders to be summarily executed, prepared by the British in May and June 1944, may provide a clue. The list included Hitler, Hermann Göring, Goebbels, Himmler, Foreign Minister Joachim von Ribbentrop, and Field Marshal Wilhelm Keitel. Some British officials wanted to add high-ranking military figures (Admirals Karl Doenitz and Erich Raeder). Deputy Prime Minister Clement Attlee suggested that political and financial accomplices to Hitler's seizure of power like Franz von

---

31. Telford Taylor, *The Anatomy of the Nuremberg Trials* (New York: Knopf, 1992), 33.

Papen and Hjalmar Schacht appear on the list. These individuals would not be tried; after arrest and identification, they would be shot by a UN firing squad.[32]

For a time Roosevelt was receptive to the "Morgenthau Plan," as it has since become known. In September 1944 Roosevelt and Churchill met in Quebec to discuss among other matters the fate of the German leaders. Churchill plied the US president with a memorandum from Lord Simon expressing the hope that top Nazis would either commit suicide or be assassinated by their own people. If such a felicitous outcome did not come to pass, Lord Simon proposed that after the war the Nazi leaders be identified and executed without trial. Approving Lord Simon's proposal as communicated by Churchill, FDR further agreed that he and Churchill would try to enlist Stalin's support of the plan. A month later, as we have seen, Churchill traveled to Moscow for that purpose, only to be told that the Soviets would not agree to execution without trial. When Churchill later wrote FDR about the Soviet position, the American president replied that he found Stalin's view "most interesting." The issue should be addressed, he suggested, at a forthcoming meeting of the three Allies.[33]

As these events were tumbling forward, an opponent of the Morgenthau Plan arose within the War Department. Secretary of War Henry Stimson had written to Roosevelt on September 9 with a thorough refutation of Morgenthau's proposal. Pastoralization of Germany would impoverish the country and sow the seeds of future conflict. Furthermore, the Allies should avoid summary justice and instead extend a fair trial to Nazi leaders, in which they would enjoy US-style procedural rights to notification of the charge, raise a defense, and call witnesses on their behalf. The Nazis would only be charged with violating the "Rules of War," and nothing unrelated to war making would be chargeable against them. By restricting the scope of charges to those associated with warfare, Stimson ruled out the possibility of prosecuting the accused for what would later be termed "crimes against humanity" unless they were the direct outgrowth of military operations. The forum in which the trial would unfold would be "an international tribunal."[34]

---

32. Taylor, *Anatomy*, 30.

33. Taylor, *Anatomy*, 30–31.

34. Henry L. Stimson, "Memorandum Opposing the Morgenthau Plan," in Michael R. Marrus, ed., *The Nuremberg War Crimes Trial, 1945–46: A Documentary History* (Boston: Bedford, 1997), 26–27; Overy, *Interrogations*, 9; Taylor, *Anatomy*, 34.

The vagueness of the Allies' plans for dealing with the Nazi war crimes problem at this stage also pervades the Moscow Declaration of November 1, 1943. Too often this document is cited in the secondary literature as evidence of a purported Allied decision to prosecute the major Nazi war criminals. In fact, the actual wording of the decree supports no such interpretation. The factual background out of which the declaration grew positively belies this view. That background was Churchill's efforts to convince his US and Soviet partners of the wisdom of summary execution. Before the meeting of the British, US, and Soviet foreign ministers in October to coordinate war crimes policy, the British prime minister had shared a draft of his plan with Roosevelt and Stalin. When the declaration was finally issued on November 1, it was based on this draft.[35] The declaration stated the Allies' intention after the war to send lower-ranking military officers and Nazi Party members "responsible for ... atrocities, massacres and executions ... back to the countries in which their abominable deeds were done in order that they may be judged and punished according to the laws of these liberated countries. ... ." This policy of extradition of suspected Nazi war criminals to the countries they had victimized for trial in their national court systems did not, however, apply to "the major criminals whose offences have no particular geographical location and who will be punished by a joint decision of the Governments of the Allies." For the British at this time, and even for the Americans until the fall of 1944, that "joint decision" would be the summary execution of Nazi leaders.[36]

While Churchill and his cabinet clung to execution, Roosevelt began to waver in his support of the Morgenthau Plan. Secretary of War Stimson's insistence that major Nazi figures be placed on trial began to win adherents throughout the government. Within the War Department itself, the commitment to an international trial received a boost from an unlikely source. An extensive summary of a book by the chief of the Soviet Extraordinary State Commission for the Investigation of German War Crimes, Professor A. N. Trainin, made the rounds within the Department. Titled "The Criminal Responsibility of the Hitlerites," Trainin argued that Nazi leaders might be prosecuted in an international tribunal for conspiracy to wage aggressive war, or crimes against

---

35. Taylor, *Anatomy*, 29.

36. The Moscow Conference; October 1943, Joint Four-Nation Declaration, http://avalon.law.yale.edu/wwii/moscow.asp (accessed September 21, 2019).

peace, as well as with violations of the law of war. As Richard Overy comments, "Trainin was seen by the War Department as a useful ally in their efforts to define how a tribunal might be established, and to isolate and outmanoeuvre those in Washington and London who favoured execution."[37] Yet again, in Overy's view, Soviet influence was decisive in persuading the Americans (and eventually the British) of the trials concept.

Other scholars support Overy's insistence on the importance of the Soviets' contributions to Nuremberg. Francine Hirsch has called for a thorough reassessment of Nuremberg in light of documentary materials in the former USSR that have now become available for study. As early as 1937, Trainin was reproving the League of Nations for its failure to create an international criminal court to prosecute violations of the "universal law of nations." Such a body, he argued, would "defend the peace." Efforts to criminalize aggressive war by means of international treaties like the Kellogg-Briand Pact and the Pan-American Conference (both in 1928) had not gone beyond the signatories' promises to renounce aggression; neither, however, contained enforceable penal provisions.[38] Trainin's 1944 book arguing that Nazi leaders could be tried for aggressive war, or crimes against peace, was cited in January 1945 with approval not only by the American author of the conspiracy theory, Lt Col Murray Bernays, but also by the head of the US trial program at Nuremberg, Robert H. Jackson, and the chief of the British delegation at the London Conference, D. Maxwell Fyfe.[39]

At a Pentagon meeting on November 9, 1944, the idea of trying the Nazis for conspiracy in an international tribunal was approved. By January 1945 Stimson had enlisted Secretary of State Edward Stettinius Jr. and Attorney General Francis Biddle in support of an international tribunal. On January 22 they sent a memorandum to Roosevelt outlining their proposal to prosecute Nazi war criminals in two stages. In the first stage the tribunal would try "the German leaders and the organizations employed by them [e.g., the SA, SS, and Gestapo]," which would "be charged both

---

37. Overy, *Interrogations*, 10.

38. Hirsch, "Soviets at Nuremberg," 705.

39. Hirsch, "The Soviets at Nuremberg," 705–7. George Ginsburgs frankly credits Trainin with inventing the crimes against peace charge in the London Charter. George Ginsburgs, *Moscow's Road to Nuremberg: The Soviet Background to the Trial* (Leiden: Brill, 1995), 78–79.

with the commission of their atrocious crimes, and also with joint participation in a broad criminal enterprise which included and intended these
crimes, or was reasonably calculated to bring them about."[40] The authors
of the memo stressed that the court would prosecute not only accused
individuals but also the organizations implicated in Nazi crimes.

In the second stage, after the international tribunal had finished its
adjudication of the major criminals' offenses, "occupation courts" would
be assembled to prosecute the next level down, that is, suspected Nazi
war criminals not tried in the first stage or sent back to formerly occupied countries under the terms of the Moscow Declaration. The memo
envisioned that these occupation courts would take judicial notice of the
international tribunals' determinations of the guilt of criminal organizations—meaning that they could convict individual defendants based
solely on their membership in a convicted group. In short, the memorandum under the signatures of Stimson, Stettinius, and Biddle con-
templated an international tribunal followed by subsequent trials of
remaining Nazi suspects. Now isolated within the administration, Morgenthau assented to the proposal. So long as Hitler (who was still alive at
the time) would have no opportunity to "reargue the theories expounded
in *Mein Kampf*," Morgenthau conceded, he, too, would support a trial.[41]

The notion of collective criminal responsibility, known as "conspiracy,"
had an ancient pedigree in Anglo-American law, reaching back to the
origins of the Common Law in the twelfth century. In US-American law,
however, the idea that organizations themselves might be deemed criminal and thus subject to punishment was of much more recent vintage.
Only in 1909 did US law recognize for the first time that a corporation
could be held criminally responsible for the acts of its agents as these were
ascribed to the corporation.[42] The Stimson/Stettinius/Biddle memorandum made corporate liability the linchpin around which the future Allied
case against the major Nazi leaders would revolve. Their approach was
significantly shaped by the legal thought of Lieutenant Colonel Murray
Bernays, the chief of the War Department's Special Projects Office, who
as a civilian had worked for the Securities and Exchange Commission

---

40. H. L. Stimson, E. R. Stettinius Jr., and F. Biddle, "Memorandum to the President,
January 22, 1945," in Marrus, *Nuremberg War Crimes Trial*, 30–32.

41. Quoted in Overy, *Interrogations*, 10.

42. *New York Central & Hudson River Railroad Co. v. U.S.*, 22 Ill.212 U.S. 481, 29 S. Ct.
304, 53 L. Ed. 613 (1909).

(SEC). Before the United States entered the war in December 1941, the American government had used conspiracy doctrine to prosecute both corporate wrongdoers and Socialists under theories of collective liability (Socialists were indicted for violating the Smith Act of 1940).

If they were to prosecute Nazi war criminals successfully, the Allies faced the problem of how to tackle the logistics of charging tens of thousands of Germans with war crimes and giving each individual defendant his day in court. Bernays thought they might follow the examples of SEC and Smith Act prosecutions by securing a legal declaration that groups like the SS, SA, and Gestapo were criminal organizations. Once this determination was made, anyone belonging to such an organization would be charged with conspiracy and held accountable for his organization's crimes. The strategy would thus involve an initial trial in which both representative figures and their organizations stood in the dock. After their conviction, subsequent trials would be held of other Nazi defendants, who could be rapidly and efficiently prosecuted based solely on their membership in the organization declared criminal in the first proceeding.[43]

Conspiracy, simply put, is an agreement by two or more people to commit a criminal act. What was the criminal act or "master plan," as Robert Jackson later called it, that would serve as the basis for the conspiracy charge against Nazi leaders? According to Richard Overy and Francine Hirsch, Soviet jurist A. N. Trainin's argument that the Nazis were guilty of waging aggressive war significantly shaped American interpretations of this question. (Bernays, as we have seen, referred to Trainin's book on charging the Nazis with aggressive war in his top secret memo in early January 1945.) In Hirsch's estimate, the Soviets were "keen proponents" of the "complicity charge." She notes that Trainin had appropriated the concept of conspiracy from the organizer of Stalin's show trials, Andrey Vyshinsky, as an accepted fixture of Soviet domestic law. Trainin attached a special importance to conspiracy in international prosecutions because, in his own words, the perpetrator did not act by himself in such a context but always "with the aid of a complicated executive apparatus" and with "the assistance of numerous human organizations."[44]

---

43. Overy, *Interrogations*, 31; Marrus, *Nuremberg War Crimes Trial*, 28; Bradley F. Smith, *Reaching Judgment at Nuremberg: The Untold Story of How the Nazi War Criminals Were Judged* (New York: Basic Books, 1977), 27–28.

44. Quoted in Hirsch, "Soviets at Nuremberg," 707–8.

Figure 6. Hermann Göring on the witness stand.
Source: NARA 238 NT 634.

By contrast, Telford Taylor's memoir credits William Chanler with devising the legal theory that the major war criminals could be charged with crimes against peace. In addition to his title of deputy director of military government, Chanler had been a close associate of Henry Stimson: before the war, he was Stimson's law partner and neighbor, and the two men were close friends. Chanler had been chief legal officer of the Allied Military Government in Italy during the Badoglio government's imprisonment of Benito Mussolini. During the latter assignment, Taylor tells us, Chanler had prepared an indictment of Mussolini for waging illegal warfare against peaceful countries.[45] After seven weeks of confinement in the Campo Imperatore Hotel, Mussolini was rescued by German paratroopers, rendering Chanler's indictment moot. Nonetheless (again according to Taylor), Chanler carried the idea of prosecution for waging unlawful warfare back to the Pentagon with him, where it surfaced

---

45. Taylor, *Anatomy*, 37.

in a memorandum given to Stimson on November 30, 1944. Admitting that aggressive warfare was perfectly legal under traditional international law, Chanler wrote that the Kellogg-Briand Pact (also called the Pact of Paris) in the latter half of the 1920s had altered the situation. Signatories to the pact, which also included Germany, had pledged to "condemn recourse to war for the solution of International controversies, and renounce it as an instrument of national policy in their relations with one another."[46] Chanler cited the 1934 resolution of the International Law Association to buttress his argument that aggressive warfare was a criminal act. The resolution stated, "A signatory State [to the Kellogg-Briand Pact] which threatens to resort to armed force for the solution of an international dispute or conflict is guilty of a violation of the Pact."[47] From this bedrock premise of modern international law, Chanler derived the conclusion that, lacking the rights of a lawful belligerent under international law, the Nazis' violent acts in the countries they had attacked were criminal homicide and aggravated assaults, that is, crimes justiciable under the domestic law of the nations Hitler had invaded.

According to Taylor, Chanler's strong advocacy of the criminality of aggressive warfare struck a chord with his superior and friend, Henry Stimson. So far as we know, however, Stimson never approached FDR about adding the charge to a future indictment of Nazi leaders. In his memoir Taylor states that Chanler sent a summary of his position to the president by way of his son-in-law, John Boetigger. Whether the summary reached FDR or not is unknown; what we do know is that FDR later urged that charges "brought against Hitler and the chief Nazi war criminals . . . should include an indictment for waging war, in violation of the Kellogg Pact."[48] FDR's reference to the illegal war charge appears in a memo to Secretary of State Edward Stettinius, dated January 3, 1945. Although Taylor's thesis is plausible, it does not emphatically prove that Chanler was the originator of the aggressive war crimes/crimes against

---

46. Taylor, *Anatomy*, 37; William Chanler, "Memorandum: Subject: Can Hitler and the Nazi Leadership Be Punished for Their Acts of Lawless Aggression, Thus Implementing the Kellogg Pact and Outlawing Wars of Aggression?," in *The American Road to Nuremberg: The Documentary Record, 1944–45*, ed. Bradley F. Smith (Palo Alto, CA: Hoover Institution Press, 1982), 69–74.

47. Chanler, "Memorandum," 69–74.

48. Quoted in Taylor, *Anatomy*, 38. Taylor's discussion of Chanler's aggressive warfare thesis and its likely impact on FDR are found on pp. 37–39.

Figure 7. Robert Jackson, the head of the US prosecution team,
addresses the court at Nuremberg.

peace idea. Rather, the circulation of the summary of Trainin's book outlining a case against the Nazis based on aggressive war, which made the
rounds in the War Department weeks before Chanler's memorandum to
Stimson, strongly suggests direct influence of the Soviet view on Chanler.
The irony of this influence is not lost on Richard Overy, who comments,
"The 'trial' lobby in America [favoring prosecution over execution] relied
for its success on a strange alliance with a Soviet system almost entirely at
odds with American conceptions of justice."[49]

By February 1945 the pro-trial lobby centered in the War Department had gained a decisive upper hand. At this time, and with the Soviets already onboard the trial idea, the Allies met at the Crimean holiday
resort on the Black Sea, Yalta, to plan the final phases of the war and the
occupation of a defeated Germany. Churchill arrived at Yalta still advocat-
ing summary execution of Nazi leaders. The British prime minister met,
however, with a cold reception of his proposal from the Americans and

---

49. Overy, *Interrogations*, 10.

the Soviets. Contrary to assertions in the secondary literature (including the entry on the Yalta Conference in the online Encyclopedia Britannica), the Allies did not agree at Yalta to a war crimes trial of accused German leaders.[50] Instead, the Americans moved forward in April and May with their commitment to prosecution, a commitment that solidified even further after FDR's death on April 12 and the succession of his pro-trial vice-president, Harry S. Truman, to the presidency. Facing entrenched opposition from Churchill and Lord Simon, who continued to espouse execution without trial, US officials were prepared to hold an international trial with or without British support. On May 2 Truman appointed Supreme Court Justice Robert Jackson as the head of the US prosecution team. On the same day, the new US president announced his intention "to establish . . . an international military tribunal; and to provide a trial procedure . . . in keeping with our tradition of fairness toward those accused of crime."[51] He then ordered presidential special counsel Samuel Rosenman to meet with the British and Soviet representatives at the forthcoming meeting in San Francisco to establish the United Nations and persuade them to agree to trials in an international tribunal of accused Nazis.

Rosenman and Secretary of State Stettinius presented to the British and Soviet foreign ministers a draft proposal for the trial of war criminals before an international tribunal. In the weeks leading up to their meeting, a cascade of events had begun to soften British insistence on summary execution. Italian partisans shot and killed Mussolini on April 28; Hitler died by his own hand in his Berlin bunker on April 30. A day later Joseph Goebbels, named Hitler's successor as chancellor of the Reich in the Führer's last will and testament, followed Hitler into death by suicide after murdering his entire family. In light of these developments, Eden arrived in San Francisco to argue that, with the top leaders of the European Axis dead, the remaining war criminals should be extradited to the countries they had victimized in accordance with the Moscow decree.[52] On the same day that Rosenman and Stettinius presented the American draft, members of the British War Cabinet began to defect from the summary execution plan. Why this was the case is not clear; Overy speculates that

---

50. Overy, *Interrogations*, 10; Marrus, *Nuremberg War Crimes Trial*, 33.

51. Quoted in Overy, *Interrogations*, 14.

52. The Czechs in particular wished to try Hermann Göring. Had the US and Soviets agreed to the British plan, he would have stood trial in Prague. Overy, *Interrogations*, 14.

the British may have wanted to avoid alienating the Americans and Soviets in a high-profile, widely publicized international meeting. Whatever the reasons, the British about-face on the trials issue was communicated to Anthony Eden in San Francisco:

> The position as regards the major war criminals has greatly changed since this matter was last considered. Many of these have already been killed, and the same fate may well overtake others before the fighting is over.
>
> The War Cabinet still see objections to having formal state trials for the most notorious war criminals whose crimes have no geographical location. But if our two major Allies remain convinced that this is necessary, we are willing to accept their views on principle.[53]

From this point forward, the Allies were united on the plan to subject the major war criminals to judicial prosecution in an international tribunal.

## Converting the Plan into Law: The Charges against the Nazis

From the moment the Allies decided to try Nazi leaders, the Americans emerged as the driving force in the creation of the tribunal and preparation of the indictment. The US trial team under Supreme Court Justice Robert H. Jackson arrived in London to meet with their British, French, and Soviet counterparts on June 20, 1945. Their goal was to write a charter to establish the International Military Tribunal, define its jurisdiction, and flesh out its charges. Further, the charter would set forth the procedure to be observed during the trial.

The US dedication to the trials concept in San Francisco was matched by its material support of the American prosecution team. At its maximum strength, by contrast, British trial personnel did not exceed thirty-four members. The French, strapped by the privations of the war, committed even fewer resources to the trial than the British. In contrast,

---

53. Quoted in Taylor, *Anatomy*, 33.

Jackson commanded a legal staff by September of more than two hundred. Given the preponderance of US manpower and resources, it is little wonder that the Americans were the prime movers of war crimes policy in London. Thus Jackson prevailed in demanding that the trial be held in Nuremberg, a war-scarred city in the American zone of occupation, rather than in Berlin as the Soviet representative, Iona Nikitchenko, had desired. The Americans also succeeded in winning Allied agreement to center the trial on the crime of aggression, subsequently termed "crimes against peace," as well as to construct the case against the Germans around the charge of conspiracy—a charge foreign to Continental law and international law alike. Finally, the United States convinced the Allies that organizations involved in the worst of the Nazis' crimes might themselves be prosecuted and convicted as criminal organizations. Thereafter, German defendants could be tried and convicted in later proceedings for membership in such organizations.[54]

Unanimity on these issues, however, could not banish disagreement between the Allies over other matters. Despite their early advocacy of trials over summary execution, the Soviets' conception of due process differed markedly from the Anglo-American view. For the Soviets (represented by Nikitchenko), the guilt of the Nazi leadership was a foregone conclusion; all that remained was to assess the degree of each defendant's guilt and mete out the punishment it deserved. This task, and nothing more, would reside with the international tribunal. Jackson expressed his exasperation with the Soviet view to the War Department in July, repining that Nikitchenko's conception of due process clashed with Anglo-American standards.[55] The Allies also sparred over the notion of prosecuting Nazi groups as criminal organizations. From the Soviet perspective, the criminality of groups like the SS had already been decided at Yalta. In any event, they reasoned, prosecuting such groups was an absurdity because the Allies had already abolished them; hence, they no longer existed. On a related issue, Nikitchenko impugned the very concept that an organization could be declared criminal. The French delegates agreed with the Soviets as did the British, who were wary the

---

54. Overy, *Interrogations*, 16–17; Marrus, *Nuremberg War Crimes Trial*, 39, 46; David M. Crowe, *War Crimes, Genocide, and Justice: A Global History* (New York: Palgrave MacMillan, 2014), 162–63.

55. Taylor, *Anatomy*, 59; Overy, *Interrogations*, 18; Marrus, *Nuremberg War Crimes Trial*, 47.

Americans might implicate Anglo-American firms in the prewar crimes of German businesses.[56]

The criticism of ex post facto has dogged the trials of Nazi war criminals from the 1940s until today. It is noteworthy that the criticism had already arisen in the planning phases of the trial during these summer months of 1945. An ex post facto law is one that criminalizes acts that were not illegal at the time of their commission. The US Constitution forbids ex post facto laws in Article I, Section 10, Clause 1. So, too, does the Continental European legal family, in which the prohibition of retroactive punishment is a sacred tenet. The American draft of a proposed trial program circulated among the delegates contained novel potential charges against the Nazis like waging wars of aggression. Moreover, it defined international law as comprising not only treaties but principles originating in "the dictates of public conscience." While the Soviets raised no objections to such language, the British and French were dismayed that "public conscience" might be deemed a source of international criminal law. For them, this was ex post facto—as was the notion that "aggressive war" could be a crime.[57]

According to Bradley Smith, the disputes over criminal organizations and ex post facto were a kerfuffle compared with the brass-knuckled street fight over conspiracy. Battle lines were drawn between Great Britain and the United States, in the pro-conspiracy camp, and France and the USSR, in the anti-conspiracy camp. The French-Soviet criticism focused on the absence of conspiracy doctrine from Soviet and Continental law, arguing that its usage would produce confusion. The Americans could not back down in this fight: their entire theory of Nazi crime hinged on conspiracy. As Jackson had written to President Truman on June 6, 1945, "Our case against the major defendants is concerned with the Nazi master plan, not with individual barbarities and perversions which occurred independently of any central plan."[58]

Without conspiracy as a means of soldering Nazi crimes into a unified criminal enterprise, the Allies would be forced to adjudicate every one of the multitudinous "individual barbarities and perversions," an undertaking that might prove practically unworkable. The Americans understood

---

56. Smith, *Judgment*, 50–51.

57. Smith, *Judgment*, 51.

58. Robert H. Jackson, Report to the President, June 6, 1945, in Marrus, *Nuremberg War Crimes Trial*, 41.

Figure 8. Roman Andrejewitsch Rudenko, chief prosecutor of the
Soviet team at Nuremberg, addresses the court at Nuremberg.
Source: NARA RG 238 NT 426.

this and therefore did a full-court press to sell the idea of conspiracy to
their reluctant opponents. Although Jackson and his team were successful in this endeavor, the French and Soviets remained skeptical. The
French alternate judge at Nuremberg, Professor André Gros, stated the
French position: "We do not consider as a criminal violation the launching of a war of aggression."[59] Criminalizing crimes against peace was a
brazen instance of ex post facto law. Nikitchenko thought the Americans
were giving undue weight to illegal warfare when the evidence of Nazi
wrongdoing was so abundant.

Bradley Smith's narrative of a pro-conspiracy United States overcom-
ing French and Soviet reluctance has been challenged by George Ginsburgs and Francine Hirsch, who argue that, far from opposing collective
liability, the Soviets in London agreed wholeheartedly with inserting a

59. Taylor, *Anatomy*, 66. Taylor speculates that the Soviet position might have been
influenced by their own attack and occupation of Poland and war with Finland.

conspiracy charge into the International Military Tribunal (IMT) charter. Soviet support for the charge was straightforward: it had proven
enormously helpful in convicting defendants charged with "Trotskyism"
at the show trials of the 1930s. For Hirsch in particular, "triumphalist"
scholars like Bradley Smith "overstate their case" when they acclaim the
Americans as the sole creators of the legal novelties at Nuremberg without mentioning the invaluable contributions of the USSR.[60]

A four-power agreement eventually emerged on August 8 for the creation of an international military tribunal. A charter enumerating the
charges against the major Nazi leaders would serve as its legal foundation
and touchstone (Document 1.3). The charges were crimes against peace,
war crimes, crimes against humanity, and common plan or conspiracy
to commit these offenses. In addition, the charter opened the door to
the tribunal's declaring Nazi organizations criminal (Art. 9). If the court
made this determination, then members of the criminal organization
could be tried in other Allied courts (Art. 10).

## Prosecuting Nazi Leaders: The International Military Tribunal at Nuremberg

Now that the Allies had agreed to the substantive charges the Nazis
would face, who would they prosecute? The Allies had known for some
time about the gravity and scale of Nazi violations of the law of war. In
the fall of 1941, reprisal shootings for attacks on German forces had pro-
voked statements from Churchill and Roosevelt, warning the German
government of unspecified future punishment. Apprehensive that concrete threats might lead to retaliation against their own soldiers in German captivity, the Allies were reluctant to be more precise about the form
retribution would take. By September 1942, however, the British were
demanding inclusion of a war crimes proviso in any armistice with the
Germans. The proviso would stipulate the "immediate capture or surrender of wanted criminals" after Germany's defeat. In October both Great
Britain and the United States announced that the future armistice with
Germany would require surrender of Germans accused of war crimes.[61]

---

60. Hirsch, "Soviets at Nuremberg," 709–10; Ginsburgs, *Moscow's Road to Nuremberg*, 79–80.

61. Bryant, *World History*, 170–71.

Figure 9. Hans Frank, the former Nazi governor-general of Poland,
leaving the Nuremberg courtoom for lunch.
Souce: NARA RG 238 NT-687.

By November 1943 Churchill, still ruminating on his summary execution plan, said that the list of major war criminals would fall between fifty
and one hundred persons. His list included not only Germans but also
Italian and Japanese policymakers, among them Mussolini. By June 1944
the British Foreign Office had drafted a list of thirty-three Germans and

eight Italians. It was based on a binary classification scheme, consisting of (1) obvious war criminals (Hitler, Göring, Himmler, Ribbentrop, Martin Bormann) and (2) possible war criminals, whose culpability was still in question. (This second category contained the name of Erwin Kraus, the obscure chief of the Nazi Party Automobile Corps.) One year later the Italian names had been removed from the British list. When the Americans and British consolidated official lists in June 1945, no Italian name appeared on them. Mussolini was dead by this time, of course, and the United States and Britain wanted to avoid alienating the Italians from supporting the Western Bloc. The point here is that on the cusp of the London negotiations the Allies had decided that "Axis criminality" would be synonymous with German perpetrators. By this point, moreover, four of the obvious war criminals—Hitler, Goebbels, Himmler, and Bormann—were deceased. Only Göring and Ribbentrop remained of the category 1 war criminals.

In late June the Foreign Office added to the list the names of Robert Ley, the head of the German Labor Front, and Rudolf Hess, Hitler's former deputy who had been in British captivity since his ill-fated flight to Scotland in the spring of 1941. Additional names were joined to the list, each of whose indictment would have symbolic significance. Wilhelm Keitel, chief of the German Armed Forces High Command, was a symbol of German militarism; Julius Streicher, publisher of the virulent Nazi propaganda newspaper *Der Stürmer*, represented Nazi anti-Semitism; and Ernst Kaltenbrunner, Reinhard Heydrich's successor as chief of the Reich Security Main Office, symbolized the Nazi regime of terror imposed on occupied Europe. After further debate, a final cut of names was added: Wilhelm Frick, minister of the interior; Hans Frank, governor-general of occupied Poland; and Alfred Rosenberg, a prominent Nazi Party ideologue and minister for the occupied eastern territories.

If the choice of war criminals on the British list was determined by their symbolic value, the criterion for the Americans was Murray Bernays' idea of corporate responsibility. For the Americans, to be considered a major war criminal a potential defendant must have committed crimes for which he and his organization were liable.[62] As Jackson had written to Truman, the US case was interested not in "individual barbarities and perversions" unrelated to a "central plan" but in crimes committed in pursuit of "the Nazi master plan"—the plan "to incite and commit

---

62. Overy, *Interrogations*, 31.

Figure 10. Alfred Jodl, Chief of the Operations Staff of the High Command of the German Armed Forces, testifying at the IMT in Nuremberg. Source: NARA 238 NT 761.

the aggressions and barbarities which have shocked the world." As it turned out, many of these "individual barbarities and perversions" would be handled by US Army military commissions at the site of the former Dachau concentration camp (see Document 3.2). These were the small-fry among Nazi perpetrators. The big fish would stand trial before the International Military Tribunal. In the spring of 1945 the list of criminal organizations comprised the SS, the SA, and the Gestapo. Eventually, other Nazi organizations would be added, at one point as many as sixteen. US prosecutors trimmed the list to seven: in addition to the SS, the SA, and the Gestapo, it included the German General Staff, the leadership corps of the Nazi Party, the SD (security service), and the Reich Cabinet.

As they "closed the ring" around Nazi Germany's leaders in the final two years of the war, American and British soldiers carried with them instructions for the arrest and detention of suspected war criminals. The

Figure 11. "Class of 45." High-level Nazi leaders pose for a group
photograph in Camp Ashcan, August 1945. In the center, front
row bottom, is Hermann Göring. United States Holocaust
Memorial Museum.

arrestees would be detained and interrogated; if the results so warranted,
suspected war criminals would be forwarded up the chain of command
for further processing. The detaining authorities recorded anthropomet-
ric information on each suspect on a standardized form: fingerprints,
hair color and style, existence of tattoos, build, complexion, eye color, and
facial shape. They also attached a photograph of the suspect to the form.
By late May 1945 US and British forces had arrested an impressive cadre
of top-level Nazis. In US custody were Robert Ley, Ernst Kaltenbrunner,
Göring, Frick, Frank, Keitel, Rosenberg, Franz von Papen (Hitler's vice-
chancellor and ambassador to Austria and Turkey), Hjalmar Schacht, the
former head of the Reichsbank and German minister of economics, and
his successor, Walther Funk.

On May 22 the Americans added to their haul Julius Streicher, who
had grown a beard and adopted the identity of a Tyrolean artist. In the
hands of the British were Rudolf Hess, party deputy of the NSDAP;

Arthur Seyss-Inquart, the Reich commissioner for the Netherlands; Admiral Karl Doenitz, commander in chief of the German navy and for a brief time Hitler's successor as German chancellor; Alfred Jodl, chief of the German armed forces operations staff; and Albert Speer, Hitler's architect and minister of armaments. In mid-June they arrested the former foreign minister, Joachim von Ribbentrop, who had eluded capture for a month in Hamburg. The United States and Great Britain interned their captured Nazi leaders in two detention centers: the Americans in Central Continental Prisoner of War Enclosure No. 32, colloquially called "Camp Ashcan," located in the Palace Hotel of Mondorf-les-Bains, Luxembourg, the British in Castle Kransberg, or "Camp Dustbin," near Frankfurt. Both Ashcan and Dustbin served as interrogation centers for top Nazis before their trials in Nuremberg.[63]

Late in the war the Allies were aided in their evidence gathering by a new international organization, the United Nations War Crimes Commission. Its origins lay in October 1942, when Roosevelt and Lord Simon in parallel statements announced their intention to establish an agency to document war crimes. The United Kingdom thereafter invited the United Nations to create such an agency. Australia, Belgium, Canada, China, Czechoslovakia, France, Greece, India, Luxembourg, the Netherlands, New Zealand, Norway, Poland, South Africa, the United Kingdom, the United States, and Yugoslavia all agreed and pledged to send representatives to support its work. The commission finally came into existence on October 20, 1943. Its remit was to investigate war crimes committed against the United Nations across the globe. UN governments were urged to create their own national offices to investigate alleged war crimes committed on their citizens. These national offices would then send the results of their investigations to the UN War Crimes Commission, which would sift through the documentation and, where appropriate, place the names of suspected war criminals on a list. These lists as well as all supporting documentation would then be forwarded to the affected governments and their militaries, which would presumably arrest the suspects appearing on the list in preparation for trial. Throughout this process, the commission would enjoy no independent authority to conduct its own investigations into allegations of war crimes. That authority resided solely with the war crimes offices of the governments liaising with the commission.

---

63. Overy, *Interrogations*, 32–35.

It received the first wave of some 340 cases for evaluation on February 1, 1944.[64]

The cohort of Nazi prisoners in Soviet and French custody were by comparison with the Americans and British relatively modest. The two most notable of the USSR's Nazi prisoners were a deputy of Goebbels in the Ministry of Propaganda, Hans Fritzsche, and ex-commander in chief of the German navy, Grand Admiral Erich Raeder. The big fish in the French net was Baron Constantin von Neurath, former German foreign minister and Reich protector of Bohemia and Moravia.[65]

At the end of August 1945 the Allies announced the names of the major war criminals to be prosecuted by the International Military Tribunal. On October 6 the IMT issued its indictment. The defendants were Göring, Doenitz, Raeder, Schacht, Gustav Krupp von Bohlen und Halbach (owner-operator of the Krupp armaments conglomerate), von Neurath, Keitel, Fritzsche, Kaltenbrunner, Frick, Speer, Frank, von Ribbentrop, Hess, Funk, Rosenberg, Bormann, von Papen, Jodl, Baldur von Schirach (Hitler Youth leader), Ley, Streicher, Seyss-Inquart, and Fritz Sauckel (general plenipotentiary for labor deployment). After the indictment was published, Krupp was found mentally incompetent to stand trial, while Ley committed suicide and Bormann was likely killed months before the trial began. Hence, of the twenty-four defendants identified in the indictment, only twenty-one stood in the dock when the trial began in a Nuremberg courtroom on November 20, 1945. In addition to the names of the twenty-four Nazi defendants, the indictment also charged the Reich Cabinet, the leadership corps of the Nazi Party, the SS, the SD, the Gestapo, the SA, and the General Staff and High Command of the German Armed Forces (OKH) with being criminal organizations.

As we have seen, the cornerstone of the Allied case against the major war criminals was conspiracy to wage illegal warfare. Every crime charged

---

64. Joseph V. Hodgson, "Memorandum for the Assistant Secretary of War: Subject: The United Nations War Crimes Commission, October 24, 1944," NARA, RG 238. Generally on the history and accomplishments of the UN War Crimes Commission, see Dan Plesch, *Human Rights after Hitler: The Lost History of Prosecuting Axis War Crimes* (Washington, DC: Georgetown University Press, 2017); The United Nations War Crimes Commission, *History of the UN War Crimes Commission and the Development of the Laws of War* (London: His Majesty's Stationery Office, 1948). Significantly, on account of irreconcilable disputes over representation of the various Soviet Republics in the Commission, the USSR never joined it.

65. Overy, *Interrogations*, 33, 35.

against the defendants was, in the reckoning of the prosecution, an out-growth of this criminal plan. It may seem strange to readers today that the case was not focused on the more viscerally repugnant actions of the Nazis, namely the Holocaust. Why didn't the Allies center their case on Nazi genocide rather than on aggressive warfare? We will recall Secretary of War Henry Stimson's memorandum to FDR in September 1944 in opposition to the Morgenthau Plan. In this memo, Stimson confessed his doubt that Nazi crimes committed within Germany unrelated to illegal warfare could be prosecuted by military commissions. "I would be prepared to construe broadly what constituted a violation of the Rules of War," Stimson wrote, "but there is a certain field in which I fear that external courts cannot move." He went on: "Such courts would be without jurisdiction in precisely the same way that any foreign court would be without jurisdiction to try those who were guilty of, or condoned, lynching in our own country. . . ."[66]

In fact, what we today would call acts of genocide were taken seriously at Nuremberg by at least one upper-echelon US official, Robert Jackson. He had written the word in the margins of draft proposals for the charter that had considered the mass murder of minorities and nations as potential crimes against the Nazis. Jackson also inserted the word, which was otherwise never charged at Nuremberg, in Count Three—War Crimes, VIII.(A), as we read: "[The defendants] conducted deliberate and systematic genocide, viz., the extermination of racial and national groups, against the civilian populations of certain occupied territories in order to destroy particular races and classes of people and national, racial, or religious groups, particularly Jews, Poles, and Gypsies and others."[67] However, in London Jackson declared his unwavering opposition to prosecuting atrocities within Germany that lacked a connection to the master plan of waging aggressive war. The minutes of the London Conference for July 23, 1945, register his view:

> MR. JUSTICE JACKSON: We have some regrettable circumstances at times in our own country in which minorities are unfairly treated. We think it is justifiable that we interfere or attempt to bring retribution to individuals or states only because the concentration camps and deportations were

---

66. Excerpted in Marrus, *Nuremberg War Crimes Trial*, 27.

67. International Military Tribunal Indictment, excerpted in Marrus, *Nuremberg War Crimes Trials*, 65.

in pursuance of a common plan or enterprise of making an unjust or illegal war in which we became involved. We see no other basis on which we are justified in reaching the atrocities which were committed inside Germany, under German law, or even in violation of German law, by authorities of the German state. Without substantially this definition, we would not think we had any part in the prosecution of those things...."[68]

In other words, high-ranking US policymakers were concerned that prosecuting attacks on minorities within Germany proper or the nations allied with it would establish dangerous precedents for the United States—precedents that might result in Americans being hauled in front of foreign courts for mistreating their own citizens.

There was no such uneasiness about prosecuting war crimes or crimes against humanity committed on the combatants and civilians of the nations invaded by Germany. These offenses were considered patent violations of the conventional law of war as codified in the Hague and Geneva Conventions, as the IMT judges made clear:

The crimes defined by Article 6, section (b) of the charter were already recognized as War Crimes under international law. They were covered by Articles 46, 50, 52, and 56 of the Hague Convention of 1907, and Articles 2, 3, 4, 46, and 51 of the Geneva Convention of 1929. That violations of these provisions constituted crimes for which the guilty individuals were punishable is too well settled to admit of argument.[69]

The US concern with preempting international trials of Southern lynch mobs later reappeared in the American position on the UN Genocide Convention. US delegates to the UN Council responsible for drafting the convention, Ernest Gross and Dean Rusk, worried that "sporadic outbreaks against the Negro population of the United States" might become an object of international law unless genocide were legally defined as being "part of an overall plan to destroy a human group." If

---

68. Minutes of the London Conference for the Preparation of the Trial, July 23, 1945, in Marrus, *Nuremberg War Crimes Trials*, 45.

69. IMT, "Judgement: The Law Relating to War Crimes and Crimes Against Humanity," https://avalon.law.yale.edu/imt/judlawre.asp (accessed September 22, 2019).

Figure 12. The defendants in the dock at the International Military
Tribunal trial in Nuremberg.

genocide were defined in this fashion, Gross and Rusk reasoned, then
the United States had nothing to fear from foreign intrusion into what
amounted to domestic crimes: once the offenses were drawn to the attention of American authorities, "the Federal Government would under the
treaty acquire jurisdiction over such offenses."[70] As it turned out, their
worries were premature. The Senate refused to ratify the convention,
claiming it would expose Americans to prosecution for genocide against
African and Native Americans.[71]

The British and French were gripped by similar fears. A journalist
assigned to the Nuremberg trials, R. W. Cooper, wrote that they were
apprehensive about separating humanitarian crimes from illegal warfare.
Without a linkage to aggressive war, such crimes might pierce the armor
of national sovereignty even in peacetime, making French and British

70. Quoted in John Cooper, *Raphael Lemkin and the Struggle for the Genocide Convention*
(New York: Palgrave, 2008), 99.

71. Douglas Irvin-Erickson, *Raphael Lemkin and the Concept of Genocide* (Philadelphia:
University of Pennsylvania Press, 2017), 160.

Figure 13. Allied judges presiding over the trial of the major war criminals at Nuremberg.

officials criminally liable for mistreating colonial peoples and the US government for liquidating "red Americans."[72] Allied concerns to protect themselves from interference by foreign or international courts played a considerable role in their aversion to charging genocide at Nuremberg.

The indictment of the major war criminals was filed in Berlin on October 18, 1945, and then moved to Nuremberg, where the trial began on November 15 in front of a panel of four judges representing each of the victorious Allied countries. It would last nine months, culminating in the announcement of the tribunal's verdict on October 1, 1946. Nineteen of the twenty-four defendants were convicted of crimes against peace, war crimes, crimes against humanity, and conspiracy. The only acquittals were Schacht, von Papen, and Fritzsche. Doenitz, von Schirach, Speer, and von Neurath were sentenced to prison terms of ten to twenty years, while Hess, Funk, and Raeder received life sentences. Frank, Frick, Streicher, Rosenberg, Kaltenbrunner, Ribbentrop, Sauckel, Jodl, Keitel, and Seyss-Inquart

---

72. R. W. Cooper, *The Nuremberg Trial* (Harmondsworth, UK: Penguin, 1947), quoted in Irvin-Erickson, *Raphael Lemkin*, 150.

Figure 14. Allied forces on the alert outside the Nuremberg Palace of Justice shortly before the verdicts were announced.

were sentenced to death, a punishment carried out on October 16, 1945. Bormann, whose body was never found, was convicted and sentenced to death in absentia. Göring cheated the hangman's noose by taking a cyanide capsule in his prison cell before his scheduled execution.

As the trial of the major war criminals was winding down, the Americans were preparing a new round of trials in the same Nuremberg building in which the major war criminals had been prosecuted. These so-called subsequent trials would unfold in a series of twelve proceedings lasting from 1946 to 1949.

## Prosecuting the Second Tier War Criminals: The American Subsequent Trials in Nuremberg

The IMT Charter, Article 22, envisioned a series of international trials ensuing after the prosecution of the major war criminals had concluded.

Logistical difficulties—among them, US fears that the USSR would insist on holding a successor trial in the Soviet zone—persuaded the Allies to abandon this plan. Instead, they decided each national power would conduct trials within its own occupation zone. Just as the London Charter (Document 1.3) was the legal basis of the IMT, the legal foundation of the Allied "subsequent" proceedings was Control Council Law No. 10, issued by the Allied Control Council[73] in December 1945 (Document 1.4). Control Council Law No. 10 authorized the four commanders in their zones of occupation to arrest Germans suspected of war crimes and prosecute them. Among the four occupying powers, the United States organized the most ambitious and important trial program based on Control Council Law No. 10. In October 1946 the Office of Military Government-US (OMGUS) issued Military Government Ordinance No. 7, an order that implemented the terms of Law No. 10 in the American zone. Ordinance No. 7 created the immediate basis for a new round of trials to be conducted solely by US authorities. Around the same time, Robert Jackson resigned as the head of the US trial program to return to the US Supreme Court. He was succeeded by his deputy, Brigadier General Telford Taylor, who became the head of the US prosecution team for the duration of the twelve subsequent trials the Americans would hold in Nuremberg.

Law No. 10 was closely modeled on the London Charter. As in the charter, in Law No. 10 we encounter the familiar charges of crimes against peace, war crimes, crimes against humanity, and conspiracy. While there was considerable overlap in the language describing the charges in each document, Law No. 10 did not merely reproduce the charter's exposition of the crimes word for word but introduced novel changes destined to have long-term consequences in international criminal law. The defendants were the second tier of Nazi war crimes suspects, most of whom were already in US custody, although the British, French, and Poles delivered some defendants to the Americans for trial. Perhaps even more so than at the IMT, the Americans were intent on prosecuting Nazi defendants as representatives of organizations deeply implicated in Hitler's crimes. Hence, the United States targeted for prosecution German professionals (physicians and lawyers in Cases 1 and 3, involving thirty-nine defendants); the SS and police (Cases 4, 8, and 9, involving fifty-six defendants); industrialists and financiers (Cases 7 and 12, involving

---

73. The Allied Control Council was the four-power military occupation government that officially superseded the defunct Nazi government in August 1945.

Figure 15. Defendants in the first case tried by an American National Tribunal at Nuremberg, the Doctors Case (*U.S. v. Karl Brandt et al.*). Karl Brandt, the lead defendant wearing headphones, sits to the far left in the first row.

twenty-six defendants); and government ministers (Cases 2 and 11, involving twenty-two defendants). The twelve cases were the following:

1.  The "doctors case" (*U.S. v. Karl Brandt et al.*), accusing twenty-three medical professionals of "euthanasia," illegal human experimentation, and murdering concentration camp prisoners in order to skeletonize their bodies for research purposes.

2.  Prosecution of Field Marshal Erhard Milch, head of aircraft production for the Luftwaffe, for the mistreatment and murder of slave laborers during the war.

3.  The "justice case" (*U.S. v. Josef Altstoetter et al.*), charging sixteen members of the German judiciary with "judicial murder" through their participation in drafting discriminatory laws in occupied Europe and their contributions to the homicidal "special courts" of the Third Reich.

Figure 16. Otto Ohlendorff, commander of Einsatzgruppe C, beams at the camera in the defendants' gallery at the *Einsatzgruppen* trial.

4.  The case against eighteen members of the SS Economic Administrative Office (*United States v. Oswald Pohl et al.*), the organization responsible for administering the concentration camp system.

5.  The trial of German industrialist Friedrich Flick and five of his colleagues (*U.S. v. Friedrich Flick et al.*) for plunder and slave labor.

6.  The prosecution of twenty-three senior members of the I. G. Farben chemical and pharmaceutical conglomerate, consisting of eight prominent manufacturers, such as Bayer, Hoechst, and BASF (*The United States of America v. Carl Krauch et al.*), for conspiracy to wage aggressive war, plunder, and exploitation of slave labor.

7.  The "hostages case" (*U.S. v. Wilhelm List et al.*) targeting twelve high-ranking military officers for executing hostages in Yugoslavia and Greece.

8.  The "RuSHA case" (Race and Settlement Main Office of the SS—*U.S. v. Ulrich Greifelt et al.*) prosecuting fourteen members

of various SS agencies—the Race and Settlement Main Office, the office of the Reich Commissar for Consolidation of the German People, and Lebensborn—for kidnapping, deportation of civilians in occupied territory, and plunder.

9. The *"Einsatzgruppen* case" (*U.S. v. Otto Ohlendorff et al.*), charging twenty-four former *Einsatzgruppen* commanders with the mass murder of Eastern European Jews.

10. The "Krupp case" (*U.S. v. Alfried Krupp von Bohlen und Halbach et al.*), accusing Alfried Krupp, the son and successor of his father Gustav, and eleven of his underlings with plunder and exploitation of slave labor.

11. The "Ministries Trial" (*U.S. v. Ernst von Weizsäcker et al.*), accusing twenty-one Reich ministers, state secretaries, and prominent Nazi

Figure 17. Mug shot of Special Court/Nuremberg judge Oswald Rothaug, who was prosecuted at the jurists trial.

Figure 18. Map of Allied occupation zones in Germany.

government officials of participating in wars of aggression, plunder, exploitation of slave labor, and mass murder.

12. The "High Command case" (*United States v. Wilhelm von Leeb et al.*), charging fourteen senior commanders within the German military of waging aggressive warfare, plunder, exploitation of slave labor, racial persecution, mistreatment and murder of POWs, and conspiracy.

In these twelve cases, 184 defendants were tried. Of this number, seven either died or were declared unfit to stand trial before a verdict could be pronounced against them. Ninety-eight received prison terms from eighteen months to twenty years, while twenty were sentenced to life terms and twenty-four to be executed. However, capital punishment was only meted out to the accused in the doctors case (seven defendants), the SS Economic Administrative Office case (three defendants), and the *Einsatzgruppen* trial (fourteen defendants).

# Trials of Nazi Crimes by Allied Courts, 1943–1950

## The American Trials

Students of Nazi war crimes trials should be aware that the Nuremberg proceedings were not by any means exhaustive of Allied justice. Both Great Britain and the USSR were unwilling to subsume all of their prosecutions under the Nuremberg trials, particularly as they related to atrocities perpetrated in recently liberated concentration camps.[74] The desire for national prosecution independent of Nuremberg was the impetus for passage in December 1945 of Control Council Law No. 10, which aimed to create a uniform judicial policy in the four occupation zones. As historian Martin Broszat has pointed out, however, the discretion of each Allied commander within his own zone to charge and prosecute cases tended to undercut this aim.[75] This was as true in the American zone as it was in the three others.

As Allied forces advanced across Western Europe in the summer of 1944 toward the German border, they were under orders to collect

---

74. Martin Broszat, "Siegerjustiz oder Strafrechtliche 'Selbstreinigung'? Aspekte der Vergangenheitsbewältigung der deutschen Justiz während der Besatzungszeit 1945–1949," *Vierteljahrhefte für Zeitgeschichte* 29/4 (1981), 485.

75. Broszat, "Siegerjustiz," 486.

evidence of Nazi war crimes. The focus of these early efforts was on crimes committed by lower-ranking Germans on Allied soldiers. In fact, the US Army did not at this time want to investigate war crimes unless the victims were their own soldiers. The Combined Chiefs of Staff, on the other hand, disallowed prosecution of suspected German war criminals until the war was over, possibly out of fear that trials of Germans might invite retaliation against Allied POWs in German hands. On June 19, 1945, this policy was reversed when the Combined Chiefs revoked their prohibition and authorized SHAEF (Supreme Headquarters–Allied Expeditionary Forces) to prosecute German war crimes in military courts. Through the spring of 1945 and coinciding with liberation of the German concentration camps, pressure had mounted to punish the perpetrators for their atrocities. The Combined Chiefs' greenlighting of military trials against lower-ranking offenders was a byproduct of this demand for justice, a gesture indicative of American and British willingness to prosecute Nazi crimes committed not only on their own soldiers but on nonmilitary victims as well. In response to their orders, SHAEF instructed the commanding generals in the Eastern and Western territories of Europe to erect "specially appointed military government courts" for this purpose. Jurisdiction over these courts would reside with the theater judge advocate (the army official in charge of the US military legal system in the European theater).[76]

A sea change was under way in the US Army's handling of accused war criminals in its zone of occupation. On July 8, 1945, the US Joint Chiefs issued a directive to the US commander in Europe that defined in closer detail the scope of offenses and kinds of offenders to be tried in "appropriate military courts." These included lower-ranking Germans suspected of either committing or belonging to organizations that committed the following acts:

(a)    Atrocities and offenses against persons or property constituting violations of international law. . . .

(b)    Initiation of invasions of other countries and of wars of aggression. . . .

---

76. Michael Bryant, "Dachau Trials-Die rechtlichen und historischen Grundlagen der US-amerikanischen Kriegsverbrecherprozesse, 1942–1947," *Historische Dimensionen von Kriegsverbrecherprozessen nach dem Zweiten Weltkrieg*, H. Tadtke/D.Rössner/T. Schiller/W. Form, ed. (Baden-Baden, Germany: Nomos, 2007), 115.

(c) . . . atrocities and persecutions on racial, religious or political grounds, committed since January 30, 1933.[77]

The directive, which bore the title "JCS 1023/10" (Document 1.2), authorized the US commander to investigate and arrest all persons suspected of involvement in such crimes. They would be prosecuted in special military courts that differed from the "normal" courts of the military occupation, which typically dealt only with offenses against the US occupation authorities. Dwight Eisenhower, at the time the commander of the American zone, subsequently authorized US commanders to set up these special military courts for the prosecution of war crimes. The courts would consist of not fewer than five members, one of whom had to be a "legally trained officer." The court members, sitting without a jury, would convict based on evidence that a "reasonable man" would find compelling, including hearsay. Procedure would be laxer in these courts than in conventional proceedings: the members could alter procedural rights so long as the change did not disadvantage whatever rights the defendant enjoyed.[78]

Efforts to streamline military government trials of Nazi war criminals were motivated by the fear that the army was embarking on a Herculean task that might overwhelm the limited resources available to tackle it. For this reason, the Americans chose to center their prosecution of lower-level atrocities on the site of the former concentration camp of Dachau. Prior to this decision, the army had held a small handful of war crimes trials in other German cities—Freising, Darmstadt, and Ludwigsburg, among a handful of others. These scattershot early trials, all of them related to attacks by German civilians on downed American flyers, eventually gave way to consolidated trials in Dachau. Much like the decision to try the major war criminals at Nuremberg, the choice to centralize the army's trial program in Dachau was pragmatic: its grounds and buildings could accommodate the fifteen thousand suspected war criminals and witnesses hitherto assembled there. In October 1945 the army did conduct a major trial in a different venue. The prosecution of seven former staff

---

77. JCS 1023/10-Directive on the Identification and Apprehension of Persons Suspected of War Crimes or Other Offenses and Trial of Certain Offenders, July 8, 1945, NARA RG 549, General Admin., box 1.

78. JCS 1023/10, 117–18; Letter to the commanding generals of the eastern and western military districts, August 25, 1945, NARA RG 549 (unmarked box).

Figure 19. Martin Gottfried Weiss takes the stand in the Dachau trial.
United States Holocaust Memorial Museum, courtesy of
Vincent Paul Donaghue.

members for the murder of disabled Eastern European workers at the Hadamar psychiatric hospital was held in Wiesbaden. The trial lasted one week (August 8–15) and resulted in the convictions of all of the defendants, who received punishments from hanging to confinement. The bulk of what would be called the "Dachau trials," however, truly began only on November 15, 1945, with the first American trial of Nazi concentration camp staff, *U.S. v. Martin Weiss et al.* (Document 3.2).

The Weiss trial became known as a "parent" case, meaning its legal concepts and holdings would guide all further prosecutions of concentration camp staff held at Dachau. The trial indicted forty Dachau camp personnel, including the commandant from 1942 to 1943, Martin Gottfried Weiss, a world-famous expert in medical diseases, Dr. Klaus Schilling, and various former guards. As the first of the US Army's trial of concentration camp staff, the Dachau trial had little precedent to draw on. (The trial began five days before the IMT trial

Figure 20. Group portrait of the defendants in the Dachau war crimes. United States Holocaust Memorial Museum, courtesy of Leslie Urch.

at Nuremberg.) For guidance in the drafting of charges, the Americans consulted a similar trial held by the British in the fall of 1945 targeting ex-personnel at the Belsen concentration camp. Convened at Lüneburg in September, the British trial wrapped up shortly after the Dachau trial had started.

The two cases were remarkably comparable: both involved concentration camps on German soil in which the SS had beaten, tortured, starved, mistreated, and sometimes killed thousands of foreign prisoners; both involved dozens of defendants (forty-five in the British trial, forty in the American) charged with violations of international law (i.e., the Geneva and Hague Conventions); both were conducted by the military authorities of each country. The Americans adopted the British idea of a "common plan" to link the accused to the war crimes committed at Dachau. Common plan bore a surface resemblance to conspiracy, but in fact the two theories were not identical. Common plan presented a lower hurdle for the prosecution, which only had to show a "community of intention" between the defendants in order to hold each of them accountable for the crimes perpetrated in the camp. All the prosecutors had to prove was that a defendant was aware of the abuses in the camp and contributed to their occurrence.[79] On December 13, the military court convicted all of the defendants of participating in a "common design" to commit war crimes on thousands of camp inmates, sentencing most of them to death by hanging. The US Army prosecuted a flood of defendants after the parent case had concluded. These proceedings included subsidiary Dachau camp trials (October 1946–September 1947) and a cluster of trials based on war crimes committed in the Buchenwald camp near Weimar (April 1947–December 1947), the Mauthausen camp in Upper Austria (March 1946–November 1947), and several other less notorious concentration camps (Dora-Nordhausen, Mühldorf, and Flossenbürg). Altogether, by the end of the army trial program in December 1947, it had held some 462 trials at Dachau; of this number, at least 225 dealt with crimes committed in Nazi concentration camps. The remainder largely concerned attacks on American soldiers and downed airmen by German civilians. Around twelve hundred defendants were tried and 73 percent convicted. By the late 1940s, as the Cold War tightened its grip on the Allies' will to pursue these cases, US authorities came to regard further prosecution of Nazi offenders as inimical to gaining West German support for an anti-Soviet coalition in central Europe. They established a War Crimes Modification Board in November 1949, which recommended reduced sentences in 392 of the 512 applications under consideration. Many of the accused convicted in the Dachau trials were released in 1950 and 1951. Subsequent proceedings before other American agencies (namely, the Interim Mixed Parole and Clemency Board, created in 1953, and the Mixed Parole and Clemency Board, founded in 1955) led to further releases. In 1957 the last defendant to be tried, convicted, and imprisoned by the military courts at Dachau walked out of Landsberg prison in Bavaria a free man.[80]

## British Trials

If the cornerstone of the Nazi war crimes trial program in the American zone was JCS Directive 1023/10, the legal foundation of trials in the

---

79. Michael S. Bryant, "Punishing the Excess: Sadism, Bureaucratized Atrocity, and the U.S. Army Concentration Camp Trials, 1945–47," in *Nazi Crimes and the Law*, ed. N. Stoltzfus and H. Friedlander (New York: GHI/Cambridge University Press, 2008), 69.

80. Tomaz Jardim, *The Mauthausen Trial: American Military Justice in Germany* (Cambridge, MA: Harvard University Press, 2012), 211–12.

British zone was the Royal Warrant of June 14, 1945 (Document 1.1). This document supplied the regulations that would govern the more than five hundred trials held in the British zone from 1945–1949. The first of these cases was the Belsen trial (*Trial of Josef Kramer and others*, September 17, 1945–November 17, 1945; Document 3.1), involving forty-five ex-staff members from the Belsen and Auschwitz camps. The lead defendant, Josef Kramer, had worked at Sachsenhausen and Mauthausen before becoming Rudolf Höß's deputy at Auschwitz. He went on to stints as commandant at Dachau, Natzweiler, and a return to Auschwitz before his transfer to Belsen. Nearly half of the accused were women, among them Irma Grese, a women's camp guard at Belsen. The British military court convicted thirty of the defendants of war crimes, twelve of whom received the death penalty, among them Kramer and Grese. The prison terms of the remainder varied from three to fifteen years, although all of them would be reduced later on.[81]

In a Hamburg trial that lasted just over a week, the British prosecuted another Holocaust-related proceeding in March 1946, the so-called Zyklon B case. The defendants were the owner of Tesch & Stabenow, Bruno Tesch, and two of his managers, Karl Weinbacher and Dr. Joachim Drösihn. In 1942 and 1943 the Tesch firm had distributed Zyklon B to SS camps like Groß Rosen and Majdanek. Tesch and Weinbacher's defense of ignorance was rejected by the court on the ground that they had to have known their shipments of Zyklon B were being used to kill camp prisoners. They were convicted of war crimes and sentenced to death. Drösihn's lower position within the Tesch hierarchy meant that, in the court's estimate, he was not able to affect the shipments. He was therefore acquitted of all charges. Likewise, a mixture of convictions and acquittals was the result of seven trials held under the Royal Warrant from December 5, 1946, to February 3, 1947, that targeted thirty-eight staff members of the Ravensbrück concentration camp. Eighteen of them were convicted and hanged, while some were given prison terms of from life to two years. Three of the accused were found not guilty.[82]

The British also prosecuted General Nikolaus von Falkenhorst, former commander of German forces in Norway, in a five-day trial by military court (July 29 to August 2, 1946). Falkenhorst was charged with

---

81. David M. Crowe, *The Holocaust: Roots, History, and Aftermath* (Philadelphia: Westview, 2008), 407–8.

82. Crowe, *Holocaust*, 408.

war crimes for circulating the "commando order," a Hitler decree issued in October 1942 to the German military in Europe and Africa, which ordered that all captured Allied commandos be executed without trial. Convicted and condemned to death, Falkenhorst's sentence was commuted to a twenty-year prison term. (He was released from prison in 1953.) The British hauled another German general into the dock in 1947, the former commander of German forces in Italy, Luftwaffe Field Marshal General Albert Kesselring, for war crimes committed in connection with the "Ardeatine massacre" in 1944. The massacre consisted of shootings of Italian hostages in reprisal for a partisan attack on German occupation troops. The British court, rejecting his defense that shooting ten civilian hostages for every German soldier killed in partisan attacks was permissible under the law of war, convicted him of war crimes on May 6, 1947. Sentenced to die by firing squad (considered more honorable than hanging), Kesselring, like Falkenhorst, was granted a commuted sentence of life in prison. Like Falkenhorst, too, Kesselring was finally released from prison in 1952 for health reasons.[83]

Although the Falkenhorst and Kesselring trials had at best a tenuous connection with the Holocaust, the British trial of Field Marshal General Erich von Manstein held in Hamburg in 1949 involved an amalgam of conventional war crimes and Holocaust-specific atrocities. He was charged with mistreating POWs, supporting Einsatzgruppe D in its murder of Jewish civilians in the Crimea, and ignoring the effects of his scorched earth tactics on civilians during his retreat from Soviet territory. Manstein was acquitted of the most serious charges—those relating to the extermination of Crimea's Jewish population—but convicted of failure to protect civilians in a war zone. His prison sentence of eighteen years ended with parole on medical grounds in 1953.[84]

## French Trials

France was unique among the leading Western Allies for suffering military defeat *and* occupation at Germany's hands. The division of the country between a zone under German occupation and a nominally

83. Crowe, *Holocaust*, 408.

84. Crowe, *Holocaust*, 409; Robert S. Wistrich, *Who's Who in Nazi Germany* (New York: Routledge, 1995), 166.

independent, pro-German Vichy regime under Marshal Philippe Pétain opened the door to widespread collaboration. Unsurprisingly, after liberation in 1944 French nationals accused of collaboration were prosecuted in dubious trial proceedings, many of them administered by resistance groups possessing motives for revenge. Well before the end of the European war in May 1945, these summary trials contributed to the killing of nine thousand French citizens suspected of being collaborators. This anti-collaborationist policy was eventually reduced to law, giving rise to a formal trial program focused solely on collaboration. Defendants were accused of "acts harmful to national defence . . . secret dealings with the enemy . . . attacks against national security . . . informing" and "shameful acts against the nation." Special courts were erected to hear these cases. They prosecuted 555,100 French nationals, of whom 127,063 were convicted. Three of the convicted collaborators were executed.[85]

Subsequent trials in the mid-1940s tackled high-ranking officials within the Vichy government. Pierre Laval, the Vichy prime minister in 1940 and 1942–1944, was convicted of collaboration and executed by firing squad on October 15, 1945. The leader of the fascist political group Action française, Charles Maurras, was also convicted of collaboration and sentenced to death, a punishment commuted on appeal to life in prison. Other former Vichy officials prosecuted during this time for collaboration were Joseph Darnand, the head of Vichy's paramilitary force Milice implicated in the SS roundup and deportation of Jews, who was tried, convicted, and executed in 1945; Marshal Philippe Pétain, whose death sentence in 1945 for treason was commuted to life imprisonment by French president Charles de Gaulle; and René Bousquet, chief of the Vichy police and a contributor to the roundup and deportation of Jews, who was convicted of "national indignity" and sentenced to a five-year prison term. The court presiding over his trial suspended the sentence based on his work with the resistance. Much later, in 1991, Bousquet would be indicted again and charged with deporting 194 Jewish children in 1942. He was assassinated before the trial began.[86]

Within the French zone of occupation itself, the French military government erected a mélange of tribunals at various administrative levels

---

85. Crowe, *Holocaust*, 414–15; Henry Rousso, "Did the Purge Achieve Its Goals?" in *Memory, the Holocaust and French Justice: The Bousquet and Touvier Affairs*, ed. Richard J. Golsan (Hanover, NH: University Press of New England, 1996), 101.

86. Crowe, *Holocaust*, 415–17.

(regency, county, and state), the most important of which, at least in the history of Nazi trials, was the Tribunal général in Rastatt (Baden-Württemberg). The French created the tribunal in 1946 as a means of fulfilling the zonal trial policy of Control Council Law No. 10.[87] Accordingly, among its most prominent cases was the trial of German steel magnate Hermann Röchling, convicted of crimes against humanity under Law No. 10 for the exploitation of slave labor. Other trials dealt chiefly with crimes in concentration camps like Neue Bremm near Saarbrucken.[88] Although the tribunal's jurisdiction was technically restricted to crimes perpetrated within the territorial boundaries of the French zone, there were exceptions to this rule. An example was the tribunal's prosecution of staff members from the Ravensbrück camp located within the Soviet zone. The French were especially interested in Ravensbrück because of the numbers of French nationals deported to it, including Charles de Gaulle's niece Geneviève de Gaulle Anthonioz.[89]

## Soviet Trials

The USSR's judicial confrontation with Nazi crimes was conditioned by several factors peculiar to that country's plight during the war: the unexpected German invasion in defiance of the German-Soviet nonaggression pact, the staggering loss of life (twenty-six to twenty-eight million people killed, most of them civilians), and Josef Stalin's murderous paranoia. Other factors, as David Crowe observes (quoting historian Mark Elliot), were the service of one million Soviet citizens in the German war effort, often recruited from POW camps, and the use of 1.8 million Soviets as German slave laborers beginning in late 1942. Crowe writes that between 1943 and 1947 more than 5.6 million of these unfortunates were repatriated to the USSR; of this number, 60 to 65 percent were put on trial for collaboration and convicted. Twenty percent of the convicted

87. Donald Bloxham, *Genocide on Trial: War Crimes Trials and the Formation of Holocaust History* (New York: Oxford, 2001), 5–6.

88. Adalbert Rückerl, *The Investigation of Nazi Crimes 1945–1978* (Hamden, CT: Archon, 1980), 29.

89. Claudia Moisel, "Résistance und Repressalien: Die Kriegsverbrecherprozesse in der französischen Zone und in Frankreich," in *Transnationale Vergangenheitspolitik: Der Umgang mit deutschen Kriegsverbrechern in Europa nach dem Zweiten Weltkrieg*, ed. Norbert Frei (Wallstein: Göttingen, 2006), 264.

were executed or sentenced to lengthy prison terms, while others received shorter sentences or were exiled.[90]

The Soviets' experience with Nazi crimes was remarkable, too, for the extraordinary earliness of their war crimes trials. Rather than join the Allies' war crimes investigative organization, the UN War Crimes Commission, Stalin relied on a Soviet counterpart created under Alexander Vyshinsky in November 1942, the State Extraordinary Commission for the Determination and Investigation of Nazi and their Collaborators' Atrocities in the USSR (ChGK), to collect evidence of Axis war crimes. In the spring of 1943 the Soviet government adopted a policy of severe punishment of enemy combatants and their collaborators for crimes against Soviet nationals and POWs. The accused would be tried in military courts and, if convicted, publicly hanged. By summer and fall 1943 there ensued three multidefendant trials in Krasnodar, Krasnodon, and Mariupol. In the northern Caucasian city of Krasnodon, a military court tried eleven Soviet defendants on charges of treason and collaboration in the mass murder of civilians by Einsatzgruppe D, Sonderkommando 10a. All of the accused were convicted; eight were given the death penalty and three were sentenced to twenty years of hard labor.[91]

The Krasnodar trial was not a public event. However, in late 1943 Stalin held his first public trials of accused Nazi war criminals. In Kharkov from December 15 to 18, 1943, a military court prosecuted three German military members (SS, Wehrmacht, and police) for mass murder under Soviet law and a Soviet citizen for collaboration and treason (Sec. 5, Trials by Soviet Courts). The charges were related to the German occupation of Kharkov in late October 1941, during which the German army and the *Einsatzgruppen* murdered tens of thousands of civilians (primarily Jews) and POWs by mass shooting, hanging, and gas vans. While the indictment referred to the Nazis' ghettoization of Kharkov's Jews, in this trial as well as in other Soviet military proceedings the identities of Jewish victims were rarely mentioned. Rather, the indictments charged defendants with the "massacre of Soviet citizens."[92]

---

90. Crowe, *Holocaust*, 425.

91. Crowe, *Holocaust*, 426.

92. Alexander V. Prusin, "'Fascist Criminals to the Gallows!'; The Holocaust and Soviet War Crimes Trials, December 1945–February 1946," *Holocaust and Genocide Studies* 17/1 (2003): 3.

Well before the end of the war, the Soviets, much like the French, were embroiled in prosecuting suspected collaborators with the Germans. Military courts condemned fifty-two hundred alleged collaborators to hard labor between April 1943 and July 1944. As the war drew to a close in the spring of 1945, secret police and military courts convicted five thousand Soviet citizens of collaboration and sentenced them to death.[93] In the months after the war's end (December 1945–February 1946), the Soviets turned their attention to cases against German defendants implicated in atrocities against Soviet civilians (primarily Soviet Jews) and POWs. The trials were held in Bryansk, Kiev, Leningrad, Minsk, Riga, Smolensk, and Velikiye Luki. These were public trials resulting in maximum punishment for most of the defendants. Of the ten accused tried in Smolensk (December 16–21, 1945), seven were sent to the gallows, one to twenty years of hard labor, and the remaining two to hard labor terms of fifteen and twelve years.[94] The outcome of the Smolensk trial was typical of these military courts in the immediate postwar period.

The Soviet trials of German perpetrators and Soviet collaborators ground on until the end of the decade. Proceedings against Soviet collaborators concluded by 1947, those against Nazi defendants by 1949. A lull in prosecutions persisted through the 1950s into the 1960s due to Stalin's death and a general amnesty in 1955 given to many Soviet nationals incarcerated for collaboration. This amnesty did not extend to crimes of murder or torture, an exemption that launched a fresh wave of trials in the Ukraine and the Baltic countries in the 1960s. These trials dealt with the mass slaughter of Jews at Babi Yar, Kovno, Riga, and Vilna. In comparison with the avalanche immediately after the war, however, these later proceedings and their results were negligible. Historians have estimated that, from late 1945 to 1949, Soviet military tribunals convicted approximately 2.5 million people of crimes related to the German invasion.[95]

---

93. Crowe, *Holocaust*, 427.

94. George Ginsburgs, "The Nuremberg Trial: Background," in *The Nuremberg Trial and International Law*, ed. George Ginsburgs and Vladimir Nikolaevich Kudriavtsev (Amsterdam: Martinus Nijhoff/Kluwer, 1990), 29. For the sobering outcomes of the other military trials held in this period, see Ginsburgs, 29n41.

95. Rain Liivoja, "Competing Histories: Soviet War Crimes in the Baltic States," in *The Hidden Histories of War Crimes Trials*, ed. Kevin Heller and Gerry Simpson (New York: Oxford University Press, 2013), 251–52.

Figure 21. Dina Pronicheva, a Jewish survivor of the Babi Yar massacre, testifies about her experiences during a war crimes trial in Kiev. United States Holocaust Memorial Museum, courtesy of Babi Yar Society.

## Polish Trials

In contrast with the United States and Great Britain, who were reticent to make a public commitment to trials until late in the war, the Polish government in exile in London announced its support for judicial prosecution of Nazi crimes on December 15, 1939. Similarly, while the other Allies only began gathering evidence of such crimes in 1943, the Poles were already amassing it in 1940. On March 30, 1943, the Polish president in exile, Władysłav Raczkiewicz, issued a proclamation declaring Nazi perpetrators criminally liable for war crimes based on their violation of international law and the Polish Criminal Code of 1932. Up until this time, however, the only Polish trials related to the crimes of the German occupation were proceedings against suspected Polish collaborators held in underground "special courts."[96] As the end of the war hove into

---

96. Crowe notes that these "Home Army" trials conducted by the Polish underground convicted 5,000 Poles for war crimes and sentenced some 3,500 to death; of this number, 2,500 of the sentences were carried out. Crowe, *Holocaust*, 423.

view in May 1944, the war council of the Polish military in the USSR issued a "Decree concerning the Punishment of War Crimes and Treason against the Polish Nation." While this decree was never adopted as policy, it did go on to influence the most important document in the postwar Polish trials of Nazi war criminals—the "Decree of August 31, 1944" by the Polish Committee of National Liberation (Document 1.5). This law would serve as the subsequent legal charter of the Polish trials of accused Nazis.[97]

In late March 1945 the Main Commission for the Investigation of German Crimes in Poland was formed within the Ministry of Justice. The thirteen district commissions that it comprised interviewed witnesses, exhumed the bodies of victims, and gathered evidence of Nazi criminality for both the looming Nuremberg trials and proceedings to be held by the Poles themselves. The commission partnered with another organization created in February 1946, the Polish Military Mission for the Investigation of German War Crimes, which hunted for war criminals in all the German zones of occupation and liaised with the Polish member of the UN War Crimes Commission. By 1949 the Military Mission had succeeded in securing the extradition of 1,817 Germans suspected of war crimes in Poland.[98]

Although the best known of the Polish trials of Nazi war criminals would commence in 1946, the first of the trials actually started two years before these blockbuster cases, and it related to the Majdanek concentration/extermination camp. The inaugural Majdanek trial took place before a "special criminal court" in Lublin from November 27, 1944, to December 2, 1944. The defendants were four low-ranking guards and two *Kapos*,[99] who were nearly lynched on their way to the courtroom. Charged with violations of Section 1(a) of the Decree of August 31, 1944, which enabled the prosecution and punishment of any person involved in the German "murder, ill treatment or persecution against the civilian population or prisoners of war," the defendants were convicted and sentenced to death. Lacking a right of appeal, they were hanged in a field adjoining the Majdanek crematorium just one day after announcement

---

97. Crowe, *Holocaust*, 423; Włodzimierz Borodziej, "'Hitleristische Verbrechen': Die Ahndung deutscher Kriegs- und Besatzungsverbrechen in Polen," in Frei, *Transnationale Vergangeheitspolitik*, 409–10.

98. Borodziej, "Verbrechen," 412.

99. I.e., prisoners who functioned as guards in German concentration camps.

Figure 22. The makeshift gallows in Auschwitz I (main camp) on which Rudolf Höß, former commandant of Auschwitz, was hanged in April 1947. Photo by Michael Bryant.

of the verdict, on December 3, 1944.[100] In the four years supervening on this first Majdanek trial, the special court in Lublin prosecuted ninety-five other staff members from Majdanek, meting out capital punishment to seven of them.[101]

---

100. Andrzej Selerowicz and Winfried Garscha, "Die strafrechtliche Ahndung in Polen," in *Das KZ Lublin-Majdanek und die Justiz: Strafverfolgung und verweigerte Gerechtigkeit: Polen, Deutschland und Österreich im Vergleich* (Graz, Austria: Clio, 2011), 88–96.

101. Crowe, *Holocaust*, 423.

By far the most famous of the Polish trials were administered by what the late historian Alexander Prusin has termed "Poland's Nuremberg," the "Supreme National Tribunal" (Najwyższym Trybunale Narodowym, or "NTN").[102] The NTN was established in January 1946 by Poland's new provisional government to try significant Nazi functionaries responsible for atrocities in Poland during the war. Its first trial shortly after its founding was the prosecution of Arthur Greiser, the Reich governor of the Wartheland charged with a miscellany of war crimes. Among them were genocide (Chelmno and the Łódź ghetto were both within the Wartheland), torture, destruction of Polish culture, deportations of hundreds of thousands of Jews and non-Jewish Poles to the General Government, murder, and the kidnapping of Polish children. Greiser was convicted and sent to the gallows. Six further trials followed on the heels of Greiser. Amon Göth, commandant of the Płaszów concentration camp near Kraków, faced charges for his actions at Płaszów and for the murders of thousands of Jews when the ghettos at Kraków, Tarnow, and Szebnie were closed under his direction in 1943 and 1944 (Document 4.1). Jews who escaped death as the ghettos were liquidated were sent to Belzec for gassing (some 6,000 Jews in the Tarnow ghetto were dealt with in this manner; the rest were shot on the spot). In September 1946 he was convicted of war crimes, murder, and genocide and hanged near the site of the Płaszów camp.[103] Three months after Göth's conviction, the NTN heard the case of the former German governor of Warsaw, Ludwig Fischer, and three of his underlings. The trial lasted from December 1946 until February 1947, ending with capital punishment for all the defendants save one, Ludwig Leist.

After appearing as a defense witness at the Nuremberg IMT in April 1946, the former commandant of Auschwitz, Rudolf Höß, was sent back to Poland under the Moscow Declaration to stand trial before the NTN in Warsaw. He was convicted in March 1947 of, among other offenses, genocide—a concept broadly construed by the NTN to mean not just physical killing but cultural extermination—and sentenced to

---

102. Alexander V. Prusin, "Poland's Nuremberg: The Seven Court Cases of the Supreme National Tribunal, 1946–1948," *Holocaust and Genocide Studies* 24/1 (2010): 1–25.

103. The U.N. War Crimes Commission, *Law Reports of Trials of War Criminals*, Vol. VII: "Case No. 37: Trial of Haupsturmführer Amon Leopold Goeth" (London: His Majesty's Stationery Office, 1948), 1–10.

death. On April 16, 1947, Höß was hanged on a gallows adjacent to the morgue/crematorium in Auschwitz I; the gallows still stands today (see Figure 22).

Where Höß's trial involved only himself as the sole defendant, this was not the case of a much larger and, in the final analysis, more important proceeding held before the NTN in Kraków from November to December 1947. The defendants were led by Arthur Liebehenschel, Höß's successor as camp commandant, and thirty-nine other members of the camp staff. At this second of the Polish Auschwitz trials (Höß's was the first), the NTN declared the Auschwitz camp administration to be a "criminal group," membership in which gave rise to a presumption of criminality. With this finding of law, the NTN explicitly reserved the right to declare Nazi organizations criminal independently of the IMT's verdict at Nuremberg on the legal theory that the Poles could enlarge the definition of what counted as a criminal organization, so long as they did not contradict the IMT. Thus, mere membership in the SA and Nazi Party carried an automatic punishment of not less than three years in prison. All of the defendants except one were convicted. Twenty-one of the twenty-three death sentences were carried out, including Liebehenschel's; the rest were sentenced to prison terms ranging from several years to life.[104]

**Table 1. Convictions based on the Decree of August 31, 1944**

| Year | Death penalty | Life prison term | Prison term of more than 10 years | Prison term of less than 10 years | Total number of persons punished |
|------|------|------|------|------|------|
| 1946 | 303 | 31 | 92 | 1,812 | 2,238 |
| 1947 | 143 | 80 | 182 | 3,285 | 3,690 |
| 1948 | 258 | 92 | 301 | 2,576 | 3,227 |
| 1949 | 187 | 46 | 127 | 1,318 | 1,678 |
| 1950 | 222 | 35 | 169 | 1,633 | 2,059 |

Adapted from Borodziej, "Verbrechen," 431.

---

104. The U.N. War Crimes Commission, *Law Reports of Trials of War Criminals*, Vol. VII: "Case No. 38: Trial of Obersturmbannführer Rudolf Franz Ferdinand Hoess" (London: His Majesty's Stationery Office, 1948), 20; Borodziej, "Verbrechen," 421.

Figure 23. Josef Bühler is brought in handcuffs to the airport
to be flown to Poland for trial as a war criminal. United States
Holocaust Memorial Museum, courtesy of Colleen A. Picchi.

The coda to the NTN proceedings were the trials of the Danzig-West
Prussian governor and gauleiter Albert Forster (April 1948) and Hans
Frank's deputy governor, Josef Bühler (June–August 1948). Both men
were ardent Nazis heavily implicated in genocide and mass murder during the war, and after its conclusion both were extradited to Poland under
the terms of the Moscow Declaration to stand trial. Both were convicted
and executed—Bühler on August 8, 1948, Forster on February 28, 1952.
With these two trials, the work of the NTN drew to a close.

The seven trials conducted by the NTN were not the only ones tried
by Polish courts between 1945 and 1950. Other postwar trials were held
by Polish district courts, such as the October 1947 trial of Majdanek
guard Wilhelm Reinartz by the District Court of Lublin (Document 4.2).

In sum, from 1944 to 1951 the Poles convicted eighteen thousand defendants of war crimes, among them five thousand Germans. As David Crowe cautions, however, it has become clear since Polish judicial records became more available in 1989 that some Poles convicted of war crimes and collaboration were in fact innocent of these charges. Rather, the accused were railroaded into convictions because they opposed communism in Poland.[105]

# Trials by German Courts

## German Courts in the Western Zones

In order to fully grasp the daunting challenges facing German courts in their trials of Nazi war criminals immediately after the war, we should recall the crippling restrictions imposed on their jurisdiction. The Allies were concerned that a German judiciary sympathetic to ex-Nazis might exonerate them or mete out lenient sentences much as had occurred after World War I. The Western powers' decision in 1920 to entrust prosecution of German war criminals to the Reich Supreme Court in Leipzig had ultimately led to acquittals and laughably negligible punishment. This example of thwarted justice lingered in the minds of Allied policymakers as World War II ended and attention turned to the postwar reconstruction of Germany. After momentarily shutting down the German court system, the Allies reopened the ordinary courts as they had existed before 1933. The Allies denied to them, however, any authority to try offenses committed by Germans against the Allied occupation or citizens of Allied nations. This limitation effectively prevented German courts from prosecuting most Holocaust-based crimes insofar as these were overwhelmingly committed on non-German nationals.[106]

By December 1945 the Allies had a change of heart. Article III.1.d of Control Council Law No. 10 (issued on December 20), for the first time, allowed German courts to charge Nazi war crimes suspects with crimes against humanity, so long as both the perpetrator and the victim were

---

105. Crowe, *Holocaust*, 424–25.

106. Henry Friedlander, "The Judiciary and Nazi Crimes in Postwar Germany," *Simon Wiesenthal Center Annual* 1 (1984): 34.

German. Thereafter the British and French authorized German courts within their occupation zones to try such cases under Law No. 10. The United States, by contrast, declined granting their indigenous courts this leeway, ostensibly because of the American concern that German application of Law No. 10 in Nazi trials would raise issues of retroactivity.[107] The approach of the British was diametrically opposite: under British Order No. 47, German courts had no choice but to apply Law No. 10 and its definition of crimes against humanity in suitable cases.[108] The result was an unevenness in the outcomes of Nazi trials across occupation zones.

Under the thumb of close Allied supervision, the German judiciary focused on the Nazi crimes that fell within their jurisdiction, that is, offenses by Germans on other Germans (or stateless victims), chargeable in the American zone as crimes under German law and in the British and French zones as both domestic violations and crimes against humanity. This amounted to trials dealing with attacks on Jews and their property during the *Kristallnacht* (Night of Broken Glass) pogrom of November 1938 (Document 6.4); political killings committed in the year after the Nazis seized power (Document 6.5); and murders of alleged "defeatists" as the Third Reich reeled toward defeat in the spring of 1945. Due to Allied constraints on German courts, none of these cases could be prosecuted until the end of 1945 at the earliest.

One strain of cases that proved especially troublesome for the Germans involved the so-called grudge informers—persons who had informed on the July 20 bomb plot conspirators or had reported their neighbors to the Gestapo for listening to forbidden foreign radio broadcasts. From a legal standpoint, these cases were problematic. At Nuremberg the ex post facto issue was less knotty because the trials were generally viewed as an expression of the conquerors' sovereign authority as occupiers of Germany. When Law No. 10's definitions of crimes against humanity were applied by German courts to German cases, however, the retroactivity objection reared its head. This was a subject of intense debate among German jurists in the immediate postwar period.[109] The issue stalked the

---

107. Broszat, "Siegerjustiz," 496.

108. Broszat , "Siegerjustiz," 518.

109. See the discussion in Broszat, "Siegerjustiz," 486ff.; D. O. Pendas, "Retroactive Law and Proactive Justice: Crimes against Humanity in Germany, 1945–1950," *Central European History* 43 (2010): 432.

German trials based on Control Council Law No. 10 until August 1951, when German courts were no longer able to charge their Nazi defendants with crimes against humanity.

As historian Henry Friedlander has written, due to the limits placed on the range of cases German judges might hear, the most notorious of the Nazis' crimes were adjudicated in Allied courts. Deportations, mass shootings by the *Einsatzgruppen*, genocide in Nazi death camps, and murders committed in concentration and labor camps were reserved for non-German courts right after the war because nearly all of the victims were non-German.[110] There was a notable exception to this rule, however: the trials dealing with Nazi "euthanasia." This program, also called "T-4" because it was headquartered at Tiergartenstrasse 4 in Berlin, was launched in the fall of 1939 and carried out by Hitler's own chancellery. A full-fledged homicidal program took shape that transferred designated mental patients from their home institution to one of six killing centers, where they were murdered in gas chambers disguised as shower rooms. Disabled children selected for the program were sent to children's wards for killing through starvation, lethal injection, or overdoses of medicine. Most of the victims were German citizens, and for this reason T-4 fell within the jurisdiction allowed to German courts by Control Council Law No. 10 (German perpetrators and German victims).

The first euthanasia case tried by a German court involved the murder of disabled patients at the Obrawalde institution near Meseritz (Pomerania) in 1943–1944. The defendants were a physician, Hilde Wernicke, and a nurse, Helene Wieczorek. Wernicke had given orders to administer the lethal injections and Wieczorek had obeyed them. In March 1946 a Berlin district court in the Soviet zone of occupation convicted both women of murdering hundreds of patients in this manner and sentenced them to death, a punishment upheld on appeal (Document 6.1). Like other euthanasia defendants tried in succeeding years, the two women had been charged under the German Penal Code, Section 211, which defined murder under German law as follows:

> The murderer shall be punished by death. A murderer is someone who kills a human being out of blood-thirst, for

---

110. Henry Friedlander, "After Nuernberg: German Law and Nazi Crimes" (lecture presented at the American Historical Association Annual Meeting, Los Angeles, CA, December 28–30, 1981).

the satisfaction of sexual desires, for greed or any other base motives, in a cunning or cruel manner or by means causing common danger, or to make possible or conceal another felony.

For the Berlin District Court, the women's participation in euthanasia satisfied Section 211's elements of "cruelty" (inflicting severe physical or mental pain on the victim), "treacherous" (exploiting the defenselessness of the victim), and "base motives," a vague term having to do with the grossly unethical nature of the killing.[111]

German courts in other districts adhered to much the same interpretation of homicide in their euthanasia cases. In a pair of trials (December 1946 and January 1947), a Frankfurt district court convicted health care personnel implicated in euthanasia killings in Hessen of murder. The medical staff of another Hessian facility, the Hadamar psychiatric hospital, were tried for killing patients and convicted of murder in March 1947. The will to convict was emblematic of the first wave of Nazi euthanasia cases tried by German courts in Western occupation zones. In these proceedings, judges rejected the defense of "superior orders" as well as the contention that Hitler's authorization of the killing program was legal under German law. Instead, they sometimes resorted to natural law arguments to affirm that the defendants must have understood the patent wrongfulness of their actions. On this basis, German courts found euthanasia killers guilty as perpetrators of murder under Section 211.[112]

There was an exception to this willingness to convict killers as perpetrators, one that would prove fateful in later efforts to prosecute Nazi war crimes. Under German criminal law, once a defendant was found guilty of murder, an additional determination had to be made about the extent of the defendant's participation in the crime. If the killer carried out the crime without personally supporting or benefiting from it, such as a killing done on behalf of or on the orders of another person, then she or he was an accomplice; if the offender either subjectively endorsed the crime or controlled the circumstances of the murder, then she or he was a perpetrator. The distinction was important because a perpetrator of murder was often punished more severely than an accomplice. Until

---

111. Friedlander, "After Nuernberg," 10–11.

112. Broszat, "Siegerjustiz," 500.

the late 1940s, German courts usually rejected this "subjective" theory, preferring instead to convict those who killed with their own hands as perpetrators. This was true of both Hessian euthanasia cases mentioned above. In the Hadamar trial, however, the court—while convicting Hadamar doctors as perpetrators and sentencing them to death—convicted the nursing staff as accomplices on the grounds that they "[acted] weakly and without will" (Document 6.2). They were then sentenced to prison terms of three to eight years. In the aftermath of the Hadamar case, German courts began to apply the rationale of subjective theory to euthanasia doctors, characterizing them as accomplices to homicide rather than perpetrators.[113] Growing endorsement of subjective theory worked in concert with another German legal doctrine, necessity, to mitigate the guilt of proven killers and, in some instances, to justify their acquittals outright (Document 6.3).

It was through their investigations into Nazi euthanasia at the tag end of the 1940s that West German authorities stumbled over Operation Reinhard as a distinct, self-contained program. The investigation that launched the German judiciary's first serious encounter with the genocide of European Jews involved a mechanic arrested for participation in euthanasia at Hadamar. During his police interrogations, he talked about his assignment to the Treblinka death camp, where Jews were killed in gas chambers. Frankfurt prosecutors traced the names he provided, all of whom had served with him at Hadamar before their transfer to Poland in support of Operation Reinhard. Three of these suspects were located and indicted in 1950 for murder. The first trial ended in conviction and a death sentence (subsequently commuted to life in prison); the second, which jointly prosecuted two former guards at Sobibor, resulted in the acquittal of one defendant and the conviction of the other, who was sentenced to a life term. The crucial difference in the fates of the two men was the availability of witnesses to the second guard's actions. Witnesses were able to attest to his sadism and cruelty in the camp, enabling the court to find he had acted with "base motives" and in a "cruel" manner and convict him of murder as a perpetrator.[114]

---

113. Michael S. Bryant, *Confronting the "Good Death": Nazi Euthanasia on Trial, 1945–1953* (Boulder: University Press of Colorado, 2005), 128–35.

114. Michael S. Bryant, *Eyewitness to Genocide: The Operation Reinhard Death Camp Trials 1955–1966* (Knoxville: University of Tennessee Press, 2014), 36–37.

### German Courts in the Eastern Zone

Nowhere in any of the Allied occupation zones was denazification pursued with more rigor than in the Soviet zone. One of the first official acts of the Soviet government in Eastern Germany was to remove 390,478 former Nazis from their jobs. Within the German judiciary, any membership whatsoever by a German judge in the Nazi Party was disqualifying; there was no interest in rehabilitating former Nazi judges as was often done in the British, French, and US zones. Such action led to a grave scarcity in trained legal personnel, which the Soviets briefly considered supplying by appointing so-called people's judges—that is, nonprofessional laymen—to the bench after a crash course in the basics of law. Although the plan was later shelved, it is highly revealing of the occupiers' mentality at the time. Martin Broszat concludes that this episode demonstrates the upper hand of politics over the professional competence of the newly reorganized judiciary in Germany.[115] It presaged the future direction of Nazi trials in the eastern part of the divided country.

After Soviet authorities conducted their own trials of accused Nazi war criminals, convicting more than 12,500, they released 14,202 suspected war criminals into East German custody in 1950. Some of these suspects had worked in the concentration camps of Bautzen (a subcamp of Größ Rosen), Buchenwald, and Sachsenhausen, all of them within the Soviet zone. The East Germans were already embroiled in war crimes trials well before these suspects landed in their hands. Nonetheless, the chief of the Soviet Military Administration (SMAD) informed Deputy Prime Minister Walter Ulbricht that the East Germans should determine who among the prisoners released to them were suitable for prosecution by their own courts. German legal scholar Günther Wieland writes that an additional 10,513 persons convicted in military trials were sent to the East Germans for punishment, along with 649 others accused by the Soviets of "especially severe crimes committed against the USSR."[116] According to Wieland, a total of 29,632 accused war criminals had been remanded to

---

115. Broszat, "Siegerjustiz," 489.

116. Günther Wieland, "Die Ahndung von NS-Verbrechen in Ostdeutschland 1945–1990," introduction to *DDR-Justiz und NS-Verbrechen: Sammlung Ostdeutcher Strafurteile Wegen Nationalsozialistischer Tötungsverbrechen* (Amsterdam: University of Amsterdam Press, 2002), 55. Wieland is quoting a letter from the commander in chief of Soviet Forces in Germany, Vasily Chuikov, to the East German authorities, dated January 14, 1950.

the East Germans by early 1950 with explicit instructions for their judicial punishment. Given the large number of defendants, it is little wonder that, from 1948 until 1964, the East German government convicted 12,807 accused war criminals—nearly all of them between 1948 and 1950.[117]

The East Germans interned their war crimes suspects in the Waldheim prison thirty kilometers north of Chemnitz. Instructions from Ulbricht were relayed down the chain of command that the trials of the hapless prisoners should be "wrapped up" within the following six weeks and should conclude with "fair" but "harsh" verdicts. For the East Germans, the six-week deadline was critical in view of impending elections. Punishment of less than ten years should be avoided, regardless of time already served for the offense. With this mandate in hand, a panel consisting of politically reliable judges belonging to the East German Communist Party (SED) convicted 3,324 defendants of war crimes between April 26 and June 29, 1950. Thirty-three were sentenced to death (twenty-four were executed), 146 to life in prison, 1,901 to prison terms of fifteen to twenty-five years, 947 to prison terms of ten to fourteen years, and 290 to terms of five to nine years. Four of the convicted were sentenced to prison terms of less than five years. Not all of the defendants were convicted of the reprehensible crimes we typically identify with Nazism; some were found guilty of acting in concert with the Werewolf terror group, unauthorized possession of weapons, disseminating Nazi propaganda, espionage, and making anti-Soviet statements.

The quality of justice dispensed in these proceedings was not only tainted by overtly political factors. The lack of procedural safeguards for the defendants proved to be a warped burlesque of the very concept of a fair trial. Only ten of the proceedings were held in public, and the spectators to them were a select group prepared by the government. Most of the trials occurred beyond the public eye in strangely nonlegal environments: some were held in an administrative building, others in a former hospital. In neither space did the court allow defendants access to defense counsel of their choice or exculpatory witnesses. Prosecutors entered documents into evidence against the defendants bearing signatures by persons unavailable for questioning. Remarkably, such irregularities produced only five reductions of sentence on appeal. Rather than reductions, 1,317 appeals actually led to an increase in the convicts' sentences.[118]

---

117. Wieland, "Die Ahndung"; Crowe, *Holocaust*, 420.

118. Wieland, "Ahndung," 55–56.

It would be a gross simplification to dismiss the Waldheim trials as pure kangaroo courts railroading innocent people into convictions. Unquestionably, some of the defendants were war criminals who would likely have been convicted in any Allied court. This notwithstanding, other defendants were accused of little more than being in a bad odor with the East German government. David Crowe's critical assessment of denazification in the Soviet zone applies with equal force to the Waldheim trials: both "should be seen as a contribution to the creation of the one-party dictatorship in [East Germany]."[119]

# Epilogue: Assessing the Achievements and Legacies of the Trials

The period bracketing this short introduction—1943 to 1950—was not arbitrarily chosen: 1943 marks the first Holocaust-related trials conducted by an Allied court, the prosecution of Soviet collaborators with the *Einsatzgruppen* in Krasnodar, Krasnodon, Mariupol, and Kharkov. These trials were a harbinger of other Holocaust-based proceedings in Poland in 1944, including the first death camp trial targeting staff members of Majdanek. The five years after the war's end were the most significant in the history of Nazi war crimes prosecutions, in terms of both sheer numbers of trials and convictions and the development of novel legal theories to facilitate their punishment. This was the era of the great international trials held at Nuremberg, in which the charges of war crimes, crimes against peace, crimes against humanity, conspiracy, and membership in a criminal organization were pioneered. The hundreds of US and British Army prosecutions that unfolded before military commissions between 1945 and 1950 minted a variation of conspiracy doctrine, the theory of a common plan, to hold perpetrators accountable who might otherwise have escaped conviction. Similarly, Poland's "Nuremberg," the Supreme National Tribunal, enjoyed its brief moment in the sun during the immediate postwar period, in the course of which it became the first judicial body to prosecute a charge of genocide and to designate the Auschwitz camp staff a criminal organization.

---

119. Crowe, *Holocaust*, 421.

Moreover, the statistics bear out this era's importance in the history of Nazi war crimes trials. As historian Mary Fulbrook asserts, the "vast majority" of Nazi trials conducted in West and East Germany and in Austria (the "successor states" to the Third Reich) were held in the five-year period after the war's end. In East Germany 95 percent of all sentences for Nazi crimes were meted out between 1945 and 1950. In Austria in excess of 99 percent of convictions for such crimes had concluded by 1955. In West Germany 70 percent of convictions for Nazi crimes were achieved between 1945 and 1949; 55 percent of all cases and upward of 90 percent of all sentences were processed in the 1940s and 1950s.[120] Most of the trials in the successor states during this time applied the domestic law of their own country and were thus immune to allegations of "victor's justice"[121] and ex post facto[122] leveled at the Allies' international tribunals. Hence, they enjoyed a level of legitimacy in the view of their public. As several scholars have observed,[123] this aspect of domestic trials, which were conducted by the judiciary of the defeated states in their own language and under their own law, had a significant impact on transitional justice as Germans and Austrians sought to build democratic societies from the ruins of a defunct tyranny.

The critical five-year period after the war also witnessed the direct international effects of Nazi trials—the human rights provision of the UN Charter, the UN Declaration of Human Rights, the UN Genocide

---

120. Mary Fulbrook, *Reckonings: Legacies of Nazi Persecution and the Quest for Justice* (New York: Oxford University Press, 2018), 231, 235. For additional statistics on German trials of Nazi offenders immediately after World War II, see Pendas, "Retroactive Law," 429; Dick de Mildt, *In the Name of the People: Perpetrators of Genocide in the Reflection of their Post-War Prosecution in West Germany* (Amsterdam: Martinus Nijhoff, 1996), 18ff.

121. A charge voiced by many observers of the allied trials at the time, among them German defense counsel Otto von Kranzbühler, *Rückblick auf Nürnberg* (Hamburg, Germany: Zeit-Verlag E. Schmidt, 1949).

122. The newly reopened German courts were preoccupied by the retroactivity issue, leading to clashes between regional court judges and the appellate courts of the occupation. See Broszat, "Siegerjustiz," 493ff. (exploring this conflict against the backdrop of the postwar Tillessen and euthanasia cases).

123. See, e.g., Pendas, "Retroactive Law and Proactive Justice," 430; Jon Elster, *Closing the Books: Transitional Justice in Historical Perspective* (Cambridge: Cambridge University Press, 2004); Anna J. and Richard L. Merritt, eds., *Public Opinion in Germany: The HICOG Surveys, 1949–1955* (Urbana: University of Illinois Press, 1980).

Convention, and the fourth Geneva Convention. The international framework erected by these documents is now a permanent fixture of the postwar order. Lucius Clay, the US military governor of Germany between 1945 and 1949, said in an interview given in the mid-1980s that the Nuremberg trials "were a good thing, and that without them you would have a different Germany today."[124] The same might be said of the impact of postwar Nazi trials on geopolitics: without them, the international order today would be different, perhaps radically so.

What are we to make of these trials after the passage of some seventy years? Even today one hears the jeremiad that Nazi war criminals escaped punishment after the war. In his recent book *Why? Explaining the Holocaust*, historian Peter Hayes puts paid to this myth of Nazi impunity. He rebuts the myth with recourse to the impressive statistics documenting postwar Nazi trials. In sum, US, Soviet, British, and French courts convicted 8,812 Germans and Austrians in the immediate postwar period. Between 1945 and 1947 the American trial program at Dachau prosecuted 1,030 concentration camp staff, convicting 885 of them. Of the 432 convicted Nazis sentenced to death either for camp atrocities or attacks on downed airmen, 261 were hanged, among them forty-eight staff members of the Mauthausen camp, who were sent to the gallows at Dachau on May 27–28, 1947. Their hangings rank as the largest single execution carried out by the US government in its history. The Americans also executed Otto Moll, chief of the Auschwitz crematoria and supervisor of a forced march of Auschwitz prisoners to Dachau, in May 1946 at Landsberg prison. Great Britain prosecuted 989 accused war criminals and executed eleven ex-staff members of the Belsen camp in December 1945, including SS-Obersturmführer Franz Hössler, commander of the first gas chambers at Auschwitz, who ultimately landed at Belsen after stints in Dachau, Auschwitz-Birkenau, and Natzweiler.[125]

Throughout Europe, recently liberated nations hauled thousands of former Nazi offenders and collaborators into the dock. From 1945 to 1957 the Poles prosecuted 5,358 Germans, executing prominent Nazi figures in the three years after the war. We have already discussed some

---

124. Quoted in Paul Betts, "Germany, International Justice and the 20th century," *History and Memory* 17(1/2) (2005): 76.

125. Peter Hayes, *Why? Explaining the Holocaust* (New York: W. W. Norton, 2017), 306–7.

of them: men like Rudolf Höß, Amon Göth, and the other headline defendants tried by the Supreme National Tribunal during its fleeting existence. The Poles also hanged Hans Biebow, chief of the German administration of the Łódź ghetto, in June 1947; Ludwig Fischer, governor of the Warsaw district in the General Government, in March 1947; Ernst Boepple, deputy to Josef Bühler, in December 1950; Heinrich Josten, commander of the Auschwitz SS guard detail, in January 1948; and Maximilian Grabner, the Gestapo chief in Auschwitz and architect of the Block 11 torture chamber, in January 1948.[126]

The Dutch pursued their own trials in the six-year period after the war's end, prosecuting sixteen thousand accused collaborators and convicting most of them. At the same time, Dutch courts convicted 241 German war criminals, including the SS police leader of the occupied Netherlands, Hanns Rauter, and the German officials in charge of deporting Dutch Jews to the death camps, Willy Lages and Ferdinand aus der Fünten. Forty of the convicted were hanged, although the death sentences of Rauter and aus der Fünten were commuted.[127] Similar judicial reckonings with war crimes unfolded in Romania, France, Norway, Slovakia, and Hungary. Hayes emphasizes that all the German envoys to Croatia, Slovakia, Hungary, Bulgaria, and Romania involved in the Final Solution in those countries were killed either before or after trial between 1945 and 1947.[128] In Czechoslovakia, 18,496 accused war criminals and collaborators had been prosecuted by 1948.[129]

The record of justice for Nazi crimes was far from unblemished. Of the fifty thousand policemen serving in German police battalions implicated in the murder of 500,000 people, only sixty-four faced prosecution and forty-one were punished. A mere 10 percent of the Germans employed at Auschwitz were ever put on trial. The infamous Josef Mengele, an SS doctor who performed selections on the ramp and gruesome medical experiments in Birkenau, escaped a criminal trial through flight to South

---

126. Hayes, *Why?*, 307–8.

127. Dick de Mildt and Joggli Meihuizen, "'Unser Land muss tief gesunken sein . . .' Die Aburteilung deutscher Kriegsverbrecher in den Niederlanden," in Frei, *Transnationale Vergangenheitspolitik*, 283.

128. Hayes, *Why?*, 310.

129. David M. Crowe, *War Crimes, Genocide, and Justice: A Global History* (New York: Palgrave Macmillan, 2014), 243.

America, where he remained in hiding until his death in 1979.[130] These failures aside, the incidence of effective prosecution and punishment is striking. "In general," Hayes writes, "the chances of high-ranking perpetrators being punished were quite high. . . . Though not a perfect record, this is hardly a terrible one."[131] Not perfect, but not terrible, either. In an imperfect world, this may be as good as it gets.

In fact, the record of Nazi war crimes trials has bequeathed a legacy far richer than the statistics of convictions, punishment, and acquittals. The main legacy of the Nuremberg trials is unmistakable: for the first time, the leaders of a modern government were prosecuted for crimes under the international law of nations. The hoary immunity of "reasons of state" (*raisons d'état*) was lifted and aggressive warfare declared to be a crime under international law. While crimes against peace have not quite risen to the level of international customary law, the pressure that virtually all governments face today to couch their military actions as "self-defense" is arguably conditioned by the Nuremberg jurisprudence on aggressive war.

Furthermore, and despite its emphasis on the doctrine of criminal conspiracy, Nuremberg remains relevant in our own time because its architects insisted on the principle of individual responsibility. As Robert Jackson phrased it during the trial, "The idea that a state, any more than a corporation, commits crimes, is a fiction. Crimes always are committed only by persons." Jackson went on to emphasize that citizens everywhere had "international duties which transcend the national obligations of obedience imposed by the individual state . . . if the state in authorizing actions moves outside its competence in international law."[132] State actors high or low could no longer—at least in theory—invoke superior orders or their position within a complex hierarchy to dodge legal responsibility for what they did.

A true innovation introduced by the Nuremberg trials was the concern to protect civilians as codified in the crimes against humanity charge of the charter. According to historian Paul Betts, "unprotected civilians were now given center stage, since they had become the very objects of terror and war policy in World War II."[133] The desire to protect human

---

130. Hayes, *Why?*, 310–11.

131. Hayes, *Why?*, 308–9.

132. Quoted in Betts, "Germany," 60.

133. Betts, "Germany," 64.

rights became a mainstay of the UN Charter, Declaration of Human Rights, and the Genocide Convention. The promise of human rights enforcement, however, would have to await a later day because none of these documents was ultimately enforceable, either because they lacked an enforcement provision or the governments of powerful countries declined to ratify them. Legal scholar Geoffrey Robertson has argued that the UN Charter sought to promote human rights yet contained no guarantee of them because "no Great Power was prepared in 1945 to be bound by international law in respect of the treatment of its own subjects."[134] Not until the creation of the International Tribunal for the Former Yugoslavia (ICTY) in the midst of the Balkan wars of the 1990s was the promise of international human rights enforcement issued in Nuremberg partially fulfilled.

The legal legacy of Nuremberg may be contrasted with that of the trials of Nazi defendants in German courts. A salient aspect of the latter was the use of national law to prosecute heinous offenses. The refusal of the West German government to pass legislation enabling prosecution of accused Nazis under "special law" (such as genocide, conspiracy, or crimes against humanity, none of which existed in the German Penal Code during the war) meant that prosecutors were obliged to pursue their defendants using the staid categories of conventional German criminal law. This was also the case during the immediate postwar era, when the Allies largely controlled the actions of German courts within their occupation zones. In other words, the law used to convict pickpockets and petty thieves would also be employed to charge euthanasia doctors, denouncers, concentration camp killers, and SA arsonists. Numerous commentators have assailed the Germans for applying in their trials of Nazi offenders a form of law inadequate to dealing with state criminality. However, given the Allied and German unwillingness to recognize an exceptional category of criminal wrongdoing to which extraordinary law might be applied in German trials, the Federal Republic had little choice but to charge accused Nazis with violations of their own domestic penal code.[135]

For decades after the end of the war, German courts often hesitated to hold Nazi defendants fully responsible for their actions insofar as they

---

134. Quoted in Betts, "Germany," 65.

135. An important exception to this aversion to special law was the requirement in the British and French zones that crimes against humanity under Control Council Law No. 10 be charged by German courts, where appropriate, alongside violations of domestic law.

were merely carrying out the orders of their superiors. Such a defense was inadmissible at Nuremberg, as we have seen, but it was a significant hurdle to conviction and punishment in German trials, particularly by the late 1940s. The idea emerged that a defendant who merely followed his or her orders had not been proven to have the requisite intent of a perpetrator, a characterization that virtually ensured a lesser punishment. By the 1960s this "subjective" theory led to negligible punishment, acquittals, and even the quashing of proceedings against rafts of defendants (such as the aborted trial planned for former members of the Reich Security Main Office). The Germans would eventually swing around to a very different view of accomplice liability in the first two decades of the twenty-first century, but by then most of the perpetrators who had eluded trial were dead and beyond the reach of earthly justice. The lesson here is that, when confronted by unparalled atrocities, governments might be advised to pass special laws recognized as extraordinary one-off measures to deal with them. Such legislation would no doubt invite ex post facto objections, but the commonsensical retort—namely, that punishing uniquely reprehensible crimes unimagined by the criminal law is a higher value than avoiding the exposure of hardened war criminals to unfair legal jeopardy—would, I think, prove convincing to a great many people.

The final legacy of these trials is the ineluctability of politics in legal affairs. A half-century of pro-Western scholarship on Nuremberg has framed the IMT as a halcyon moment when Western and Eastern European governments put politics aside in the interests of meting out punishment for appalling German crimes. A more recent generation of scholars has called this interpretation into question, pointing out the ways in which the United States and USSR instrumentalized the trials to promote their foreign policy agendas. Thus, despite the tu quoque prohibition of the charter (forbidding German defendants from arguing they should be held harmless because the Allies had engaged in the same or similar behavior), the Western judges permitted German defense counsel to raise counteraccusations based on Soviet malfeasance: its involvement in the attack on Poland, the Franco-Soviet Pact that allegedly forced the Nazis to repudiate the Locarno treaty, and Soviet actions that supposedly prompted Hitler to invade Yugoslavia in 1941. From the USSR's point of view, the most galling deviation from the prohibition of tu quoque may have been the success of German defense counsel in blaming the Red Army for the Katyn forest massacre. The

Soviets perceived these suspensions of the tu quoque rule as betrayals of the USSR by its Allies—a perception that historian Francine Hirsch believes was justified and indicative of the West's anti-Soviet agenda at Nuremberg.[136]

The USSR itself viewed the IMT proceeding as a magnificent show trial similar to Stalin's prosecution of so-called counterrevolutionaries in the 1930s. The Nuremberg trial was to be a Communist morality play featuring evil warmongering fascists preying on peaceable and heroic Soviet peoples. Denunciation of Nazi wickedness on a world stage would confirm Soviet political theories and enhance the USSR's international prestige. The fiasco of these aims at Nuremberg—as the USSR's trial team watched German defense counsel demolish their country's image as an innocent and unwitting victim of Hitler's aggression, all with the apparent connivance of the Western Allies—was bad enough. The situation grew even darker when Winston Churchill delivered his "Iron Curtain" speech in Fulton, Missouri, likening the Soviet government to the Nazis. We ought not overlook the curious timing of Churchill's speech, which coincided with the Soviet trial team wrapping up its case against the major war criminals in Nuremberg. A day after the speech, headlines in US newspapers read, "Unite to Stop the Russians," and the Nazi defendants in the Nuremberg dock rejoiced at the prospect of the alliance unraveling. Not only had events skidded out of the control of Soviet propaganda; they had actually produced the diametrically opposite result from what Stalin, Vyshinsky, and Trainin had intended. Instead of burnishing the reputation of the Soviets for courage and decency and vindicating the Communist system, the trial had portrayed them as clumsy, mendacious, vicious, and belligerent. The USSR's bruising experience at Nuremberg rendered it yet more suspicious of the West and of international organizations as a whole. In 1948 the acrid taste of its political failures at Nuremberg would stiffen Soviet opposition to an international criminal court to enforce the proposed Genocide Convention. The reason for Soviet opposition, according to historian Anton Weiss-Wendt, was its abhorrence of "being in a situation in which it could not exercise

---

136. Hirsch, "Soviets at Nuremberg," 725–27. Significantly, the USSR and United States jousted in other proceedings at roughly the same time, such as at the Tokyo trials. See, e.g., Valentyna Polunina, "From Tokyo to Khabarovsk: Soviet War Crimes Trials in Asia as Cold War Battlegrounds," in Kerstin von Lingen, ed., *War Crimes Trials in the Wake of Decolonization and Cold War in Asia, 1945–1956* (New York: Palgrave, 2016), 239–60.

direct control."[137] Smarting from the recent debacle at the IMT, the lack of "direct control" over another international criminal tribunal caused Soviet leaders to reject it.

The point is that politics were not suspended in the interest of rendering justice for Nazi crimes at Nuremberg. Rather, the Arctic breath of Cold War politics was already pouring through the somber, wainscoted chambers of Courtroom 600 when the trial began in late 1945. In the aftermath of the trial and for the next half-century, the United States and USSR weaponized human rights discourse in their global struggle against each other. Soviet officials endeavored with little success to assert a continuity between Nazi Germany and the Anglo-Americans. The crux of their indictment against the West were British colonialism and anti-black racism in the United States, two charges leveled at the Western powers in the negotiations surrounding both the Genocide Convention and the Universal Declaration of Human Rights.[138] Similarly, at the trial of U-2 pilot Francis Gary Powers in 1960 for espionage, the former chief prosecutor for the USSR at Nuremberg, Roman Rudenko, lacerated the US government for inciting "monstrous crimes against peace."[139]

The Americans gave as well as they took. Director of the FBI J. Edgar Hoover equated the Nazis with the Soviets *sans phrases*, dismissing Soviet communism as nothing but "red fascism." The identification of the USSR with Nazi Germany became a commonplace of American political rhetoric during the Cold War. In June 1950 US president Harry S. Truman made a speech to persuade Congress to ratify the Genocide Convention. In it he warned that the lack of due process under Soviet law was a serious deprivation of human rights and insinuated that the Americans might be able to use the Genocide Convention as a weapon against the Communists.[140] Through the 1960s and 1970s mutual charges of human rights outrages, including crimes against humanity, flowed between the two superpowers. The origins of this politicization of human rights language by both Cold War antagonists lay in the rivalries between East and West already on display at the Nuremberg trials.

---

137. Anton Weiss-Wendt, *The Soviet Union and the Gutting of the UN Genocide Convention* (Madison: University of Wisconsin Press, 2017), 7.

138. Weiss-Wendt, *Gutting*, 107, 123.

139. Hirsch, " Soviets at Nuremberg," 728–29.

140. Weiss-Wendt, *Gutting*, 211.

# Brief Historiographical Essay

The secondary literature on Nazi criminality and postwar trials is oceanic in its vastness. Here we can only touch on some of the more important works relevant to the themes discussed in this short introduction to Nazi crimes and their punishment.

The dominant theory of Nazi criminality at Nuremberg, which traced the Third Reich's crimes to a prewar conspiracy led by Hitler and his followers but embracing leading sectors of the Nazi state and society, was influenced by Franz Neumann's *Behemoth: The Structure and Practice of National Socialism, 1933–1944* (1942; expanded, 1944). In his book, Neumann argued that the mainsprings of policymaking within the National Socialist state were a conspiratorial "power cartel" consisting of three interdependent blocs: Nazi government offices, big business, and the army. By 1936 a fourth bloc had joined the cartel: the SS (including the police and the SD). Neumann's study contributed to the "Nuremberg paradigm"[141] of Nazi criminality, which traced the worst of the Nazis' crimes to the machinations of this power cartel.

The interpretive school of intentionalism arose from the evidence presented at the IMT as filtered through the reducing valve of the Nuremberg paradigm. In the "conspiracy" of groups involved in launching the Holocaust, early intentionalists like Lucy Dawidowicz emphasized the central directorial role of Hitler, whose plans to murder the Jews, in her view, dated back to 1918 and Germany's loss of World War I.[142] Similarly, Gerald Fleming's 1986 book *Hitler and the Final Solution* portrayed a straight line extending from Hitler's pre–World War I anti-Semitism to the eruption of the Final Solution in 1941. For Dawidowicz, Fleming, and other intentionalists,[143] Hitler's role in converting his lifelong hatred of the Jews into genocidal policy by late 1941 was essential: he was the planner and initiator of the Holocaust from beginning to end, molding

---

141. See Erich Haberer, "History and Justice: Paradigms of the Prosecution of Nazi Crimes," *Holocaust and Genocide Studies* 19/3 (2005), 491ff.

142. Lucy S. Dawidowicz, *The War Against the Jews 1933–45* (New York: Holt-Rinehart-Winston, 1975).

143. See, e.g., John Toland, *Adolf Hitler: The Definitive Biography* (New York: Doubleday, 1976); Sebastian Haffner, *Anmerkungen zu Hitler* (Frankfurt: Fischer Taschenbuch, 1981); Joachim Fest, *Hitler: Eine Biographie* (Berlin: Ullstein Taschenbuch, 1998); Klaus Hildebrand, *Das Dritte Reich* (Munich: Oldenbourg Wissenschaftsverlag, 2003).

the process of destruction in accordance with his all-consuming malice toward the Jews. The clay of Nazi Jewish policy was shaped into the Final Solution by his hands.

The "functionalist" (or "structuralist") interpretive school, by contrast, rejected the centrality of Hitler's influence or the existence of a long-term plan to murder the Jews en masse. Instead, functionalists stressed the improvisation of Nazi leaders scattered across occupied Eastern Europe as the decisive factor in unleashing the Final Solution rather than a top-down order from Hitler to commence genocide. A preeminent functionalist was German historian Hans Mommsen, who deemphasized the impact of ideology and Hitler's involvement on the decisions that eventuated in the Final Solution, tracing them instead to local initiatives by German satraps acting on their own initiative albeit with the knowledge of and tacit approval of Hitler.

In this account, set forth in a number of essays written by Mommsen,[144] Hitler emerges as a weak dictator who set general policy directions but exerted little actual control over Nazi racial policy (an area he left for the most part to his lieutenants, such as Göring and Goebbels). Responding to crises of Jewish overcrowding in the summer and fall of 1941, the gauleiters, police chiefs, SS leaders, and members of the civilian administration in the occupied eastern territories resorted to ever more extreme measures to solve their Jewish "problem" in a manner they thought Hitler would endorse. A process of "cumulative radicalization" set in motion by local Nazi leaders but approved by Hitler drove Nazi policy toward genocide; as the "Holocaust by bullets" gave way to the "Holocaust by gas" with the erection of the first death camps in late 1941–early 1942, radicalization became institutionalized. The unfathomable moral obscenity of murdering all the Jews of Europe was sewn as it were into the fabric of Nazi foreign policy. For Mommsen and other functionalists, none of this was actuated by an order from Hitler. Although the Führer became aware of the descent into genocide and gave it a retroactive green light, he was not its originator. The functionalist point is that the Holocaust was

---

144. Hans Mommsen, "Hitlers Stellung im nationalsozialistischen Herrschaftssystem," in Gerhard Hirschfeld and Lothar Kettenacker, eds., *Der Führerstaat. Mythos und Realität* (Stuttgart: Klett-Cotta, 1981), 43–72; Hans Mommsen, "Die Realisierung des Utopischen: Die 'Endlösung der Judenfrage' im Dritten Reich," *Geschichte und Gesellschaft* 9 (1983), 381–420. For another classic statement of the functionalist position, see Martin Broszat, "Hitler und die Genesis der 'Endlösung.' Aus Anlaß der Thesen von David Irving," *Vierteljahrshefte für Zeitgeschichte* 25 (1977), 737–75 (arguing that the failure of the German offensive against the USSR in late 1941 stymied efforts to deport the Jews, causing Nazi officials in the Occupied Territories to turn to extermination as an alternative; local initiative was then retroactively approved by Berlin).

the outcome of local decision making by onsite German officials working more or less independently of Hitler, although drawing energy from his long-standing anti-Semitism and braced with his blessing post hoc.

More recent scholarship has tried to strike a via media between intentionalism and functionalism. Calling himself a "moderate functionalist," Christopher Browning argued in *Fateful Months: Essays on the Emergence of the Final Solution* and in a later work coauthored with Jürgen Matthäus, *The Origins of the Final Solution: The Evolution of Nazi Jewish Policy September 1939–March 1942*, that the "euphoria of victory" on the Eastern Front in the summer of 1941 emboldened Hitler to "signal" Himmler and Heydrich to begin planning for the Final Solution. The apparent chaos of German Jewish policy during this phase merely shows that parts of the government were still unacquainted with the Führer's change of heart, and for a time during the summer and fall of 1941 they continued with the former policy of emigration/expulsion. In volume 2 of his biography *Hitler: Nemesis 1936–1945*, Ian Kershaw rejects "cumulative radicalization" in favor of a view stressing Hitler's knowledge and approval of the Final Solution. While the plan may not have been clearly etched in Hitler's thinking before the war, it was latent in his mind for many years and needed only the rigors and hardships of the war to reveal it. Kershaw does, however, concede that the murder of the Jews was local and regional until December 1941. In this fashion, like Browning, Kershaw acknowledges on-the-ground decisions in conformity with perceptions of Hitler's wishes—a style of action Kershaw terms "working toward the Führer"— while upholding Hitler's indispensable role in the genocide.

The debate among academics over the origins of the Final Solution that once raged at fever pitch has largely spent itself today, with a consensus of historians tending to agree with the moderate functionalist/ moderate intentionalist positions of Browning and Kershaw.

The scholarship cited above was written by professional historians of European history. This is decidedly not the case with the early wave of writings about the Nuremberg war crimes trial, which, likely because of the contemporaneity of the IMT, was authored by participants in the trials.[145] Because they were actors in the history they relate, the authors

---

145. See, e.g., Francis Biddle, *In Brief Authority* (Garden City, NY: Doubleday, 1962); Telford Taylor, "The Nuremberg War Crimes Trials," *International Conciliation* 450 (April 1949), 243–371; Whitney Harris, *Tyranny on Trial: The Evidence at Nuremberg* (Dallas, TX: Southern Methodist University Press, 1954); G. M. Gilbert, *Nuremberg Diary* (New York: Farrar, Straus, 1947).

offer unique and highly valuable insights into the planning for and day-to-day operations of the IMT and the successor trials. Nonetheless, precisely because of their proximity to the events, their views are subject to bias and should not be handled uncritically. This is true as well for nonparticipant authors using the personal papers and reminiscences of trial participants as their sources.

We previously discussed the pro-Western scholarship on Nuremberg that may be classified as "triumphalist" and its tendencies to lionize the West while either ignoring or belittling the Soviets. The triumphalist works on Nuremberg include Bradley Smith, *Reaching Judgment at Nuremberg* (1977) and *The American Road to Nuremberg: The Documentary Record, 1944–1945* (1981) and Lawrence Douglas, *The Memory of Judgment: Making Law and History in the Trials of the Holocaust* (2001). Accounts leaning heavily on either British or US archival materials and memoirs, and thus telling the story of the trials from the Anglo-American viewpoint, include Ann Tusa and John Tusa, *The Nuremberg Trial* (1983), Joseph E. Persico, *Nuremberg: Infamy on Trial* (1994), Telford Taylor, *The Anatomy of the Nuremberg Trials* (1992), Airey Neave, *Nuremberg: A Personal Record of the Trial of the Major Nazi War Criminals in 1945–6* (1978), and Gary J. Bass, *Stay the Hand of Vengeance: The Politics of War Crimes Tribunals* (2000). Media representations of Nuremberg are saturated with pro-Western triumphalism: the 2006 PBS documentary *The Nuremberg Trials*, for example, extolled US chief prosecutor Robert Jackson while ignoring Soviet contributions to the trial.

Although objections to the triumphalist bias have been raised, Nuremberg triumphalism is still the dominant orthodoxy today. Dissidents from this orthodoxy in Anglo-American scholarship are, among others, Donald Bloxham, *Genocide on Trial: War Crimes Trials and the Formation of Holocaust History and Memory* (2001); Michael Bazyler, "The Role of the Soviet Union in the International Military Tribunal at Nuremberg" (2006); George Ginsburgs, *Moscow's Road to Nuremberg: The Soviet Background to the Trial* (1995); and Francine Hirsch, "The Soviets at Nuremberg" (2008). Among the prominent defenders of Soviet contributions to the IMT within the USSR or its successor states are Yuri Zorya and Natalia Lebedeva, "The Year 1939 in the Nuremberg Files" (1989); Marina Sorokina, "People and Procedures: Toward a History of the Investigation of Nazi Crimes in the USSR" (2005); and N. S. Lebedeva, *Podgotovka Niurnbergskogo protsessa* (1975).

# DOCUMENTS

## Section 1
## Enabling Laws: The Legal Foundations of Postwar Courts Trying Nazi Crimes

### 1.1

### The British Royal Warrant of June 18, 1945[1]

*In September 1944 the British judge advocate general, the official in charge of courts-martial within the British Royal Navy, Army, and Air Force, recommended that lower-tier German war criminals in British custody be tried under Royal Warrant by military courts after the war. Trial procedures would be drawn from British court-martial practice but adapted to the peculiar circumstances of war crimes trials. The Royal Warrant was eventually issued in mid-June 1945 as Army Order 81/1945. It would serve as the legal authority for the five hundred trials held by British military courts dealing with Nazi crimes.*

### GEORGE R. I.

WHEREAS WE deem it expedient to make provision for the trial and punishment of violations of the laws and usages of war committed during any war in which WE have been or may be engaged at any time after the second day of September, nineteen hundred and thirty-nine;

OUR WILL AND PLEASURE IS that the custody, trial and punishment of persons charged with such violation of the laws and usages

---

1. Source: https://avalon.law.yale.edu/imt/imtroyal.asp (accessed July 6, 2019).

of war as aforesaid shall be governed by the Regulations attached to this Our Warrant

Given at Our Court at St. James's, this 14th day of June, 1945, in the 9th year of our Reign. By His Majesty's Command,

P. J. GRIGG

## Regulations for the Trial of War Criminals

1.  In these Regulations if not inconsistent with the context and subject to any express provision to the contrary the following expressions have the following meanings namely:

    "War Crime" means a violation of the laws and usages of war committed during any war in which His Majesty has been or may be engaged at any time since the 2nd September, 1939. . . .

2.  (a) The following officers shall have power to convene Military Courts for the trial of persons charged with having committed war crimes and to confirm the findings and sentences of such Courts namely:-

    (i) Any officers authorized so to do by His Majesty and His Warrant

    (ii) Any officers authorized so to do by delegation under the Warrant of any officer referred to under (i) above whom His Majesty has authorized to make such delegation by His Warrant.

    . . .

3.  . . . [T]he provisions of the Army Act and the Rules of Procedure made pursuant thereto so far as they relate to Field General Courts-Martial . . . shall apply so far as applicable to Military Courts under these Regulations and any matters preliminary or incidental thereto or consequential thereon in like manner as if the Military Courts were Field General Courts-Martial and the accused were persons subject to military law charged with having committed offences on active service.

    . . .

4.  If it appears to an officer authorized under the Regulations to convene a Military Court that a person then within the limits of his command has . . . committed a war crime he may direct that such person if not already in military custody shall be taken into

and kept in such custody pending trial in such manner and in the charge of such military unit as he may direct. . . . But such commanding officer shall have no power to dismiss the charge or deal with the accused summarily for a war crime. . . .

5.    A Military Court shall consist of not less than two officers in addition to the President, who shall be appointed by name, but no officer, whether sitting as President or as a member, need have held his commission for any special length of time. . . .

    In default of a person deputed by H. M. Judge Advocate General to act as Judge Advocate, the Convening Officer may by order appoint a fit person to act as Judge Advocate at the trial. If no such Judge Advocate is deputed or appointed, the Convening Officer should appoint at least one officer having one of the legal qualifications mentioned in Rule of Procedure 93 (B) as President or as a member of the Court. . . .

6.    The accused shall not be entitled to object to the President or any member of the Court or the Judge Advocate or to offer any special plea to the jurisdiction of the Court.

7.    Counsel may appear on behalf of the Prosecutor and accused in like manner as if the Military Court were a General Court-Martial. . . .

8.    (i) At any hearing before a Military Court convened under these regulations the Court may take into consideration any oral statement or any document appearing on the face of it to be authentic, provided the statement or document appears to the Court to be of assistance in proving or disproving the charge notwithstanding that such statement or document would not be admissible as evidence in proceedings before a Field General Court-Martial, and without prejudice to the generality of the foregoing in particular:

    (a) If any witness is dead or is unable to attend or to give evidence or is, in the opinion of the Court, unable so to attend without undue delay, the Court may receive secondary evidence of statements made by or attributable to such witness;

    (b) any document purporting to have been signed or issued officially by any member of any Allied or enemy force or by any official or agency of any Allied, neutral or enemy government, shall be admissible as evidence without proof of the issue or signature thereof;

···

(d) the Court may receive as evidence of the facts therein stated any depositions or any record of any Military Court of Inquiry or (any Summary) of any examination made by any officer detailed for the purpose by any military authority;

(e) the Court may receive as evidence of the facts therein stated any diary, letter or other document appearing to contain information relating to the charge;

(f) if any original document cannot be produced or, in the opinion of the Court, cannot be produced without undue delay, a copy of such document or other secondary evidence of its contents may be received in evidence;

It shall be the duty of the Court to judge of the weight to be attached to any evidence given in pursuance of this Regulation which would not otherwise be admissible.

(ii) Where there is evidence that a war crime has been the result of concerted action upon the part of a unit or group of men, then evidence given upon any charge relating to that crime against any member of such unit or group may be received as prima facie evidence of the responsibility of each member of that unit or group for that crime.

In any such case all or any members of any such unit or group may be charged and tried jointly in respect of any such war crime and no application by any of them to be tried separately shall be allowed by the Court [Army Order 127, 1945].

(iii) The Court shall take judicial notice of the laws and usages of war.

(iv) Unless the Convening Officer otherwise directs a finding of guilty and the sentence shall be announced in Open Court by the President, who shall at the same time state that such finding and sentence are subject to confirmation. . . . A finding of acquittal, whether on all or some of the offences with which the accused is charged, shall not require confirmation or be subject to be revised and shall be pronounced at once in Open Court, but the Court shall not thereupon release the accused, unless otherwise entitled to be released.

(v) The sittings of Military Courts will ordinarily be open to the public so far as accommodation permits. But the Court may on the ground that it is expedient so to do in the national interest or in the interests of justice, or for the effective prosecution of war crimes generally, or otherwise, by order prohibit the publication of any evidence to be given or of any statement to be made in the course of the proceedings before it, or direct that all or any portion of the public shall be excluded during any part of such proceedings as normally take place in Open Court, except during the announcement of the finding and sentence pursuant to paragraph (iv) above.

(vi) A record shall be made of the Proceedings of every Military Court.

9.   A person found guilty by a Military Court of a war crime may be sentenced to and shall be liable to suffer any one or more of the following punishments, namely:-

(i) Death (either by hanging or by shooting);

(ii) Imprisonment for life or for any less term;

(iii) Confiscation;

(iv) A fine.

· · ·

Sentence of death shall not be passed on any person by a Military Court without the concurrence of all those serving on the Court if the Court consists of not more than three members, including the President, or without the concurrence of at least two-thirds of those serving on the Court if the Court consists of more than three members, including the President.

10.  The accused may within 14 days of the termination of the Proceedings in Court submit a Petition to the Confirming Officer against the finding or sentence or both provided that he gives notice to the Confirming Officer within 48 hours of such termination of his intention to submit such a Petition. The accused shall have no right to submit any Petition otherwise than as aforesaid.

Provided that if such Petition is against the finding it shall be referred by the Confirming Officer, together with the Proceedings of the trial, to His Majesty's Judge Advocate General or to any Deputy of his approved by him for that purpose in the Command overseas where the trial took place for advice and report.

11. The finding and any sentence which the Court had jurisdiction to pass may be confirmed and, if confirmed, shall be valid, notwithstanding any deviation from these Regulations, or the Rules of Procedure or any defect or objection, technical or other, unless it appears that a substantial miscarriage of justice has actually occurred.

12. When a sentence passed by a Military Court has been confirmed, the following authorities shall have power to mitigate or remit the punishment thereby awarded or to commute such punishment for any less punishment or punishments to which the offender might have been sentenced by the said Court; that is to say the rank of

    (i) The secretary of State for War or any officer not below the Major-General authorized by him; and

    (ii) ... (a) the Secretary of State for Foreign Affairs, or (b) where an offender convicted by a military court is undergoing sentence in the British Zone of Germany, or in the British Zone of Austria, the High Commissioner in Germany or in Austria ... designated by His Majesty's Government, if authorized by the Secretary of State for Foreign Affairs, or any other person, so authorized, who may, for the time being, be discharging the functions of the High Commissioner as aforesaid. ...

13. In any case not provided for in these Regulations such course will be adopted as appears best calculated to do justice.

By Command of the Army Council, [signature illegible]
LONDON

# 1.2

# Joint Chiefs of Staff Directive 1023/10, July 15, 1945[2]

*As the British moved forward with their plans for military trials of lower-tier war criminals in the summer of 1945, the Americans were advancing along a parallel track. The first concrete authority given US forces to prosecute war criminals was the Joint Chiefs*

---

2. Source: https://avalon.law.yale.edu/imt/imtjcs.asp (accessed September 23, 2019).

*of Staff Directive 1023/10, issued on July 8, 1945. It defined the term "war crimes" and authorized the US commander in chief to take measures to investigate, identify, arrest, and imprison suspected war criminals. Most important, it empowered the commander to try suspected war criminals in "appropriate military courts," which had to be separate from courts that prosecuted offenses against the American occupation. The directive remained in effect until December 1945, when it was superseded by Control Council Law No. 10.*

## DIRECTIVE ON THE IDENTIFICATION AND APREHENSION OF PERSONS SUSPECTED OF WAR CRIMES OR OTHER OFFENSES AND TRIAL OF CERTAIN OFFENDERS

1.    This directive is issued to you as Commander in Chief of the U. S. (U. K.), (U. S. S. R.) (French) forces of occupation. As a member of the Control Council[3] you will urge the adoption by the other occupying powers of the principles and policies set forth in this directive and, pending Control Council agreement, you will follow them in your zone.

2.    The crimes covered by this directive are:

     a. Atrocities and offenses against persons or property constituting violation of international law, including the laws, rules and customs of land and naval warfare.

     b. Initiation of invasions of other countries and of wars of aggression in violation of international laws and treaties.

     c. Other atrocities and offenses, including atrocities and persecutions on racial, religious or political grounds, committed since 30 January 1933.

3.    The term "criminal" as used herein includes all persons, without regard to their nationality or capacity in which they acted, who have committed any of the crimes referred to in paragraph 2 above, including all persons who (1) have been accessories to

---

3. I.e., the allied body governing the four Allied occupation zones set up in Germany and Austria after World War II. It consisted of representatives from the United States, United Kingdom, France, and the USSR.

the commission of such crimes, (2) have taken a consenting part therein, (3) have been connected with plans or enterprises involving their commission, or (4) have been members of organizations or groups connected with the commission of such crimes. With reference to paragraph 2b, the term "criminal" is intended to refer to persons who have held high political, civil or military (including General Staff) positions in Germany or in one of its allies, co-belligerents or satellites or in the financial, industrial or economic life of any of these countries.

4.    The Control Council should coordinate policies with respect to the matters covered by this directive.

5.    Subject to the coordination of such matters by the Control Council and to its agreed policies:

a. . . . [Y]ou will take all practicable measures to identify, investigate, apprehend and detain all persons whom you suspect to be criminals as defined in paragraph 3 above and all persons whom the Control Council, any one of the United Nations, or Italy notifies to you as being charged as criminals.

b. You will take under your control pending decision by the Control Council or higher authority as to its eventual disposition, property, real and personal found in your zone and owned or controlled by the persons referred to in subparagraph a above.

c. You will report to the Control Council the names of suspected criminals, their places of detention, the charges against them, the results of investigations and the nature of the evidence, the names and locations of witnesses, and the nature of locations of the property so coming under your control.

d. You will take such measures as you deem necessary to insure that witnesses to the crimes covered by this directive will be available when required.

e. You may require the Germans to give you such assistance as you deem necessary.

6.    Subject to the coordination of such matters by the Control Council and to its agreed policies:

a. You will promptly comply with a request by any one of the United Nations or Italy for the delivery to it of any person who is stated in such request to be charged with a crime to which this directive is applicable, subject to the following exceptions:

(1) Persons who have held high political, civil or military position in Germany or in one of its allies, co-belligerents, or satellites will not be delivered to any one of the United Nations or Italy, pending consultation with the Control Council to ascertain whether it is desired to try such persons before an international military tribunal. Suspected criminals desired for trial before international military tribunals or persons desired as witnesses at trials before such tribunals will not be turned over to the nation requesting them so long as their presence is desired in connection with such trials.

(2) Persons requested by two or more of the United Nations or one or more of the United Nations and Italy for trial for a crime will not be delivered pending determination by the Control Council of their disposition.

The Control Council should take all practicable measures to insure the availability of such persons to the several United Nations concerned or Italy, in such priority as the Control Council shall determine. If in any case the Control Council fails to make such determination within a reasonable period of time, you will make your own determination based on all the circumstances, including the relative seriousness of the respective charges against such person and will deliver the requested person to the United Nations or Italy accordingly.

b. Compliance with any request for the delivery of a person shall not be delayed on the ground that other requests for the same person are anticipated.

c. Delivery of a person to requesting nation shall be subject to the condition that if such person is not brought to trial, tried and convicted within six months from the date he is so delivered, he will be returned to you upon request for trial by any of the other United Nations or Italy.

d. In exceptional cases in which you have a doubt as to whether you should deliver a person demanded under subparagraph a above, you should refer the matter for decision to the Control Council with your recommendations.

The Control Council should determine promptly any dispute as to the disposition of any person detained within Germany in accordance with this directive.

7. Appropriate military courts may conduct trials of suspected criminals in your custody. In general these courts should be separate

from the courts trying current offenses against your occupation, and, to the greatest practicable extent, should adopt fair, simple and expeditious procedures designed to accomplish substantial Justice without technicality. You should proceed with such trials and the execution of sentences except in the following cases:

a. Trials should be deferred of suspected criminals who have held high political, civil or military positions in Germany or in one of its allies, cobelligerents, or satellites, pending consultation with the Control Council to ascertain whether it is desired to try such persons before an international military tribunal.

b. Where charges are pending and the trial has not commenced in your zone against a person also known to you to be wanted elsewhere for trial, the trial in your zone should be deferred for a reasonable period of time, pending consultation with the Control Council as to the disposition of such person for trial.

c. Execution of death sentences should be deferred when you have reason to believe that the testimony of those convicted would be of value in the trial of other criminals in any area whether within or without your zone.

# 1.3

# London Charter of August 8, 1945[4]

*While the decision to prosecute major Nazi war criminals was made in the late spring of 1945, not until the United States, USSR, Great Britain, and France signed an agreement on August 8 to convene a trial was the judicial solution formally adopted. The allies attached to this agreement a charter enumerating the charges against the upper-echelon Nazis. This document, called the "London Charter" or "London Agreement," became the legal basis of the indictment filed in Berlin on October 6. Article 6 of the Charter set forth the charges of crimes against peace, war crimes, crimes against humanity, and conspiracy. Articles 9 and 10 contained the criminal organizations charge.*

---

4. Source: https://avalon.law.yale.edu/imt/imtchart.asp (accessed July 7, 2019).

# I. CONSTITUTION OF THE INTERNATIONAL MILITARY TRIBUNAL

*Article 1.*

In pursuance of the Agreement signed on the 8th day of August 1945 by the Government of the United States of America, the Provisional Government of the French Republic, the Government of the United Kingdom of Great Britain and Northern Ireland and the Government of the Union of Soviet Socialist Republics, there shall be established an International Military Tribunal (hereinafter called "the Tribunal") for the just and prompt trial and punishment of the major war criminals of the European Axis.

*Article 2.*

The Tribunal shall consist of four members, each with an alternate. One member and one alternate shall be appointed by each of the Signatories. The alternates shall, so far as they are able, be present at all sessions of the Tribunal. In case of illness of any member of the Tribunal or his incapacity for some other reason to fulfill his functions, his alternate shall take his place.

*Article 3.*

Neither the Tribunal, its members nor their alternates can be challenged by the prosecution, or by the Defendants or their Counsel.[5] Each Signatory may replace its members of the Tribunal or his alternate for reasons of health or for other good reasons, except that no replacement may take place during a Trial, other than by an alternate.

*Article 4.*

(a)   The presence of all four members of the Tribunal or the alternate for any absent member shall be necessary to constitute the quorum.

(b)   The members of the Tribunal shall, before any trial begins, agree among themselves upon the selection from their number of a

---

5. This provision of the charter arguably precluded the *tu quo que* (you, too) defense subsequently raised by German defense counsel at Nuremberg.

President, and the President shall hold office during the trial, or as may otherwise be agreed by a vote of not less than three members. The principle of rotation of presidency for successive trials is agreed. If, however, a session of the Tribunal takes place on the territory of one of the four Signatories, the representative of that Signatory on the Tribunal shall preside.

(c) Save as aforesaid the Tribunal shall take decisions by a majority vote and in case the votes are evenly divided, the vote of the President shall be decisive: provided always that convictions and sentences shall only be imposed by affirmative votes of at least three members of the Tribunal.

*Article 5.*

In case of need and depending on the number of the matters to be tried, other Tribunals may be set up; and the establishment, functions, and procedure of each Tribunal shall be identical, and shall be governed by this Charter.

## II. JURISDICTION AND GENERAL PRINCIPLES

*Article 6.*

The Tribunal established by the Agreement referred to in Article 1 hereof for the trial and punishment of the major war criminals of the European Axis countries shall have the power to try and punish persons who, acting in the interests of the European Axis countries, whether as individuals or as members of organizations, committed any of the following crimes. The following acts, or any of them, are crimes coming within the jurisdiction of the Tribunal for which there shall be individual responsibility:

(a) **CRIMES AGAINST PEACE**: namely, planning, preparation, initiation or waging of a war of aggression, or a war in violation of international treaties, agreements or assurances, or participation in a common plan or conspiracy for the accomplishment of any of the foregoing;

(b) **WAR CRIMES**: namely, violations of the laws or customs of war. Such violations shall include, but not be limited to, murder, ill-treatment or deportation to slave labor or for any other purpose of civilian population of or in occupied territory, murder or ill-treatment of prisoners of war or persons on the seas, killing of hostages, plunder of public or private property, wanton destruction of cities, towns or villages, or devastation not justified by military necessity;

(c) **CRIMES AGAINST HUMANITY**: namely, murder, extermination, enslavement, deportation, and other inhumane acts committed against any civilian population, before or during the war; or persecutions on political, racial or religious grounds in execution of or in connection with any crime within the jurisdiction of the Tribunal, whether or not in violation of the domestic law of the country where perpetrated.

Leaders, organizers, instigators and accomplices participating in the formulation or execution of a common plan or conspiracy to commit any of the foregoing crimes are responsible for all acts performed by any persons in execution of such plan.

## Article 7.

The official position of defendants, whether as Heads of State or responsible officials in Government Departments, shall not be considered as freeing them from responsibility or mitigating punishment.

## Article 8.

The fact that the Defendant acted pursuant to order of his Government or of a superior shall not free him from responsibility, but may be considered in mitigation of punishment if the Tribunal determines that justice so requires.

## Article 9.

At the trial of any individual member of any group or organization the Tribunal may declare (in connection with any act of which the individual may be convicted) that the group or organization of which the individual was a member was a criminal organization.

After the receipt of the Indictment the Tribunal shall give such notice as it thinks fit that the prosecution intends to ask the Tribunal to make such declaration and any member of the organization will be entitled to apply to the Tribunal for leave to be heard by the Tribunal upon the question of the criminal character of the organization. The Tribunal shall have power to allow or reject the application. If the application is allowed, the Tribunal may direct in what manner the applicants shall be represented and heard.

*Article 10.*

In cases where a group or organization is declared criminal by the Tribunal, the competent national authority of any Signatory shall have the right to bring individuals to trial for membership therein before national, military or occupation courts. In any such case the criminal nature of the group or organization is considered proved and shall not be questioned.

. . .

*Article 13.*

The Tribunal shall draw up rules for its procedure. These rules shall not be inconsistent with the provisions of this Charter.

. . .

## IV. FAIR TRIAL FOR DEFENDANTS

*Article 16.*

In order to ensure fair trial for the Defendants, the following procedure shall be followed:

(a)   The Indictment shall include full particulars specifying in detail the charges against the Defendants. A copy of the Indictment and of all the documents lodged with the Indictment, translated into a language which he understands, shall be furnished to the Defendant at reasonable time before the Trial.

(b)   During any preliminary examination or trial of a Defendant he will have the right to give any explanation relevant to the charges made against him.

(c)   A preliminary examination of a Defendant and his Trial shall be conducted in, or translated into, a language which the Defendant understands.

(d)   A Defendant shall have the right to conduct his own defense before the Tribunal or to have the assistance of Counsel.

(e)   A Defendant shall have the right through himself or through his Counsel to present evidence at the Trial in support of his defense, and to cross-examine any witness called by the Prosecution.

. . .

*Article 18.*

The Tribunal shall

(a)   confine the Trial strictly to an expeditious hearing of the cases raised by the charges,

(b)   take strict measures to prevent any action which will cause reasonable delay, and rule out irrelevant issues and statements of any kind whatsoever,

(c)   deal summarily with any contumacy, imposing appropriate punishment, including exclusion of any Defendant or his Counsel from some or all further proceedings, but without prejudice to the determination of the charges.

*Article 19.*

The Tribunal shall not be bound by technical rules of evidence. It shall adopt and apply to the greatest possible extent expeditious and nontechnical procedure, and shall admit any evidence which it deems to be of probative value.

. . .

*Article 22.*

The permanent seat of the Tribunal shall be in Berlin. The first meetings of the members of the Tribunal and of the Chief Prosecutors shall be held at Berlin in a place to be designated by the Control Council for Germany. The first trial shall be held at Nuremberg, and any subsequent trials shall be held at such places as the Tribunal may decide.

. . .

## VI. JUDGMENT AND SENTENCE

*Article 26.*

The judgment of the Tribunal as to the guilt or the innocence of any Defendant shall give the reasons on which it is based, and shall be final and not subject to review.

*Article 27.*

The Tribunal shall have the right to impose upon a Defendant, on conviction, death or such other punishment as shall be determined by it to be just.

# 1.4

# Control Council Law No. 10, December 20, 1945[6]

*Control Council Law No. 10 was largely based on its predecessor decree, the London Charter. Thus, its definitions of the substantive charges against the second tier of Nazi war criminals strongly resemble those of its precursor document. Similarity is not identity, however, and Law No. 10's definition of crimes against humanity deleted the charter's "war nexus" clause ("in execution of or in connection with any crimes," etc.), thereby detaching crimes against humanity from their dependence on crimes against peace and war crimes. Henceforth, despite some inconsistency in courts' interpretations, crimes against humanity could be charged against state actors even when their actions had no connection to armed conflict.*

In order to give effect to the terms of the Moscow Declaration of 30 October 1943 and the London Agreement of 8 August 1945, and the Charter issued pursuant thereto and in order to establish a uniform legal basis in Germany for the prosecution of war criminals and other similar

---

6. Source: https://avalon.law.yale.edu/imt/imt10.asp (accessed July 7, 2019).

offenders, other than those dealt with by the International Military Tribunal, the Control Council enacts as follows:

## Article I

The Moscow Declaration of 30 October 1943 "Concerning Responsibility of Hitlerites for Committed Atrocities" and the London Agreement of 8 August 1945 "Concerning Prosecution and Punishment of Major War Criminals of European Axis" are made integral parts of this Law. Adherence to the provisions of the London Agreement by any of the United Nations, as provided for in Article V of that Agreement, shall not entitle such Nation to participate or interfere in the operation of this Law within the Control Council area of authority in Germany.

## Article II

1.    Each of the following acts is recognized as a crime:

(a) Crimes against Peace. Initiation of invasions of other countries and wars of aggression in violation of international laws and treaties, including but not limited to planning, preparation, initiation or waging a war of aggression, or a war of violation of international treaties, agreements or assurances, or participation in a common plan or conspiracy for the accomplishment of any of the foregoing.

(b) War Crimes. Atrocities or offenses against persons or property constituting violations of the laws or customs of war, including but not limited to, murder, ill treatment or deportation to slave labour or for any other purpose, of civilian population from occupied territory, murder or ill treatment of prisoners of war or persons on the seas, killing of hostages, plunder of public or private property, wanton destruction of cities, towns or villages, or devastation not justified by military necessity.

(c) Crimes against Humanity. Atrocities and offenses, including but not limited to murder, extermination, enslavement, deportation, imprisonment, torture, rape, or other inhumane acts committed against any civilian population, or persecutions on political, racial or religious grounds whether or not in violation of the domestic laws of the country where perpetrated.

(d) Membership in categories of a criminal group or organization declared criminal by the International Military Tribunal.

. . .

2. Any persons found guilty of any of the crimes above mentioned may upon conviction be punished as shall be determined by the tribunal to be just. Such punishment may consist of one or more of the following:

(a) Death.

(b) Imprisonment for life or a term of years, with or without hard labor.

(c) Fine, and imprisonment with or without hard labour, in lieu thereof.

(d) Forfeiture of property.

(e) Restitution of property wrongfully acquired.

(f) Deprivation of some or all civil rights.

. . .

4. (a) The official position of any person, whether as Head of State or as a responsible official in a Government Department, does not free him from responsibility for a crime or entitle him to mitigation of punishment.

(b) The fact that any person acted pursuant to the order of his Government or of a superior does not free him from responsibility for a crime, but may be considered in mitigation.

. . .

## Article III

1. Each occupying authority, within its Zone of Occupation,

(a) shall have the right to cause persons within such Zone suspected of having committed a crime, including those charged with crime by one of the United Nations, to be arrested and shall take under control the property, real and personal, owned or controlled by the said persons, pending decisions as to its eventual disposition.

(b) shall report to the Legal Directorate the name of all suspected criminals, the reasons for and the places of their detention, if they are detained, and the names and location of witnesses.

(c) shall take appropriate measures to see that witnesses and evidence will be available when required.

(d) shall have the right to cause all persons so arrested and charged, and not delivered to another authority as herein provided, or released, to be brought to trial before an appropriate tribunal. Such tribunal may, in the case of crimes committed by persons of German citizenship or nationality against other persons of German citizenship or nationality, or stateless persons, be a German Court, if authorized by the occupying authorities.

2.   The tribunal by which persons charged with offenses hereunder shall be tried and the rules and procedure thereof shall be determined or designated by each Zone Commander for his respective Zone. Nothing herein is intended to, or shall impair or limit the Jurisdiction or power of any court or tribunal now or hereafter established in any Zone by the Commander thereof, or of the International Military Tribunal established by the London Agreement of 8 August 1945.

. . .

# 1.5

# Decree of 31 August 1944 concerning the punishment of Fascist-Hitlerite criminals guilty of murder and ill-treatment of civilian population and of prisoners of war, and the punishment of traitors to the Polish Nation[7]

*The Polish Government-in-Exile's Decree of August 31, 1944 set forth the procedures and charges for the future trial of war criminals by special Polish courts. After consulting with the minister of justice, the Presidium of the National Council would appoint one professional and two lay judges to these courts, the verdicts of which would be nonappealable. In December 1946 the decree*

---

7. Source:   http://www.worldcourts.com/imt/eng/decisions/1948.07.10_Poland_v _Buhler.pdf (accessed July 16, 2019).

*was amended to include the language contained in Article 4 relating to criminal organizations. The change was inspired by the London Charter's Article 9 and the IMT's recognition that organizations whose very purpose was to commit acts in violation of international law could be declared criminal organizations.*

Article 1, Para. 1: Any person who, assisting the German authorities of occupation:

(a) took part in committing acts of murder, ill-treatment or persecution against the civilian population or prisoners of war;

(b) acted to the detriment of persons wanted or persecuted by the authorities of occupation for whatever reason it may be (with the exception of prosecution for common law crimes), by sentencing, detaining or deporting them—is liable to the death penalty.

Article 2. Any person who, assisting the authorities of the German State, or of a State allied with it, acted in any other manner or in any other circumstances than those indicated in Article 1 to the detriment of the Polish State, of a Polish corporate body, or of civilians, members of the armed forces and prisoners of war—is liable to imprisonment for a period of not less than three years, or for life, or to the death penalty.

Article 3, Para. 1. Any person who, taking advantage of the conditions created by the war, compelled persons to act under threat of persecution by the authorities of the German State, or by a State allied with it, or acted in any other manner to the detriment of persons wanted or persecuted by the said authorities—is liable to imprisonment for a period of not less than three years, or for life.

Article 4, Para. 1. Any person who was a member of a criminal organization established or recognized by the authorities of the German State or of a State allied with it, or by a political association which acted in the interest of the German State or a State allied with it is liable to imprisonment for a period of not less than three years, or for life, or to the death penalty.

Para. 2. A criminal organization in the meaning of para. 1 is a group or organization:

(a) which has as its aims the commission of crimes against peace, war crimes or crimes against humanity; or

(b) which while having a different aim, tries to attain it through the commission of crimes mentioned under (a).

Para. 3. Membership of the following organizations especially is considered criminal:

(a) the German National Socialist Workers' Party (National Sozialistische Deutsche Arbeiter Partei-NSDAP) as regards all leading positions,

(b) the Security Detachments (Schutzstaffeln-SS),

(c) the State Secret Police (Geheime Staats-Polizei-Gestapo),

(d) the Security Service (Sicherheitsdienst-SD).

Article 5, Para. 1. The fact that an act or omission was caused by a threat or order, or arose out of obligation under municipal law, does not exempt from criminal responsibility.

. . .

# 1.6

# Reich Penal Code, sec. 211 (murder), RStGB, as revised on September 4, 1941[8]

*Before 1941 murder under German law was straightforward: anyone who illegally killed another person with premeditation was guilty of murder. In 1941 the homicide statute was changed. Henceforth murder was defined as a killing actuated by an itemized list of reprehensible motives. The manner of killing, moreover, became an important factor: killings that were particularly socially harmful qualified as murder under the statute. From the mid-1940s until today, section 211 has been the law most frequently applied by German courts to the Nazis' worst crimes.*

(1)  The murderer will be punished with death.

---

8. Source:  https://www.jura.uni-bonn.de/fileadmin/Fachbereich_Rechtswissenschaft /Einrichtungen/Lehrstuehle/Stuckenberg/Materialien/UEbersicht211_Historie_ Rechtsvergleich.pdf (accessed July 7, 2019).

(2)   A murderer under this provision is any person who kills a person for pleasure, for sexual gratification, out of greed or otherwise base motives, treacherously or cruelly or by means that pose a danger to the public or in order to facilitate or to cover up another offence.

(3)   In special cases of exception in which the death penalty is not appropriate, the sentence shall be imprisonment for life.

# Section 2
# The Nuremberg War Crimes Trials:
# Selected Trial Documents

## 2.1

## The Verdict of the International Military Tribunal: Crimes against Peace and Conspiracy, September 30, 1946[9]

*Count One of the indictment at Nuremberg charged all of the accused with participating in "a common plan or conspiracy to commit . . . Crimes against Peace, War Crimes, and Crimes against Humanity." As the bedrock on which the allied case was built, conspiracy was for allied prosecutors the source of all Nazi crimes. Robert Jackson's assistant, Sydney Alderman, declared shortly after the trial began that "planning . . . illegal and aggressive war" was "the heart of the case." In its verdict of September 30–October 1, 1945, the tribunal agreed with the prosecution that the defendants had conspired to commit crimes against peace as early as November 1937. The tribunal refused, however, to endorse the prosecution's claim of a conspiracy to commit war crimes or crimes against humanity.*

### The Common Plan or Conspiracy and Aggressive War

The Tribunal now turns to the consideration of the Crimes against Peace charged in the Indictment. Count One of the Indictment charges the defendants with conspiring or having a common plan to commit crimes against peace. Count Two of the Indictment charges the defendants with committing specific crimes against peace by planning, preparing, initiating, and waging wars of aggression against a number of other states. . . .

---

9. Source: https://avalon.law.yale.edu/imt/09-30-46.asp (accessed July 7, 2019).

The charges in the Indictment that the defendants planned and waged aggressive wars are charges of the utmost gravity. War is essentially an evil thing. Its consequences are not confined to the belligerent states alone, but affect the whole world.

To initiate a war of aggression ... is not only an international crime; it is the supreme international crime differing only from other war crimes in that it contains within itself the accumulated evil of the whole.

The first acts of aggression referred to in the Indictment are the seizure of Austria and Czechoslovakia; and the first war of aggression charged in the Indictment is the war against Poland begun on 1 September 1939.

Before examining that charge it is necessary to look more closely at some of the events which preceded these acts of aggression. The war against Poland did not come suddenly out of an otherwise clear sky; the evidence has made it plain that this war of aggression, as well as the seizure of Austria and Czechoslovakia, was premeditated and carefully prepared, and was not undertaken until the moment was thought opportune for it to be carried through as a definite part of the preordained scheme and plan.

For the aggressive designs of the Nazi Government were not accidents arising out of the immediate political situation in Europe and the world; they were a deliberate and essential part of Nazi foreign policy.

From the beginning, the National Socialist movement claimed that its object was to unite the German people in the consciousness of their mission and destiny, based on inherent qualities of race, and under the guidance of the Führer.

For its achievement, two things were deemed to be essential; the disruption of the European order as it had existed since the Treaty of Versailles, and the creation of a Greater Germany beyond the frontiers of 1914. This necessarily involved the seizure of foreign territories.

War was seen to be inevitable, or at the very least, highly probable, if these purposes were to be accomplished. The German people, therefore, with all their resources, were to be organized as a great political-military army, schooled to obey without question any policy decreed by the State.

## Preparation for Aggression

In *Mein Kampf* Hitler had made this view quite plain. ... Over and over again Hitler asserted his belief in the necessity of force as the means of solving international problems, as in the following quotation:

"The soil on which we now live was not a gift bestowed by Heaven on our forefathers. They had to conquer it by risking their lives. So also in the future our people will not obtain territory, and therewith the means of existence, as a favor from any other people, but will have to win it by the power of a triumphant sword."

. . .

The precise objectives of this policy of force are also set forth in detail. The very first page of the book asserts that "German-Austria must be restored to the great German Motherland," not on economic grounds, but because "people of the same blood should be in the same Reich."

The restoration of the German frontiers of 1914 is declared to be wholly insufficient, and if Germany is to exist at all, it must be as a world power with the necessary territorial magnitude.

*Mein Kampf* is quite explicit in stating where the increased territory is to be found:

"Therefore we National Socialists have purposely drawn a line through the line of conduct followed by prewar Germany in foreign policy. . . . We put an end to the perpetual Germanic march towards the South and West of Europe, and turn our eyes towards the lands of the East. We finally put a stop to the colonial and trade policy of the prewar times, and pass over to the territorial policy of the future.

"But when we speak of new territory in Europe today, we must think principally of Russia and the border states subject to her."

*Mein Kampf* is not to be regarded as a mere literary exercise, nor as an inflexible policy or plan incapable of modification.

Its importance lies in the unmistakable attitude of aggression revealed throughout its pages.

## The Planning of Aggression

Evidence from captured documents has revealed that Hitler held four secret meetings to which the Tribunal proposes to make special reference because of the light they shed upon the question of the common plan and aggressive war.

These meetings took place on 5 November 1937, 23 May 1939, August 1939, and 23 November 1939.

At these meetings important declarations were made by Hitler as to his purposes, which are quite unmistakable in their terms.

. . .

## Conferences of 23 November 1939 and 5 November 1937

It will perhaps be useful to deal first of all with the meeting of November 1939, when Hitler called his supreme commanders together. A record was made of what was said, by one of those present. At the date of the meeting, Austria and Czechoslovakia had been incorporated into the German Reich, Poland had been conquered by the German armies, and the war with Great Britain and France was still in its static phase. The moment was opportune for a review of past events. Hitler informed the commanders that the purpose of the conference was to give them an idea of the world of his thoughts, and to tell them his decision. He thereupon reviewed his political task since 1919, and referred to the secession of Germany from the League of Nations, the denunciation of the Disarmament Conference, the order for rearmament, the introduction of compulsory armed service, the occupation of the Rhineland, the seizure of Austria, and the action against Czechoslovakia. He stated:

"One year later, Austria came; this step also was considered doubtful. It brought about a considerable reinforcement of the Reich. The next step was Bohemia, Moravia, and Poland. This step also was not possible to accomplish in one campaign. First of all, the western fortification had to be finished. It was not possible to reach the goal in one effort. It was clear to me from the first moment that I could not be satisfied with the Sudeten German territory. That was only a partial solution. The decision to march into Bohemia was made. Then followed the erection of the Protectorate and with that the basis for the action against Poland was laid, but I was not quite clear at that time whether I should start first against the East and then in the West or vice versa.... Basically I did not organize the Armed Forces in order not to strike. The decision to strike was always in me. Earlier or later I wanted to solve the problem. Under pressure it was decided that the East was to be attacked first."

This address, reviewing past events and reaffirming the aggressive intentions present from the beginning, puts beyond any question of doubt the character of the actions against Austria and Czechoslovakia, and the war against Poland.

For they had all been accomplished according to plan; and the nature of that plan must now be examined in a little more detail.

At the meeting of 23 November 1939 Hitler was looking back to things accomplished; at the earlier meetings now to be considered, he was looking forward, and revealing his plans to his confederates. The comparison is instructive.

The meeting held at the Reich Chancellery in Berlin on 5 November 1937 was attended by Lt. Col. Hossbach, Hitler's personal adjutant, who compiled a long note of the proceedings, which he dated 10 November 1937 and signed.

The persons present were Hitler, and the Defendants Göring, von Neurath and Raeder, in their capacities as Commander-in-Chief of the Luftwaffe, Reich Foreign Minister, and Commander-in-Chief of the Navy respectively, General Von Blomberg, Minister of War, and General Von Fritsch, the Commander-in-Chief of the Army.

Hitler began by saying that the subject of the conference was of such high importance that in other states it would have taken place before the Cabinet. He went on to say that the subject matter of his speech was the result of his detailed deliberations, and of his experiences during his four and a half years of government. He requested that the statements he was about to make should be looked upon in the case of his death as his last will and testament. Hitler's main theme was the problem of living space, and he discussed various possible solutions, only to set them aside. He then said that the seizure of living space on the continent of Europe was therefore necessary, expressing himself in these words:

"It is not a case of conquering people but of conquering agriculturally useful space. It would also be more to the purpose to seek raw-material-producing territory in Europe directly adjoining the Reich and not overseas, and this solution would have to be brought into effect for one or two generations. . . . The history of all times—Roman Empire, British Empire—has proved that every space expansion can only be effected by breaking resistance and taking risks. Even setbacks are unavoidable: neither formerly nor today has space been found without an owner; the attacker always comes up against the proprietor."

He concluded with this observation:

"The question for Germany is where the greatest possible conquest could be made at the lowest cost."

Nothing could indicate more plainly the aggressive intentions of Hitler, and the events which soon followed showed the reality of his purpose. It is impossible to accept the contention that Hitler did not actually mean war; for after pointing out that Germany might expect the opposition of England and France, and analyzing the strength and the weakness of those powers in particular situations, he continued:

"The German question can be solved only by way of force, and this is never without risk. . . . If we place the decision to apply force with risk at the head of the following expositions, then we are left to reply to the questions 'when' and 'how.' In this regard we have to decide upon three different cases."

The first of these three cases set forth a hypothetical international situation, in which he would take action not later than 1943 to 1945, saying:

"If the Führer is still living then it will be his irrevocable decision to solve the German space problem not later than 1943 to 1945. The necessity for action before 1943 to 1945 will come under consideration in Cases 2 and 3."

The second and third cases to which Hitler referred show the plain intention to seize Austria and Czechoslovakia, and in this connection Hitler said:

"For the improvement of our military-political position, it must be our first aim in every case of entanglement by war to conquer Czechoslovakia and Austria simultaneously in order to remove any threat from the flanks in case of a possible advance westwards."

He further added:

"The annexation of the two states to Germany militarily and politically would constitute a considerable relief, owing to shorter and better frontiers, the freeing of fighting personnel for other purposes, and the possibility of reconstituting new armies up to a strength of about twelve divisions."

This decision to seize Austria and Czechoslovakia was discussed in some detail; the action was to be taken as soon as a favorable opportunity presented itself.

The military strength which Germany had been building up since 1933 was now to be directed at the two specific countries, Austria and Czechoslovakia.

The Defendant Göring testified that he did not believe at that time that Hitler actually meant to attack Austria and Czechoslovakia, and that the purpose of the conference was only to put pressure on Von Fritsch to speed up the rearmament of the Army.

The Defendant Raeder testified that neither he, nor Von Fritsch, nor Von Blomberg, believed that Hitler actually meant war, a conviction which the Defendant Raeder claims that he held up to 22 August 1939. The basis of this conviction was his hope that Hitler would obtain a "political solution" of Germany's problems. But all that this means, when examined, is the belief that Germany's position would be so good, and Germany's armed might so overwhelming, that the territory desired could be obtained without fighting for it. It must be remembered too that

Hitler's declared intention with regard to Austria was actually carried out within a little over four months from the date of the meeting, and within less than a year the first portion of Czechoslovakia was absorbed, and Bohemia and Moravia a few months later. If any doubts had existed in the minds of any of his hearers in November 1937, after March of 1939 there could no longer be any question that Hitler was in deadly earnest in his decision to resort to war. The Tribunal is satisfied that Lt. Col. Hossbach's account of the meeting is substantially correct, and that those present knew that Austria and Czechoslovakia would be annexed by Germany at the first possible opportunity. . . .

· · ·

In the opinion of the Tribunal, the evidence establishes the common planning to prepare and wage war by certain of the defendants. It is immaterial to consider whether a single conspiracy to the extent and over the time set out in the Indictment has been conclusively proved. Continued planning, with aggressive war as the objective, has been established beyond doubt.

· · ·

Count One, however, charges not only the conspiracy to commit aggressive war, but also to commit War Crimes and Crimes against Humanity. But the Charter does not define as a separate crime any conspiracy except the one to commit acts of aggressive war. Article 6 of the Charter provides:

"Leaders, organizers, instigators and accomplices participating in the formulation or execution of a common plan or conspiracy to commit any of the foregoing crimes are responsible for all acts performed by any persons in execution of such plan."

In the opinion of the Tribunal these words do not add a new and separate crime to those already listed. The words are designed to establish the responsibility of persons participating in a common plan. The Tribunal will therefore disregard the charges in Count One that the defendants conspired to commit War Crimes and Crimes against Humanity, and will consider only the common plan to prepare, initiate and wage aggressive war. . . .

## The Law Relating to War Crimes and Crimes against Humanity

. . . the Charter does not define as a separate Crime any conspiracy except the one set out in Article 6(a), dealing with Crimes against Peace. . . .

The Tribunal is of course bound by the Charter, in the definition which it gives both of War Crimes and Crimes against Humanity. With respect to War Crimes, however, as has already been pointed out, the crimes defined by Article 6, section (b) of the Charter were already recognized as War Crimes under international law. They were covered by Articles 46, 50, 52, and 56 of the Hague Convention of 1907, and Articles 2, 3, 4, 46, and 51 of the Geneva Convention of 1929. That violations of these provisions constituted crimes for which the guilty individuals were punishable is too well settled to admit of argument.

. . .

With regard to crimes against humanity, there is no doubt whatever that political opponents were murdered in Germany before the war, and that many of them were kept in concentration camps in circumstances of great horror and cruelty. . . . The persecution of Jews during the same period is established beyond all doubt. To constitute crimes against humanity, the acts relied on before the outbreak of war must have been in execution of, or in connection with, any crime within the jurisdiction of the Tribunal. The Tribunal is of the opinion that revolting and horrible as many of these crimes were, it has not been satisfactorily proved that they were done in execution of, or in connection with, any such crime. The Tribunal therefore cannot make a general declaration that the acts before 1939 were Crimes against Humanity within the meaning of the Charter, but from the beginning of the war in 1939 war crimes were committed on a vast scale, which were also crimes against humanity; and insofar as the inhumane acts charged in the Indictment, and committed after the beginning of the war, did not constitute war crimes, they were all committed in execution of, or in connection with, the aggressive war, and therefore constituted crimes against humanity. . . .

## 2.2

# The Verdict of the International Military Tribunal: The Criminal Organizations Charge, September 30, 1946

*Citing Article 9 of the charter, the prosecution asked the tribunal to declare seven Nazi groups "criminal organizations." The seven were the Leadership Corps of the Nazi Party, the Security Service, the Gestapo, the Reich Cabinet, the SS, the Army High Command, and the SA. The IMT granted the prosecution's request, but only with respect to four of these groups.*

## The Accused Organizations[10]

. . .

A criminal organization is analogous to a criminal conspiracy in that the essence of both is cooperation for criminal purposes. There must be a group bound together and organized for a common purpose. The group must be formed or used in connection with the commission of crimes denounced by the Charter. Since the declaration with respect to the organizations and groups will, as has been pointed out, fix the criminality of its members, that definition should exclude persons who had no knowledge of the criminal purposes or acts of the organization and those who were drafted by the state for membership, unless they were personally implicated in the commission of acts declared criminal by Article 6 of the Charter as members of the organization. Membership alone is not enough to come within the scope of these declarations.

. . .

## The Leadership Corps of the Nazi Party

Structure and Component Parts: The Indictment has named the Leadership Corps of the Nazi Party as a group or organization which should be declared criminal. The Leadership Corps of the Nazi Party consisted, in effect, of the official organization of the Nazi Party, with Hitler as Führer at its head. The actual work of running the Leadership Corps was carried out by the Chief of the Party Chancellery (Hess, succeeded by Bormann) assisted by the Party Reich Directorate, or Reichsleitung, which was composed of the Reichsleiter, the heads of the functional organizations of the Party, as well as of the heads of the various main departments and offices which were attached to the Party Reich Directorate. Under the Chief of the Party Chancellery were the Gauleiter, with territorial jurisdiction over the major administrative regions of the Party, the Gaue. The Gauleiter were assisted by a Party Gaue Directorate

---

10. Source: https://avalon.law.yale.edu/imt/09-30-46.asp (accessed August 6, 2019).

or Gauleitung, similar in composition and in function to the Party Reich Directorate. Under the Gauleiter in the Party hierarchy were the Kreisleiter with territorial jurisdiction over a Kreis, usually consisting of a single county, and assisted by a Party Kreis Directorate, or Kreisleitung. The Kreisleiter were the lowest members of the Party hierarchy who were full-time paid employees. Directly under the Kreisleiter were the Ortsgruppenleiter, then the Zellenleiter and then the Blockleiter. Directives and instructions were received from the Party Reich Directorate. The Gauleiter had the function of interpreting such orders and issuing them to lower formations. The Kreisleiter had a certain discretion in interpreting orders, but the Ortsgruppenleiter had not, but acted under definite instructions. Instructions were only issued in writing down as far as the Ortsgruppenleiter. The Block- and Zellenleiter usually received instructions orally. . . .

· · ·

The Leadership Corps was used for purposes which were criminal under the Charter and involved the Germanization of incorporated territory, the persecution of the Jews, the administration of the slave labor program, and the mistreatment of prisoners of war. The Defendants Bormann[11] and Sauckel,[12] who were members of this organization, were among those who used it for these purposes. The Gauleiter, the Kreisleiter, and the Ortsgruppenleiter[13] participated, to one degree or another, in these

---

11. Martin Bormann (1900–1945) was Hitler's de facto deputy prior to his appointment as secretary to the Führer in April 1943. Although it is now believed he committed suicide on May 2, 1945, in Berlin, the Allies presumed he was still alive in 1945, leading to his indictment in absentia and his conviction and death sentence by the IMT on October 1, 1945. A West German court pronounced him legally deceased in April 1973.

12. Fritz Sauckel (1894–1946) was plenipotentiary-general for Labor Mobilization from 1942 to 1945 who, among other crimes, deported some five million people from German-occupied territories to slave labor in Germany. He was convicted of war crimes and executed in Nuremberg on October 16, 1946.

13. The Gauleiter, Kreisleiter, and Ortsgruppenleiter were offices within the hierarchy of the Nazi Party structure. The Gauleiter was the head of one of the forty-three Gaue, or territorial units, into which the Nazis subdivided Germany. The Gaue were in turn subdivided into Kreise, or districts, headed by a Kreisleiter. Finally, the Kreise were organized into Ortsgruppe (chapters or local groups) at the helm of which stood the Ortsgruppenleiter.

criminal programs. The Reichsleitung[14] as the staff organization of the Party is also responsible for these criminal programs as well as the heads of the various staff organizations of the Gauleiter and Kreisleiter. The decision of the Tribunal on these staff organizations includes only the Amtsleiter who were heads of offices on the staffs of the Reichsleitung, Gauleitung, and Kreisleitung. With respect to other staff officers and party organizations attached to the Leadership Corps other than the Amtsleiter referred to above, the Tribunal will follow the suggestion of the Prosecution in excluding them from the declaration. The Tribunal declares to be criminal within the meaning of the Charter the group composed of those members of the Leadership Corps holding the positions enumerated in the preceding paragraph who became or remained members of the organization with knowledge that it was being used for the commission of acts declared criminal by Article 6 of the Charter, or who were personally implicated as members of the organization in the commission of such crimes. The basis of this finding is the participation of the organization in war crimes and crimes against humanity connected with the war; the group declared criminal cannot include, therefore, persons who had ceased to hold the positions enumerated in the preceding paragraph prior to 1 September 1939.

## Gestapo and SD

. . .

The Gestapo and SD[15] were used for purposes which were criminal under the Charter, involving the persecution and extermination of the Jews, brutalities and killings in concentration camps, excesses in the administration of occupied territories, the administration of the slave labor program and the mistreatment and murder of prisoners of war. The Defendant Kaltenbrunner,[16] who was a member of this organization,

---

14. The Reichsleitung (Reich administration) consisted of eighteen offices, or Reichsleiter (Reich administrators), which were the preeminent political offices of the Nazi Party. Subordinate only to Hitler and his deputies, the eighteen Reichsleiter performed functions that spanned the entire Reich.

15. *Sicherheitsdienst,* or "security service," a department of the Reich Security Main Office responsible for foreign and domestic intelligence.

16. Ernst Kaltenbrunner (1903–1946), successor to Reinhard Heydrich as the head of the Reich Security Main Office in January 1943. Kaltenbrunner was tried, convicted, and hanged by the IMT in 1946.

was among those who used it for these purposes. In dealing with the Gestapo the Tribunal includes all executive and administrative officials of Amt IV of the [Reich Security Main Office, or RSHA],[17] or concerned with Gestapo administration in other departments of the RSHA, and all local Gestapo officials serving both inside and outside of Germany, including the members of the Frontier Police, but not including the members of the Border and Customs Protection or the Secret Field Police. . . . At the suggestion of the Prosecution the Tribunal does not include persons employed by the Gestapo for purely clerical, stenographic, janitorial, or similar unofficial routine tasks. In dealing with the SD the Tribunal includes Ämter III, VI, and VII of the RSHA and all other members of the SD, including all local representatives and agents, honorary or otherwise, whether they were technically members of the SS or not.

The Tribunal declares to be criminal within the meaning of the Charter the group composed of those members of the Gestapo and SD holding the positions enumerated in the preceding paragraph who became or remained members of the organization with knowledge that it was being used for the commission of acts declared criminal by Article 6 of the Charter, or who were personally implicated as members of the organization in the commission of such crimes. The basis for this finding is the participation of the organization in war crimes and crimes against humanity connected with the war; this group declared criminal cannot include, therefore, persons who had ceased to hold the positions enumerated in the preceding paragraph prior to 1 September 1939.

## SS

. . .

The SS was utilized for purposes which were criminal under the Charter involving the persecution and extermination of the Jews, brutalities and killings in concentration camps, excesses in the administration of occupied territories, the administration of the slave labor program, and the mistreatment and murder of prisoners of war. The Defendant Kaltenbrunner was a member of the SS implicated in these activities. In dealing with the

---

17. The Reich Security Main Office (RSHA) was a branch of the SS that comprised the Security Police and Security Service. The Security Police, in turn, consisted of the Criminal Police and the Gestapo. All of its components were active participants in the planning, organization, and execution of the Final Solution.

SS the Tribunal includes all persons who had been officially accepted as members of the SS, including the members of the Allgemeine SS, members of the Waffen-SS, members of the SS Totenkopf-verbände,[18] and the members of any of the different police forces who were members of the SS. The Tribunal does not include the so-called SS riding units.

· · ·

The Tribunal declares to be criminal within the meaning of the Charter the group composed of those persons who had been officially accepted as members of the SS as enumerated in the preceding paragraph, who became or remained members of the organization with knowledge that it was being used for the commission of acts declared criminal by Article 6 of the Charter, or who were personally implicated as members of the organization in the commission of such crimes, excluding, however, those who were drafted into membership by the State in such a way as to give them no choice in the matter, and who had committed no such crimes. The basis of this finding is the participation of the organization in war crimes and crimes against humanity connected with the war; this group declared criminal cannot include, therefore, persons who had ceased to belong to the organizations enumerated in the preceding paragraph prior to 1 September 1939.

[The tribunal declined characterizing the Reich Cabinet, SA, and High Command criminal organizations; the judges were not convinced they were specifically used to commit crimes against peace, war crimes, and crimes against humanity.]

# 2.3

# The American Military Tribunals at Nuremberg: The Judgment in the Doctors Trial, August 20, 1947

*The first of the twelve successor trials conducted by the Americans at Nuremberg, U.S. v. Karl Brandt et al. (or the "Doctors Trial"), began on November 21, 1946. The twenty-three*

---

18. SS Totenkopfverbände (SS Death's Head Units) were units assigned to guard and administer the concentration camps first set up by the Nazis in 1933.

*defendants were members of the public or military health ser-
vice implicated in harmful medical experiments conducted on
concentration camp prisoners and allied POWs without consent.
All save three of the accused were doctors. Although they faced
other charges, for example involuntary sterilization and euthanasia, the most serious charge, found in Count Two, related to
the gruesome medical experiments performed in the camps.
The judges presiding over the case were so moved by the hair-
raising accounts of medical atrocity that they expounded a set of
principles to govern permissible medical experimentation—principles that since their announcement have become known as the
"Nuremberg Code."*

## THE CHARGE[19]

The indictment is framed in four counts.

COUNT ONE—*The Common Design or Conspiracy.* The first count of
the indictment charges that the defendants, acting pursuant to a common design, unlawfully, willfully, and knowingly did conspire and agree
together to commit war crimes and crimes against humanity, as defined
in Control Council Law No. 10.

During the course of the trial the defendants challenged the first count
of the indictment, alleging as grounds for their motion the fact that under
the basic law the Tribunal did not have jurisdiction to try the crime of
conspiracy considered as a separate substantive offense. The motion
was set down for argument and duly argued by counsel for the prosecution and the defense. Thereafter, in one of its trial sessions the Tribunal granted the motion. That this judgment may be complete, the ruling
made at that time is incorporated in this judgment. The order which was
entered on the motion is as follows:

"It is the ruling of this Tribunal that neither the Charter of the International Military Tribunal nor Control Council Law No. 10 has defined
conspiracy to commit a war crime or crime against humanity as a separate substantive crime; therefore, this Tribunal has no jurisdiction to try
any defendant upon a charge of conspiracy considered as a separate substantive offense.

---

19. Source: https://www.legal-tools.org/doc/c18557/pdf/ (accessed July 8, 2019).

"Count I of the indictment, in addition to the separate charge of conspiracy, also alleges unlawful participation in the formulation and execution of plans to commit war crimes and crimes against humanity which actually involved the commission of such crimes. We, therefore, cannot properly strike the whole of count I from the indictment, but, insofar as count I charges the commission of the alleged crime of conspiracy as a separate substantive offense, distinct from any war crime or crime against humanity, the Tribunal will disregard that charge.

"This ruling must not be construed as limiting the force or effect of Article 2, paragraph 2 of Control Council Law No. 10, or as denying to either prosecution or defense the right to offer in evidence any facts or circumstances occurring either before or after September 1939, if such facts or circumstances tend to prove or to disprove the commission by any defendant—of war crimes or crimes against humanity as defined in Control Council Law No. 10."

COUNTS TWO AND THREE—*War Crimes and Crimes against Humanity.* The second and third counts of the indictment charge the commission of war crimes and crimes against humanity. The counts are identical in content, except for the fact that in count two the acts which are made the basis for the charges are alleged to have been committed on "civilians and members of the armed forces [of nations] then at war with the German Reich . . . in the exercise of belligerent control," whereas in count three the criminal acts are alleged to have been committed against "'German civilians and nationals of other countries." With this distinction observed, both counts will be treated as one and discussed together.

Counts two and three allege, in substance, that between September 1939 and April 1945 all of the defendants "were principals in, accessories to, ordered, abetted, took a consenting part in, and were connected with plans and enterprises involving medical experiments without the subjects' consent . . . in the course of which experiments the defendants committed murders, brutalities, cruelties, tortures, atrocities, and other inhuman acts." It is averred that "such experiments included, but were not limited to" the following:

"(A) *High-Altitude Experiments.* From about March 1942 to about August 1942 experiments were conducted at the Dachau concentration camp, for the benefit of the German Air Force, to investigate the limits of human endurance and existence at extremely high altitudes. The experiments were carried out in a low-pressure chamber in which the atmospheric conditions and pressures prevailing at high altitude (up to 68,000 feet) could be duplicated. The experimental subjects were placed in the low-pressure chamber and thereafter the simulated altitude therein was raised. Many victims died as a result of these experiments and others suffered grave injury, torture, and ill-treatment. The defendants Karl Brandt, Handloser, Schroeder, Gebhardt, Rudolf Brandt, Mrugowsky, Poppendick, Sievers, Ruff, Romberg, Becker-Freyseng, and Weltz[20] are charged with special responsibility for and participation in these crimes.

"(B) *Freezing Experiments.* From about August 1942 to about May 1943 experiments were conducted at the Dachau concentration camp, primarily for the benefit of the German Air Force, to investigate the most effective means of treating persons who had been severely chilled or frozen. In one series of experiments the subjects were forced to remain in a tank of ice water for periods up to 3 hours. Extreme rigor developed in

---

20. Karl Brandt (1904–1948) was for a time Hitler's personal physician and the Reich commissioner for the Emergency Medical and Health Care System (the highest ranking health care official in the Reich). He was convicted of war crimes and crimes against humanity and hanged at Landsberg prison in June 1948. Siegfried Handloser (1885–1954) was chief of the Medical Services of the German Armed Forces during the war. Convicted at the Doctors Trial in 1947, he was given a life sentence but released from prison in 1954 shortly before his death. Oskar Schroeder (1891–1959), chief of the Medical Service of the Luftwaffe, was convicted at the same trial and given a life sentence. He was released from prison in 1954. Himmler's personal physician and chief surgeon of the Staff of the Reich Physician and Police, Karl Gebhardt (1897–1948), was convicted at the Doctors Trial and executed in June 1948 at Landsberg prison. Rudolf Brandt (1909–1948) was a personal advisor to Himmler and director of the Office of Ministers in the Reich Ministry of the Interior. Convicted for his involvement in murdering eighty-six Jews for a skeleton collection in Strassburg, he was executed in Landsberg in June 1948. Joachim Mrugowsky (1905–1948) was supreme medical specialist in the office of the SS Reich Physician, in connection with which he was responsible for concentration camp medical experiments. He was convicted and executed in Landsberg in June 1948. Helmut Poppendick (1902–1994), the chief of the personal staff of the SS Reich Physician, was convicted and sentenced to a ten-year prison sentence; he was released from prison in 1951. Wolfram Sievers (1905–1948), the Reich manager of the SS-Ahnenerbe (SS-Ancestral Heritage), was convicted in August 1947 and executed in Landsberg in June 1948. Siegfried Ruff (1907–1989), director of the Aviation Medicine Department of the German Experimental Institute for Aviation, was acquitted, as were his codefendants Wolfgang Romberg (1911–1981), an aviation physician, and Georg Weltz (1889–1963), a radiologist and aviation physician. Hermann Becker-Freyseng, a Luftwaffe physician, was implicated in experiments on the Roma at the Dachau camp; he was convicted and sentenced to a twenty-year prison term, from which he was released in 1952.

a short time. Numerous victims died in the course of these experiments. After the survivors were severely chilled, rewarming was attempted by various means. In another series of experiments, the subjects were kept naked outdoors for many hours at temperatures below freezing. ". . . The defendants Karl Brandt, Handloser, Schroeder, Gebhardt, Rudolf Brandt, Mrugowsky, Poppendick, Sievers, Becker-Freyseng, and Weltz are charged with special responsibility for and participation in these crimes.

"(C) *Malaria Experiments.* From about February 1942 to about April 1945 experiments were conducted at the Dachau concentration camp in order to investigate immunization for and treatment of malaria. Healthy concentration camp inmates were infected by mosquitoes or by injections of extracts of the mucous glands of mosquitoes. After having contracted malaria the subjects were treated with various drugs to test their relative efficacy. Over 1,000 involuntary subjects were used in these experiments. Many of the victims died and others suffered severe pain and permanent disability. . . .

"(D) *Lost (Mustard) Gas Experiments.* At various times between September 1939 and April 1945 experiments were conducted at Sachsenhausen, Natzweiler, and other concentration camps for the benefit of the German Armed Forces to investigate the most effective treatment of wounds caused by Lost gas. Lost is a poison gas which is commonly known as mustard gas. Wounds deliberately inflicted on the subjects were infected with Lost. Some of the subjects died as a result of these experiments and others suffered intense pain and injury. . . .

"(E) *Sulfanilamide Experiments.* From about July 1942 to about September 1943 experiments to investigate the effectiveness of sulfanilamide were conducted at the Ravensbrueck concentration camp for the benefit of the German Armed Forces. Wounds deliberately inflicted on the experimental subjects were infected with bacteria such as streptococcus, gas gangrene, and tetanus. Circulation of blood was interrupted by tying off blood vessels at both ends of the wound to create a condition similar to that of a battlefield wound. Infection was aggravated by forcing wood shavings and ground glass into the wounds. The infection was treated with sulfanilamide and other drugs to determine their effectiveness. Some subjects died as a result of these experiments and others suffered serious injury and intense agony. . . .

"(F) *Bone, Muscle, and Nerve Regeneration and Bone Transplantation Experiments.* From about September 1942 to about December 1943 experiments were conducted at the Ravensbrueck concentration camp, for the benefit of the German Armed Forces, to study bone, muscle, and nerve regeneration, and bone transplantation from one person to another. Sections of bones, muscles, and nerves were removed from the subjects. As a result of these operations, many victims suffered intense agony, mutilation, and permanent disability. . . .

"(G) *Sea-Water Experiments.* From about July 1944 to about September 1944 experiments were conducted at the Dachau Concentration camp, for the benefit of the German Air Force and Navy, to study various methods of making sea water drinkable. The subjects were deprived of all food and given only chemically processed sea water. Such experiments caused great pain and suffering and resulted in serious bodily injury to the victims. . . .

"(H) *Epidemic Jaundice Experiments.* From about June 1943 to about January 1945 experiments were conducted at the Sachsenhausen and Natzweiler concentration camps, for the benefit of the German Armed Forces, to investigate the causes of, and inoculations against, epidemic jaundice. Experimental subjects were deliberately infected with epidemic jaundice, some of whom died as a result, and others were caused great pain and suffering. . . .

"(I) *Sterilization Experiments.* From about March 1941 to about January 1945 sterilization experiments were conducted at the Auschwitz and Ravensbrueck concentration camps, and other places. The purpose of these experiments was to develop a method of sterilization which would be suitable for sterilizing millions of people with a minimum of time and effort. These experiments were conducted by means of X-ray, surgery, and various drugs. Thousands of victims were sterilized and thereby suffered great mental and physical anguish. . . .

"(J) *Spotted Fever (Fleckfieber) Experiments.* From about December 1941 to about February 1945 experiments were conducted at the Buchenwald and Natzweiler concentration camps, for the benefit of the German Armed Forces, to investigate the effectiveness of spotted fever and other vaccines. At Buchenwald, numerous healthy inmates were deliberately infected with spotted fever virus in order to keep the virus alive; over 90 percent of the victims died as a result. Other healthy inmates were used to determine the effectiveness of different spotted fever vaccines and of various chemical substances. In the course of these experiments 75 percent of the selected number of inmates were vaccinated with one of the vaccines or nourished with one of the chemical substances and, after a period of 3 to 4 weeks, were infected with spotted fever germs. The remaining 25 percent were infected without any previous protection in order to compare the effectiveness of the vaccines and the chemical substances. As a result, hundreds of the persons experimented upon died. Experiments with yellow fever, smallpox, typhus, paratyphus A and B, cholera, and diphtheria were also conducted. Similar experiments with like results were conducted at Natzweiler concentration camp. . . .

"(K) *Experiments with Poison*. In or about December 1943 and in or about October 1944 experiments were conducted at the Buchenwald concentration camp to investigate the effect of various poisons upon human beings. The poisons were secretly administered to experimental subjects in their food. The victims died as a result of the poison or were killed immediately in order to permit autopsies. In or about September 1944 experimental subjects were shot with poison bullets and suffered torture and death. . . .

"(L) *Incendiary Bomb Experiments*. From about November 1943 to about January 1944 experiments were conducted at the Buchenwald concentration camp to test the effect of various pharmaceutical preparations on phosphorus burns. These burns were inflicted on experimental subjects with phosphorus matter taken from incendiary bombs, and caused severe pain, suffering, and serious bodily injury.

. . .

## THE PROOF AS TO WAR CRIMES AND CRIMES AGAINST HUMANITY

Judged by any standard of proof the record clearly shows the commission of war crimes and crimes against humanity substantially as alleged in counts two and three of the indictment. Beginning with the outbreak of World War II criminal medical experiments on non-German nationals, both prisoners of war and civilians, including Jews and "asocial" persons, were carried out on a large scale in Germany and the occupied countries. These experiments were not the isolated and casual acts of individual doctors and scientists working solely on their own responsibility, but were the product of coordinated policy-making and planning at high governmental, military, and Nazi Party levels, conducted as an integral part of the total war effort. They were ordered, sanctioned, permitted, or approved by persons in positions of authority who under all principles of law were under the duty to know about these things and to take steps to terminate or prevent them.

## PERMISSIBLE MEDICAL EXPERIMENTS

The great weight of the evidence before us is to the effect that certain types of medical experiments on human beings, when kept within reasonably well-defined bounds, conform to the ethics of the medical profession generally. The protagonists of the practice of human experimentation justify their views on the basis that such experiments yield results for the good of society that are unprocurable by other methods or means of study. All agree, however, that certain basic principles must be observed in order to satisfy moral, ethical and legal concepts:

1.  The voluntary consent of the human subject is absolutely essential.

    This means that the person involved should have legal capacity to give consent; should be so situated as to be able to exercise free power of choice, without the intervention of any element of force, fraud, deceit, duress, over-reaching, or other ulterior form of constraint or coercion; and should have sufficient knowledge and comprehension of the elements of the subject matter involved as to enable him to make an understanding and enlightened decision. This latter element requires that before the acceptance of an affirmative decision by the experimental subject there should be made known to him the nature, duration, and purpose of the experiment; the method and means by which it is to be conducted; all inconveniences and hazards reasonably to be expected; and the effects upon his health or person which may possibly come from his participation in the experiment.

    The duty and responsibility for ascertaining the quality of the consent rests upon each individual who initiates, directs or engages in the experiment. It is a personal duty and responsibility which may not be delegated to another with impunity.

2.  The experiment should be such as to yield fruitful results for the good of society, unprocurable by other methods or means of study, and not random and unnecessary in nature.

3.  The experiment should be so designed and based on the results of animal experimentation and a knowledge of the natural history of the disease or other problem under study that the anticipated results will justify the performance of the experiment.

4.  The experiment should be so conducted as to avoid all unnecessary physical and mental suffering and injury.

5.    No experiment should be conducted where there is an *a priori* reason to believe that death or disabling injury will occur; except, perhaps, in those experiments where the experimental physicians also serve as subjects.

6.    The degree of risk to be taken should never exceed that determined by the humanitarian importance of the problem to be solved by the experiment.

7.    Proper preparations should be made and adequate facilities provided to protect the experimental subject against even remote possibilities of injury, disability, or death.

8.    The experiment should be conducted only by scientifically qualified persons. The highest degree of skill and care should be required through all stages of the experiment of those who conduct or engage in the experiment.

9.    During the course of the experiment the human subject should be at liberty to bring the experiment to an end if he has reached the physical or mental state where continuation of the experiment seems to him to be impossible.

10.   During the course of the experiment the scientist in charge must be prepared to terminate the experiment at any stage, if he has probable cause to believe, in the exercise of the good faith, superior skill and careful judgment required of him that a continuation of the experiment is likely to result in injury, disability, or death to the experimental subject.

Of the ten principles which have been enumerated our judicial concern, of course, is with those requirements which are purely legal in nature. . . . We find from the evidence that in the medical experiments which have been proved, these ten principles were much more frequently honored in their breach than in their observance. Many of the concentration camp inmates who were the victims of these atrocities were citizens of countries other than the German Reich. They were non-German nationals, including Jews and "asocial persons," both prisoners of war and civilians, who had been imprisoned and forced to submit to these tortures and barbarities without so much as a semblance of trial. In every single instance appearing in the record, subjects were used who did not consent to the experiments; indeed, as to some of the experiments, it is not even contended by the defendants that the subjects occupied the status of volunteers. In no case was the experimental subject at liberty of his own free choice to withdraw from any experiment. In many cases experiments were performed by unqualified persons; were conducted at random for no adequate scientific reason, and under revolting physical conditions. All of the experiments were conducted with unnecessary suffering and injury and but very little, if any, precautions were taken to protect or safeguard the human subjects from the possibilities of injury, disability, or death. In every one of the experiments the subjects experienced extreme pain or torture, and in most of them they suffered permanent injury, mutilation, or death, either as a direct result of the experiments or because of lack of adequate follow-up care.

Obviously all of these experiments involving brutalities, tortures, disabling injury, and death were performed in complete disregard of international conventions, the laws and customs of war, the general principles of criminal law as derived from the criminal laws of all civilized nations, and Control Council Law No. 10. Manifestly human experiments under such conditions are contrary to "the principles of the law of nations as they result from the usages established among civilized peoples, from the laws of humanity, and from the dictates of public conscience."

. . .

## 2.4

## The American Military Tribunals at Nuremberg: The Judgment in the Justice Case, December 3–4, 1947[21]

*The 1947 trial of sixteen former members of the Reich Ministry of Justice, the People's Court, and the special courts (U.S. v. Josef Altstoetter, or the "justice case") is usefully paired with the Doctor's Trial as an example of the US prosecutorial strategy of indicting German professionals for their complicity in Nazi crimes. The Americans charged the defendants with committing "judicial*

21. Source: http://www.worldcourts.com/imt/eng/decisions/1947.12.04_United States_v_Altstoetter.pdf (accessed July 9, 2019).

*murder" by using the law to persecute, enslave, and exterminate
entire ethnic groups. The case is notable for Military Tribunal III's
interpretations of international law as it bore on German atrocities. The judges rejected the defendants' ex post facto and superior orders defenses and insisted that crimes against humanity
were not wholly reliant on warfare for their prosecution. This last
point emerged from the tribunal's probing and caustic analysis of
the crimes of Oswald Rothaug, a special court judge in Nuremberg during the war.*

. . . The defendant is charged under counts two, three, and four of the
indictment. Under count four he is charged with being a member of the
Party Leadership Corps. He is not charged with membership in the SD.
The proof as to count four establishes that he was Gauwalter of the Lawyers' League. The Lawyers' League was a formation of the Party and not a
part of the Leadership Corps as determined by the International Military
Tribunal in the case against Goering [Göring], et al.

As to counts two and four of the indictment, from the evidence submitted, the Tribunal finds the defendant not guilty. The question of
the defendant's guilt as to count three of the indictment remains to be
determined.

The evidence as to the character and activities of the defendant is volu-
minous. We shall confine ourselves to the question as to whether or not
he took a consenting part in the plan for the persecution, oppression, and
extermination of Poles and Jews.

His attitude of virulent hostility toward these races is proved from
many sources and is in no wise shaken by the affidavits he has submitted
on his own behalf.

The evidence in this regard comes from his own associates—the judges,
prosecutors, defense counsel, medical experts, and others with whom he
dealt. . . . In particular the testimony of Father Schosser is important. He
testified as to many statements made by the defendant Rothaug during
the trial of his own case, showing the defendant's hostility to Poles and
his general attitude toward them. He stated that concerning the Poles in
general, Rothaug expressed himself in the following manner:

"If he (Rothaug) had his way, then no Pole would be buried in a German cemetery, and then he went on to make the remark which everybody heard in that courtroom—that he would get up from his coffin if
there was a Pole being buried near to him. Rothaug himself had to laugh

because of this mean joke, and he went on to say, 'You have to be able to hate, because according to the Bible, God is a hating God.'"

The testimony of Elkar is even more significant. He testifies that Rothaug believed in severe measures against foreigners and particularly against Poles and Jews, whom he felt should be treated differently from German transgressors. Rothaug felt there was a gap in the law in this respect. He states that Rothaug asserted that in his own court he achieved this discrimination by interpretation of existing laws but that other courts failed to do so. Such a gap, according to Rothaug, should be closed by singling out Poles and Jews for special treatment. . . .

This animosity of the defendant to these races is further established by documents in this case which show that his discrimination against these races encompassed others who he felt lacked the necessary harshness to carry out the policy of the Nazi State and Party toward these people.

In this connection the communication of Oeschey to Deputy Gauleiter Holz, concerning Doebig, is worthy of note. In this communication many charges were made against Doebig for his failure to take action against officials under him who had failed to carry out the Nazi programs against Jews and Poles. Oeschey testified that these charges were copied from a letter submitted to him by the defendant Rothaug and that the defendant assumed responsibility for these charges. Rothaug denies that he assumed responsibility or had anything to do with the charges made, except in one immaterial instance. However, in the light of the circumstances themselves, the Tribunal accepts Oeschey's testimony in this regard, particularly in view of the unimpeached affidavit of Oeschey's secretary to the effect that these charges were copied directly by her from a letter of Rothaug's.

Documentary proof of Rothaug's attitude in this respect is further found in the records of cases tried by him which hereafter will be considered.

Proof as to his animus is not shaken by his own testimony. It is confirmed by his testimony. He states:

"In my view, by introduction of the question of the so-called incredibility of Poles, the whole problem is shifted onto another plane. It is a matter of course that a nation, which has been subjected by another nation, and which is in a state of stress—that a citizen of such a country which had been subjected to another *vis-a-vis* the victorious nation, finds himself in quite a different moral-ethical relationship. It is useless to shut your eyes against reality. Of course, he finds himself in a different moral relationship from the relationship in which a German citizen would find himself. It is so natural there is no point in ignoring it. There is no need to lie."

· · ·

Concerning his participation in the Nazi policy of persecution and extermination of persons of these races, we shall confine our discussions to three cases which were tried by Rothaug as presiding judge.

The first case to be considered is that of Durka and Struss. . . .

The essential facts are in substance as follows: Two Polish girls—one, according to the testimony of Kern, 17 years of age, the other somewhat older—were accused of starting a fire in an armament plant in Bayreuth. This alleged fire did not do any material damage to the plant, but they were in the vicinity when it started and were arrested and interrogated by the Gestapo. Both gave alleged confessions to the Gestapo. Almost immediately following this occurrence, they were brought to Nuremberg by the Gestapo for trial before the Special Court.[22]

Upon their arrival the prosecutor in the case, Markl, was directed to draw up an indictment based upon the Gestapo interrogation. This was at 11 o'clock of the day they were tried.

The witness Kern was summoned by the defendant Rothaug to act as defense counsel in the case approximately 2 hours before the case came to trial. He informed Rothaug that he would not have time to prepare a defense. According to Kern, Rothaug stated that if he did not take over the defense, the trial would have to be conducted without a defense counsel. According to Rothaug, he told Kern that he would get another defense counsel. In either event the trial was to go on at once.

The trial itself, according to Kern, lasted about half an hour; according to the defendant, approximately an hour; according to Markl, it was conducted with the speed of a court martial.

The evidence consisted of the alleged confessions which one of the defendants repudiated before the court. Rothaug states that he thereupon called the Gestapo official who had obtained these alleged confessions and questioned him under oath. According to Rothaug the Gestapo

---

22. The "special courts" were Nazi-created political courts established shortly after Hitler came to power, intended as a means to bypass the ordinary judicial system and liquidate the regime's alleged enemies. Between 1933 and 1945 Nazi special courts executed some twelve thousand people.

official stated that the interrogations were perfectly regular. There was also a letter in evidence which it was said the defendants had tried to destroy before their capture. The witness Kern stated on cross-examination that this letter had little materiality.

The defendant attempts to justify the speed of this trial upon the legal requirements in existence at this time. He states, in contradiction to the other witnesses, that a clear case of sabotage was established. This Tribunal is not inclined to accept the defendant Rothaug's version of the facts which were established. Under the circumstances and in the brief period of the trial, the Tribunal does not believe the defendant could have established those facts from evidence.

According to the witness Kern, one of the defendants was 17 years of age. This assertion as to age was not disputed. A German 18 years of age or thereunder would have come under the German Juvenile Act and would not have been subject to trial before a Special Court or to capital punishment. Whatever the age of the defendants in this case, they were tried under the procedure described in the ordinance against Poles and Jews which was in effect at this time, by a judge who did not believe the statements of Polish defendants, according to the testimony in this case. These two young Polish women were sentenced to death and executed 4 days after trial. In the view of this Tribunal, based upon the evidence, these two young women did not have what amounted to a trial at all but were executed because they were Polish nationals in conformity with the Nazi plan of persecution and extermination.

The second case to be considered is the Lopata case. This was a case in which a young Polish farmhand, approximately 25 years of age, is alleged to have made indecent advances to his employer's wife. He first was tried in the district court at Neumarkt. That court sentenced him to a term of 2 years in the penitentiary. A nullity plea was filed in this case before the Reich Supreme Court, and the Reich Supreme Court returned the case to the Special Court at Nuremberg for a new trial and sentence. The Reich Supreme Court stated that the judgment of the lower court was defective, since it did not discuss in detail whether the ordinance against public enemies[23] was applicable and stated that if such ordinance

---

23. The "Decree against Public Enemies" was passed on September 5, 1939, enabling the Nazi government to seek the death penalty when the perpetrator was convicted of exploiting the conditions of the war (such as blackouts) to carry out a crime. A copy of the

were applicable—a thing which seemed probable, a much more severe sentence was deemed necessary.

The case was therefore again tried in violation of the fundamental principles of justice that no man should be tried twice for the same offense.

In the second trial of the case, the defendant Rothaug obligingly found that the ordinance against public enemies had been violated. In its reasons, the court states the facts on which the verdict was based as follows:

"The wife of farmer Schwenzl, together with the accused and a Polish girl, chopped straw in the barn. The accused was standing on the righthand side of the machine to carry out the work. Suddenly, in the middle of the work, the accused, without saying anything, touched with his hand the genitals of the wife of farmer Schwenzl, through her skirt. When she said, after this unexpected action of the defendant, 'You hog, do you think I am not disgusted about anything; you think you can do that because my husband is sick,' the accused laughed and in spite of this dissuasion touched again the genitals of the farmer's wife above her skirt. The wife of farmer Schwenzl slapped him after that. In spite of this, the accused continued with his impertinent behavior; for a third time he touched the genitals of the farmer's wife above the skirt.

. . .

"The accused did not make a complete confession. He states that he only once, for fun, touched the farmer's wife's genitals above the skirt.

"The court is convinced, on account of the testimony given by the witness Therese Schwenzl, who makes a trustworthy impression, that the affair occurred exactly as described by the witness. Therefore, its findings were arrived at according to the testimony given by her."

The Polish woman who was present at the time of this alleged assault is not listed as a witness. Rothaug has stated in his testimony before this Court that he never had a Polish witness. As for the reasons for bringing the defendant under the public enemy ordinance, the following facts are stated in the reasons for the verdict: Lopata having had some minor difficulties with the farmer Schwenzl refused to eat his noon meal and induced the Polish servant maid to do likewise. Thereupon, farmer

decree translated into English is available at https://encyclopedia.ushmm.org/content/en/article/decree-against-public-enemies (accessed July 10, 2019).

Schwenzl, his employer, called him to account in the stable. The defendant put up resistance to the farmer's "admonitions" by arming himself with a dung fork. It is further stated that the Pole, at the threshold of the farm hallway, again turned against his employer and let him go only when attacked by the sheep dog which the farmer kept. As to the actual reasons for the sentence of this Polish farmhand to death, the following paragraphs are more significant:

"Thus, the defendant gives the impression of a thoroughly degenerate personality, which is marked by excitability and a definite trend to mendacity, or to lying. The whole inferiority of the defendant, I would say, lies in the sphere of character and is obviously based on his being a part of Polish subhumanity, or in his belonging to Polish subhumanity.

"The drafting of men into the armed forces effected a heavy labor shortage in all spheres of life at home, last but not least in agriculture. To compensate this, Polish laborers, among others, had to be used to a large extent, mainly as farmhands.

"These men cannot be supervised by the authorities to such an extent as would be necessary due to their insubordinate and criminal disposition.

· · ·

"The action of the defendant constitutes a considerable disturbance of the peace of the persons immediately concerned by his mean actions. The rural population has the right to expect that the strongest measures will be taken against such terrorization by foreign elements. But beyond disregarding the honor of the wife of farmer Schwenzl, the attack of the defendant is directed against the purity of the German blood. Looking at it from this point of view, the defendant showed such insubordination within the German living space that his action has to be considered as especially significant.

· · ·

"Accordingly, as outlined in article III, paragraph 2, second sentence of the ordinance against Poles and Jews, the crime of the defendant, which in connection with his other behavior shows a climax of unheard-of impudence, has to be considered as especially serious so that the death sentence had to be passed as the only just expiation, which is also necessary in the interest of the Reich security to deter Poles of similar mentality."

The defendant was sentenced under the ordinance against Poles and Jews in the Incorporated Eastern Territories.[24] The verdict was signed by the defendant Rothaug, and an application for clemency was disapproved by him.

When on the witness stand, the defendant Rothaug was asked the following question by the court:

". . . if Lopata had been a racial German, all other facts being the same as they were in the Lopata case, is it your judgment that the nullity plea would have been invoked and that the Supreme Court would have ordered the case sent back to you for another trial? I should like your opinion on that."

Rothaug replied as follows to this question:

"Mr. President, this question is very interesting, but I cannot even imagine that possibility even theoretically, because the very elements which are of the greatest importance could not be the same in the case of a German."

Lopata was sentenced to death and subsequently executed.

The third case to be considered is that of Leo Katzenberger. The record in this case shows that Lehmann Israel Katzenberger, commonly called Leo Katzenberger, was a merchant and head of the Jewish community in Nuremberg; that he was "sentenced to death for an offense under paragraph 2, legally identical with an offense under paragraph 4 of the decree against public enemies in connection with the offense of racial pollution." The trial was held in the public session on 13 March 1942. Katzenberger's age at that time was over 68 years.

The offense of racial pollution with which he was charged comes under article 2 of the Law for the Protection of German Blood and Honor.[25] This section reads as follows:

"Sexual intercourse (except in marriage) between Jews and German nationals of German or German-related blood is forbidden."

---

24. The "incorporated eastern territories" comprised areas seized from Poland and placed under German civilian control; these included the Gau East Prussia, Gau Silesia, the Reichsgau Danzig-West Prussia, and the Reichsgau Wartheland.

25. The "Law for the Protection of German Blood and Honor" was the second of the so-called Nuremberg Laws that Hitler announced at the Nazi party rally in Nuremberg on September 15, 1935. It banned sexual relations between Jews and non-Jewish ("Aryan") Germans. Interracial sex was deemed a crime called "racial defilement." Further, the law forbade Jews from employing non-Jewish women under the age of forty-five as domestic help. The law is available in English translation at https://encyclopedia.ushmm.org/content/en/article/nuremberg-laws (accessed July 10, 2019).

The applicable sections of the Decree against Public Enemies reads as follows:

"Section 2
"*Crimes during Air Raids*

"Whoever commits a crime or offense against the body, life, or property, taking advantage of air raid protection measures, is punishable by hard labor of up to 15 years, or for life, and in particularly severe cases, punishable by death.

...

"Section 4
"*Exploitation of the State of War as a Reason for More Severe Punishment*

"Whoever commits a criminal act exploiting the extraordinary conditions caused by war is punishable beyond the regular punishment limits with hard labor of up to 15 years, or for life, or is punishable by death if the sound common sense of the people requires it on account of the crime being particularly despicable."

The evidence in this case, aside from the record, is based primarily upon the testimony of Hans Groben, the investigating judge who first investigated the case; Hermann Markl, the official who prosecuted the case; Karl Ferber, who was one of the associate judges in the trial; Heinz Hoffmann, who was the other associate judge in the trial; Armin Baur, who was medical expert in the trial; Georg Engert, who dealt with clemency proceedings; and Otto Ankenbrand, another investigating judge.

The salient facts established in connection with this case are in substance as follows: Sometime in the first half of the year 1941 the witness Groben issued a warrant of arrest against Katzenberger, who was accused of having had intimate relations with the photographer Seiler. According to the results of the police inquiry, actual intercourse had not been proved, and Katzenberger denied the charge. Upon Groben's advice, Katzenberger agreed that he would not move against the warrant of arrest at that time but would await the results of further investigation. These further investigations were very lengthy, although Groben pressed the public prosecutor for speed. The police, in spite of their efforts, were unable to get further material evidence, and it became apparent that the way to clarify the situation was to take the sworn statement of Seiler, and this was done.

In her sworn statement she said that Katzenberger had known both her and her family for many years before she had come to Nuernberg and that his relationship to her was a friendly and fatherly one and denied the charge of sexual intercourse. The evidence also showed that Katzenberger had given Seiler financial assistance on various occasions and that he was administrator of the property where Seiler lived, which was owned by a firm of which he was a partner. Upon Seiler's statement, Groben informed Dr. Herz, counsel for Katzenberger, of the result and suggested that it was the right time to move against the warrant of arrest. When this was done, Rothaug learned of it and ordered that the Katzenberger case be transferred from the criminal divisional court to the Special Court. The first indictment was withdrawn, and another indictment was prepared for the Special Court.

The witness Markl states that Rothaug dominated the prosecution, especially through his close friendship with the senior public prosecutor, Dr. Schroeder, who was the superior of Markl.

The indictment before the Special Court was prepared according to the orders of Rothaug, and Katzenberger was not charged only with race defilement in this new indictment, but there was also an additional charge under the decree against public enemies, which made the death sentence permissible. The new indictment also joined the Seiler woman on a charge of perjury. The effect of joining Seiler in the charge against Katzenberger was to preclude her from being a witness for the defendant, and such a combination was contrary to established practice. Rothaug at this time told Marki that there was sufficient proof of sexual intercourse between Seiler and Katzenberger to convince him, and that he was prepared to condemn Katzenberger to death. Markl informed the Ministry of Justice of Rothaug's intended procedure against Katzenberger and was told that if Rothaug so desired it, the procedure would be approved.

Prior to the trial, the defendant Rothaug called on Dr. Armin Baur, medical counsellor for the Nuernberg Court, as the medical expert for the Katzenberger case. He stated to Baur that he wanted to pronounce a death sentence and that it was, therefore, necessary for the defendant to be examined. This examination, Rothaug stated, was a mere formality since Katzenberger "would be beheaded anyhow." To the doctor's reproach that Katzenberger was old, and it seemed questionable whether he could be charged with race defilement, Rothaug stated: "It is sufficient for me that the swine said that a German girl had sat upon his lap."

The trial itself, as testified to by many witnesses, was in the nature of a political demonstration. High Party officials attended, including Reich Inspector Oexle. Part of the group of Party officials appeared in uniform.

During the proceedings, Rothaug tried with all his power to encourage the witnesses to make incriminating statements against the defendants. Both defendants were hardly heard by the court. Their statements were passed over or disregarded. During the course of the trial, Rothaug took the opportunity to give the audience a National Socialist lecture on the subject of the Jewish question. The witnesses found great difficulty in giving testimony because of the way in which the trial was conducted, since Rothaug constantly anticipated the evaluation of the facts and gave expression to his own opinions.

Because of the way the trial was conducted, it was apparent that the sentence which would be imposed was the death sentence. After the introduction of evidence was concluded, a recess was taken, during which time the prosecutor Markl appeared in the consultation room and Rothaug made it clear to him that he expected the prosecution to ask for a death sentence against Katzenberger and a term in the penitentiary for Seiler. Rothaug at this time also gave him suggestions as to what he should include in his arguments.

The reasons for the verdict were drawn up by Ferber. They were based upon the notes of Rothaug as to what should be included. Considerable space is given to Katzenberger's ancestry and the fact that he was of the Mosaic faith, although that fact was admitted by Katzenberger. Such space is also given to the relationship between Katzenberger and Seiler. That there was no proof of actual sexual intercourse is clear from the opinion. The proof seems to have gone little farther than the fact that the defendant Seiler had at times sat upon Katzenberger's lap and that he had kissed her, which facts were also admitted. Many assumptions were made in the reasons stated which obviously are not borne out by the evidence. The court even goes back to the time prior to the passage of the law for the protection of German Blood and Honor, during which Katzenberger had known Seiler. It draws the conclusion apparently without evidence, that their relationship for a period of approximately 10 years, had always been of a sexual nature. The opinion undertakes to bring the case under the decision of the Reich Supreme Court that actual sexual intercourse need not be proved, provided the acts are sexual in nature.

Having wandered far afield from the proof to arrive at this conclusion as to the matter of racial pollution, the court then proceeds to go far afield in order to bring the case under the decree against public enemies. Here the essential facts proved were that the defendant Seiler's husband was at the front and that Katzenberger, on one or possibly two occasions, had visited her after dark. On both points the following paragraphs of the opinion are enlightening. . . .

"Looked at from this point of view, Katzenberger's conduct is particularly contemptible. Together with his offense of racial pollution he is also guilty of an offense under paragraph 4 of the ordinance against people's parasites. . . . It should be noted here that the national community is in need of increased legal protection from all crimes attempting to destroy or undermine its inner cohesion.

"On several occasions since the outbreak of war the defendant Katzenberger crept into Seiler's flat after dark. In those cases the defendant exploited the measures taken for the protection in air raids. His chances were further improved by the absence of the bright street lighting which exists in the street along Spittlertorgraben in peacetime. He exploited this fact fully aware of its significance because thus he instinctively escaped during his excursions being observed by people in the street.

"The visits paid by Katzenberger to Seiler under the protection of the blackout served at least the purpose of keeping relations going. It does not matter whether during these visits extramarital sexual relations took place or whether they only conversed as when the husband was present, as Katzenberger claims. The request to interrogate the husband was therefore overruled. The court holds the view the defendant's actions, done with a purpose within a definite plan, amount to a crime against the body according to paragraph 2 of the ordinance against people's parasites.[26] The law of 15 September 1935 has been passed to protect German blood and German honor. The Jew's racial pollution amounts to a grave attack on the purity of German blood, the object of the attack being the body of a German woman. The general need for protection therefore makes appear as unimportant the behavior of the other partner in racial pollution who anyway is not liable to prosecution. The fact that racial pollution occurred up to at least 1939–1940 becomes clear from statements made by the witness Zeuschel to whom the defendant repeatedly and consistently admitted that up to the end of 1939 and the beginning of 1940 she was used to sitting on the Jew's lap and exchanging caresses as described above.

---

26. I.e., the public enemies decree.

"Thus, the defendant committed an offense also under paragraph 2 of the ordinance against people's parasites.

"The personal character of the male defendant also stamps him as a people's parasite. The racial pollution practiced by him through many years grew, by exploiting wartime conditions, into an attitude inimical to the nation, into an attack on the security of the national community, during an emergency.

"This was why the defendant Katzenberger had to be sentenced both on a charge of racial pollution and of an offense under paragraphs 2 and 4 of the ordinance against people's parasites, the two charges being taken in conjunction according to paragraph 73 of the criminal code.

. . .

"In passing sentence the court was guided by these considerations: The political life of the German people under national socialism is based on the community. One fundamental factor of the life of the national community is race. If a Jew commits racial pollution with a German woman, this amounts to polluting the German race and, by polluting a German woman, to a grave attack on the purity of German blood. The need for protection is particularly strong.

"Katzenberger has been practicing pollution for years. He was well acquainted with the point of view taken by patriotic German men and women as regards racial questions, and he knew that by this conduct he insulted the patriotic feelings of the German people. Nor did he mend his ways after the National Socialist revolution of 1933, after the passing of the law for the protection of German blood, in 1935, after the action against Jews in 1938, or the outbreak of war in 1939.

"The court therefore regards it as indicated, as the only feasible answer to the frivolous conduct of the defendant, to pass death sentence, as the heaviest punishment provided by paragraph 4 of the decree against public enemies. His case takes on the complexion of a particularly grave crime as he was to be sentenced in connection with the offense of committing racial pollution, under paragraph 2 of the Decree against Public Enemies, especially if one takes into consideration the defendant's character and the accumulative nature of commission. This is why the defendant is liable to the death penalty which the law provides for only such cases. Dr. Baur, the medical expert, describes the defendant as fully responsible."

We have gone to some extent into the evidence of this case to show the nature of the proceedings and the animus of the defendant Rothaug. One undisputed fact, however, is sufficient to establish this case as being an act in furtherance of the Nazi program to persecute and exterminate Jews. That fact is that nobody but a Jew could have been tried for racial pollution. To this offense was added the charge that it was committed by Katzenberger through exploiting war conditions and the blackout. This brought the offense under the ordinance against public enemies and made the offense capital. Katzenberger was tried and executed only because he was a Jew. As stated by Elkar in his testimony, Rothaug achieved the final result by interpretations of existing laws as he boasted to Elkar he was able to do.

This Tribunal is not concerned with the legal incontestability under German law of these cases above discussed. The evidence establishes beyond a reasonable doubt that Katzenberger was condemned and executed because he was a Jew; and Durka, Struss, and Lopata met the same fate because they were Poles. Their execution was in conformity with the policy of the Nazi State of persecution, torture, and extermination of these races. The defendant Rothaug was the knowing and willing instrument in that program of persecution and extermination.

From the evidence it is clear that these trials lacked the essential elements of legality. In these cases the defendant's court, in spite of the legal sophistries which he employed, was merely an instrument in the program of the leaders of the Nazi State of persecution and extermination. That the number the defendant could wipe out within his competency was smaller than the number involved in the mass persecutions and exterminations by the leaders whom he served, does not mitigate his contribution to the program of those leaders. His acts were more terrible in that those who might have hoped for a last refuge in the institutions of justice found these institutions turned against them and a part of the program of terror and oppression.

The individual cases in which Rothaug applied the cruel and discriminatory law against Poles and Jews cannot be considered in isolation. It is of the essence of the charges against him that he participated in the national program of racial persecution. It is of the essence of the proof that he identified himself with this national program and gave himself utterly to its accomplishment. He participated in the crime of genocide.

Again, in determining the degree of guilt the Tribunal has considered the entire record of his activities, not alone under the head of racial persecution but in other respects also. Despite protestations that his judgments were based solely upon evidence introduced in court, we are firmly convinced that in numberless cases Rothaug's opinions were formed and decisions made, and in many instances publicly or privately announced before the trial had even commenced and certainly before it was concluded. He was in constant contact with his confidential assistant Elkar, a member of the criminal SD, who sat with him in weekly conferences in the chambers of the court. He formed his opinions from dubious records submitted to him before trial. By his manner and methods he made his court an instrumentality of terror and won the fear and hatred of the population. From the evidence of his closest associates as well as his victims, we find that Oswald Rothaug represented in Germany the personification of the secret Nazi intrigue and cruelty. He was and is a sadistic and evil man.

Under any civilized judicial system he could have been impeached and removed from office or convicted of malfeasance in office on account of the scheming malevolence with which he administered injustice. Upon the evidence in this case it is the judgment of this Tribunal that the defendant Rothaug is guilty under count three of the indictment. In his case we find no mitigating circumstances; no extenuation.

. . .

# Section 3
# Trials by Army Courts: The Belsen and Dachau Trials

## 3.1

## Trial of Josef Kramer and 44 Others (The Belsen Trial), September 17–November 17, 1945[27]

*The British Belsen trial, held in Lüneburg, Germany, from September 17, 1945, to November 17, 1945, was the first of more than five hundred Royal Warrant trials by British authorities between 1945 and 1949. The leading defendant was Josef Kramer, former adjutant to Rudolf Höß at Auschwitz and commandant of the Dachau, Natzweiler, and Auschwitz camps before his transfer to Belsen in 1944. The British Belsen trial merits consideration here not only due to its status as the earliest concentration camp trial but because of the theory of "common design" advanced by the prosecution and accepted by the military court. Common design, like conspiracy at Nuremberg, enabled prosecutors to hold the members of the Belsen administration criminally responsible for all the crimes committed there. The Americans would borrow common design from the Belsen trial in their own proceedings against the Dachau camp staff, a trial that followed on the heels of the Belsen case.*

---

27. Source: http://www.bergenbelsen.co.uk/pages/TrialTranscript/Trial_Contents.html (accessed July 10, 2019).

*Day 47*

CAPTAIN ROBERTS [defense counsel for Oskar Schmitz and Karl Franzioh[28]]: May it please the Court. . . . Before I start my address there is one thing I would like to say, and it is this. I am the fifth Defending Officer to address you, and although we have as well as we can, tried to coordinate our speeches, what I have to say must inevitably, to a certain degree, repeat what has already been said, but I assure the Court that I will keep that repetition to the minimum.

I raise that now because the first part of my argument concerns something which has already been mentioned by two of my learned friends, namely, what is meant by that extremely obscure regulation which the Court has spent so much time considering, Regulation 8(2).

The learned Prosecutor in his opening address said this at page 25 of the transcript of the first day's proceedings: "I shall ask the Court to view the evidence as a whole and I shall ask the Court to say that each must bear his responsibility not only for the actions of his own hand but for the actions of this criminal gang who were working together. Nevertheless, lest there should be the slightest shadow of doubt, no person has been brought before this Court against whom the Prosecution will not produce some evidence of personal acts of active and deliberate cruelty and, in many cases, individual murder. By all means, if you view these separate acts separately you must, of course, when coming to your verdict decide each individual case, the case against each individual accused, whether he is guilty or not, but in considering the separate evidence of these individual acts of cruelty I ask the Court to bear them in mind not only as individual acts, but as acts of one of the members of this group, which is evidence not only against himself but against every single one of the persons who were working in that camp as part of that group taking part in this concerted ill-treatment."

Both my accused are concerned only with the Belsen charge, and it appears to me, from that paragraph which I have just read, that any member of the SS and any prisoner in any position of authority who was in

---

28. Oskar Schmitz (1916–date of death unknown) was a senior camp inmate charged with war crimes at the Belsen trial and acquitted. Karl Franzioh (1912–1945) was an SS-Rottenführer (equivalent to an Obergefreiter, or private, in the German army) at the Belsen camp. He was convicted of shooting camp prisoners for picking up potato peels outside his window—presumably because they were starving. He was executed on December 13, 1945, in Hamelin.

Belsen for whatever period of time, no matter how short, was a member of the staff of the Belsen concentration camp, and responsible for the well-being of the persons interned there, and further, that such people formed a group within the meaning of Regulation 8(2) under the Royal Warrant and that this group participated in what the Prosecution has called the concerted ill treatment of the internees.

I do not propose to go at all into the question of whether these people did in fact form a group, nor whether they were responsible for the well-being of these internees. I propose to go straight to what I consider to be the root of the problem, and that is these two words "concerted action."

Fifty-three days ago the word "concerted" was defined in this Court as meaning "plan," "contrive," "pre-arrange," and with respect I would remind you of that definition now, because it does seem to me that upon the construction which is put upon that one word depends [on] the meaning of Regulation 8(2), and upon the meaning of that Regulation stands or falls the whole of the Prosecution's case in regard to the joint responsibility of the accused for the alleged war crime that occurred at Belsen concentration camp.

It is to my mind quite clear from what the learned Prosecutor said when replying to the Defence's applications for separate trial—that was also on the first day of this case—that the Prosecution are trying to maintain that common action is the same as concerted action.

I will read you two short passages which the learned Prosecutor said on that occasion: "I ask the Court to say that there is ample evidence on which the Court can draw the overwhelming inference that this was a common action by all these people." A few lines later he says: "I ask the Court to regard the application as a whole as being one which must fail on the ground that there is ample evidence on the summary that there was concerted action by those people at Auschwitz and Belsen."

In my submission, one of the basic rules of construction is what words should be construed according to their natural meaning. If that normal meaning is given to them and the document as a whole makes sense, then that normal meaning is the correct meaning to be put on those words.

One should not attempt to give another meaning to those words either on the ground that that other meaning is what was intended by the draughtsman, nor on the ground that that other meaning is better suited to one's purpose, and it is my submission that if it was intended that common action should be the substance of this Regulation, then the words "common action" would have been used.

Since these words "concerted action" do appear in this Regulation, then I submit that the Court must construe these words according to their normal meaning, and not in such a way as the Prosecution suggests.

In my view, whatever meaning is put upon the words "concerted action," that meaning must imply two things, firstly there must be some prior planning with a view to a definite end; secondly there must be full knowledge of the plan and of the end in view by those carrying it out.

The obvious example of concerted action, but nonetheless a good one, is that of an orchestra. There each performer in that orchestra has what is termed, I believe, a score. He not only knows which notes he has to play, but also what the other performers are playing and when the score itself one can compare with the plan, and the music which the whole orchestra produces as the definite end which the plan had in view.

Now I ask you to consider in contrast to that the concentration camp at Belsen. To my mind, from the scenes which have been so graphically described to you by Mr. Le Druillenec[29] and by Brigadier Glyn Hughes,[30] it is quite obvious that here was chaos and disorder on a colossal scale; quite the reverse from the concerted action, and it would be difficult to find anywhere a clearer example of un-concerted action.

In my submission, in order that this, what occurred at Belsen, should have been the result of concerted action, it would have been necessary, when each member of the staff arrived at Belsen, that something like this should have taken place. He would have been told: "Here in this camp we mean to kill as many people as painfully as possible. To that end we have introduced typhus into the camp; to that end we have, with the cooperation of the Royal Air Force, ensured that prisoners receive little food and no water; to that end we are asking all the other camps in the district to pour as many prisoners as possible into this camp, will you not become a partner with us in this joint enterprise?"

Now there is no evidence of any such thing or anything like it ever occurring at Belsen.

I would like to read a further extract from the learned Prosecutor's speech when he opened his case: "The case for the Prosecution is quite a definite one, it is that the people concerned are all members of an

---

29. Harold Osmund le Druillenec (1911–1985) was one of two surviving British nationals of the Belsen camp.

30. Brigadier Hugh Llewellyn Glyn Hughes (1892–1973), a British officer in the Royal Army Medical Corps, testified at the Belsen trial in September 1945.

organisation, that they served under a joint leader and that their actions are common—that each one of the persons in the dock has taken part in these cruelties."

I submit that though there may have been evidence of incidents of the same type, there has been no evidence whatsoever of concerted action on the part of that section of the staff at Belsen who are now in the dock, and therefore the Court are not justified in receiving any evidence against an individual accused than that evidence which is specifically directed to that individual.

This screen of joint responsibility which the Prosecution has sought to erect, this accumulation of horrors with which the Prosecution has tried to bespatter every one of the accused, is, in my submission, nothing but an attempt on the part of the Prosecution to cover up the weakness of their case against many of the accused who are now before you.

Now the Prosecution ask you by inference, I think it is safe to say, if not in so many words, that the mere presence of the accused during the commission of a war crime in itself makes them guilty of that crime.

Now I think the easiest way of dealing with that problem is to read you a very short extract from Archbold[31] dealing with principles in the second degree. At page 1429 it reads as follows: "There must also be a participation in the act; for even if a man is present whilst a felony is committed, if he takes no part in it and does not act in concert with those who commit it, he will not be a principle in the second degree, merely because he did not endeavour to prevent the felony, or failed to apprehend the felon."

In my submission that passage relating to felonies under English law must be adopted by this Court when trying war crimes.

May I just briefly sum up what I have said so far. Firstly, concerted action means what it says. Secondly, there was no concerted action at Belsen. Thirdly, Regulation 8(2) cannot be applied to the evidence before you regarding Belsen, and fourthly, mere presence in Belsen camp in whatever capacity is no crime in itself.

I would ask you, therefore, in considering the cases of the two accused whom I represent, to put aside all these general allegations, to turn your backs on the accusations which have been made against the other accused, and to regard only the evidence specifically affecting each one of them.

. . .

---

31. *Archbold Criminal Pleading, Evidence and Practice*, first published in 1822, was at this time (and remains today) the premier manual for criminal lawyers in England and Wales.

*Day 51*

THE JUDGE ADVOCATE [instructions to the military court members]

. . . Well, gentlemen, I want now to tell you what I think you already know, and that is that you have not got to prove everything in a charge. You have got to prove the substance, and if you are satisfied that there was ill treatment, substantial ill treatment causing death or physical suffering, to people whose names the Prosecution were not able to put before you, that would, in my view, allow you to convict the accused; even though you were not satisfied upon any particularly named person, provided you are satisfied that the substance of the charge is made out.

The case for the Prosecution is that all these people were employed on the staff at Auschwitz, and they ask you to say that all these people knew that a system and a source of conduct was in force, and that in one way or another in furtherance of that common agreement to run the camp in a brutal way, all those people were taking part in it. They suggest that if you are satisfied they were doing so, then they must, each and every one of them, assume responsibility for what happened. It is again hardly necessary for me to remind you gentlemen that when you come to consider the question of guilt and responsibility, the strongest case must surely be that of the Kommandant Kramer and then down the list according to the positions they held. You are not bound to find anything which the evidence does not establish, but that is the case for the Prosecution. They may have had different responsibilities, but the Prosecution say, looking at it clearly and fairly, is not it an irresistible inference that there was a concerted design at this camp to act in the way that has been proved? They ask you not to treat these individual acts which you may find to be proved merely as offences committed by themselves, but also as evidence clearly indicating that that particular person was a party willingly in the furtherance of this system.

. . .

I think you will appreciate what the case for the Prosecution now is. On a broad basis it is suggested that in Germany in these war years there was this system of concentration camps of which Auschwitz and Belsen were two; that in these camps it was the practice and the habit to treat people, especially the unfortunate Jews, as if they were of no account and had no rights whatsoever; that the staff of these concentration camps were deliberately taking part in a procedure which took no account of those wretched people's lives; that there was calculated mass murder such as at Auschwitz; that there was calculated disregard of the ordinary duties which fell upon a staff to look after the well-being and health of people at Belsen; that throughout all these camps the staff were made quite clearly to understand the brutalities, ill-treatment, and matters of that kind would not be punished if they took place at the expense of the Jews, and the case for the Prosecution is that there was this common concerted design of the staff to do these horrible and terrible things.

The Prosecution have brought before you in the dock a large number of persons ranging from Kramer,[32] the Kommandant who was in charge of Auschwitz [Birkenau] and Belsen (and who seems to have been such a loyal and faithful servant to his masters that he was twice decorated by them, a second time in January, 1945, after his sojourn at Auschwitz), down to the Kapo[33] or the functionary who was a tool, and whose reward for his efforts appears to have been to have the right to a bed and an extra bowl of soup. Be that as it may, the Prosecution's case is that they take the view, and they ask you to consider whether it has been established or not, that all these people in the dock in one way or another were taking part in this common concerted way to ill-treat and in some cases kill, these unfortunate Jews. If you are satisfied of that, they ask you to say that each and every one must bear their responsibility for what happened. Their responsibility must, of course, vary with their position, but the Prosecution say they are still guilty.

Now, Sir, I know you will carefully consider these matters. You may think that there is no distinction which one should give to people who are concerned in their various duties with the gas chamber. You may think that if these Aufseherinnen[34] were responsible and taking part in a concerted scheme at Belsen to ill-treat these Jews they must take the responsibility for that. On the other hand, if you think these Aufseherinnen, or some of them, were at Belsen doing a good job of work in the kitchens

---

32. Josef Kramer (1906–1945) was the commandant of Auschwitz-Birkenau (May 1944–November 1944) and Belsen (December 1944 until its liberation in April 1945). He was convicted in the British Belsen trial and hanged on the Hamelin gallows on December 13, 1945.

33. A *Kapo* was a prisoner assigned by the SS to assist in the administration of camp functions such as the supervision of slave labor details.

34. Concentration camp guards.

and trying to help as much as they could, that is a factor you will have to consider when considering their guilt or otherwise for the appalling state of affairs that arose at Belsen.

That is the issue which you have to consider, and I propose to leave it in your hands to deal with in the light of the evidence.

. . .

# 3.2

# *U.S. v. Martin Weiss et al.* (The Dachau "Parent" Case), November 15–December 13, 1945[35]

*The "common design" theory pursued—and finally adopted—at the Belsen trial caught the attention of US officials planning a parallel trial at the site of the former Dachau camp. As in the Belsen proceedings, the notion of a common design to commit atrocities in the camp became the main battleground on which the prosecutors and defense counsel sparred at Dachau.*

## Closing argument of the Prosecution (Lt. Col. Denson)[36]

. . . I would like to call the court's attention and wish to emphasize the fact that the offense with which these 40 men stand charged is not killing, beating, torturing these prisoners but the offense of aiding, abetting, encouraging, and participating in a common design to kill, to beat, to torture and to subject these persons to starvation.

It may be, because of the testimony submitted here, this court may be inclined to determine the guilt or innocence of those forty men by the number of men that they killed, or by the number of men that they beat, or the number that they tortured. That is not the test that is to be applied in this case. True enough, the testimony that has been introduced here

---

35. Source: NARA/College Park, RG 338, M 1174, Vols. 2 and 3.

36. William Denson (1913–1998) was an American military prosecutor at the Dachau, Buchenwald, Flossenbürg, and Mauthausen concentration camp trials.

stamps Moll[37] as being a murderer, Knoll[38] as being a murderer, Tempel[39] as a most brutal and sadistic murderer and Eichberger[40] as being a murderer. But we are not trying these men for specific acts of misconduct. We are trying them for their participation in this common design to subject these individuals to killings, to beatings, and to tortures. As a matter of fact, this case would have been established without showing that a single man over in that dock at any time killed a man. It would be sufficient may it please the court, to show that there was in fact a common design and that these individuals participated in it, and that the purpose of this common design was the killings, the beatings and the tortures and the subjections to starvation, and the other indignities of these prisoners. The case could be established by proof that one person might be shot by Bongarts [sic][41],

---

37. As part of the guard staff at Auschwitz-Birkenau, Otto Moll (1915–1946) was reputed to have killed thousands—and perhaps tens of thousands—of prisoners there before his transfer to a satellite camp of Dachau, and then to Dachau itself one day before its liberation by American troops. He was convicted of war crimes at the "parent" Dachau trial and hanged at Landsberg prison in May 1946.

38. Christian Knoll (1895–1946) was a *Kapo* and, beginning in February 1941, senior block leader (*Blockältester*) of the Jewish barracks as well as the correctional block (*Strafblock*) in the Dachau concentration camp. As senior block leader he accrued a reputation for beating numerous prisoners to death, for which he was prosecuted by the Americans at the parent Dachau trial. He was convicted and sentenced to death on December 13, 1945. The sentence was carried out in Landsberg on May 29, 1946.

39. Wilhelm Tempel (1908–1946), an SS member assigned to Majdanek and Auschwitz before his transfer to Dachau in August 1944, served as a work detail supervisor at a sub-camp of Dachau, Kaufering IV. He was convicted of war crimes at the Dachau parent case in December 1945 and sentenced to death for beating inmates with a rubber truncheon and shooting to death several of them. He was executed at Landsberg prison in May 1946.

40. Leonhard Eichberger (1915–1946), an SS-*Hauptscharführer* (master sergeant) and *Rapportführer* (report leader, a midlevel noncommissioned rank specific to the SS, whose main duty was the morning and evening roll calls), was prosecuted at the Dachau parent case for war crimes at the Dachau camp. He was convicted for his role in interrogating political prisoners, his participation in between 150 and 200 executions, and his preparation of reports regarding executions in the camp. Sentenced to death in December 1945 by the US Army military commission, he was executed in Landsburg prison on May 29, 1946.

41. Theodor Bongartz (1902–1945) was the chief of the crematorium in the Dachau camp responsible for numerous murders of camp prisoners, among them a member of the July 1944 bomb plot against Hitler, Georg Eiser, whom Bongartz executed with a gun-shot to the back of the neck (*Genickschuss*). He died in US custody of either tuberculosis (the official cause of death) or cirrhosis of the liver caused by hepatitis (the precise cause of death is unclear).

the counterpart of Mahl[42] at the crematorium or Zill[43] and Hoffmann [sic][44] were responsible for floggings. The evidence before this court demonstrates beyond all peradventure of a doubt the existence of this common design. It is not contended nor is it necessary to sustain the charges that this common design had its origin in Dachau nor was it first conceived in January 1942. Such contentions would be absurd on their face and manifest untruths when considered in the light of history of Nazism in Germany. We all know that Dachau has its origination in the year 1933, and we all know that the unfortunate persons who came through the gate into the camp, as prisoners, were destined for a fate worse than death itself. The operation of the camp was but one of the instrumentalities employed by the Nazi to solidify this newly acquired power by crushing those who opposed their rule. Witnesses for both the defense and prosecution testified under Pierkowski [sic],[45] a prisoner was brutally beaten or hung up by his wrists, bound with chains, for hours, and what

---

42. Emil Maul (1900–1967) was a "career criminal" (*Berufsverbrecher*) imprisoned in the Dachau camp, where he also served as the *Blockältester* (senior block leader) of the correctional block. In 1943 he was assigned to the camp crematorium to work as a *Kapo* for Theodor Bongartz until the camp's liberation in April 1945. His involvement in executions within the camp resulted in his conviction and death sentence at the US Dachau parent case in December 1945. That sentence, however, was subsequently commuted to a ten-year prison term. Maul was released from prison in February 1952.

43. Egon Zill (1906–1974) was an SS major (*Sturmbannführer*) who drifted between various concentration camps, including Dachau, before assignment as commandant at the Natzweiler-Struthof and Flossenbürg camps. He was eventually sacked from his command position for incompetence and transferred to the Eastern Front in 1943. In the 1950s he was convicted by a Munich Court of murder and sentenced to life in prison; the sentence was subsequently reduced to 15 years.

44. Franz Johann Hofmann (1906–1973) was assigned to the guard staff at Dachau shortly after its establishment in 1933. He remained there for the next nine years, rising through promotions to the rank of SS-*Obersturmfuehrer* (first lieutenant). In December 1942 he was transferred to Auschwitz, where he participated in "selections" of incoming transports before his assignment as head of the "gypsy camp" in Auschwitz-Birkenau. Living under a pseudonym after the war, he was able to elude prosecution until 1959, when he was arrested and indicted for murder by a Munich court. Hofmann was convicted of two counts of murder and sentenced to life in prison, a sentence reaffirmed by his additional conviction in the Frankfurt Auschwitz trial in August 1965. He died in prison in 1973.

45. Alexander Piorkowski (1904–1948) was Martin Weiss' predecessor as commandant of the Dachau camp, a position he held from February 1940 to September 1942. He was tried and convicted of war crimes by US military commission in 1947. A spirited

was his offense? Some slight infraction of the rules of the camp. And killed, why? Because of his leaving his place of servitude for the Nazis, more than one time and had been apprehended and sent to Dachau for execution. No, not execution, but an unlawful killing which has all the earmarks of murder.

But they argue that under Weiss,[46] and I'm sure that they will because witnesses took the stand, and testified to the effect that conditions were different. Beatings and wrist hangings were less frequent, discipline had been relaxed. Yes, conditions in Dachau were different under Weiss. Conditions in Germany were different at that time, when Weiss came here, Germany was entering her fourth year of war, and man power, labor, was sorely needed to satisfy her demands for a war that was to rage on more than one front. Why waste this pool of man power that was kept in protective custody? The frugal, yet sadistic mind of the Nazis again exerted itself, and we even find witnesses, who have appeared before this court, testifying that more emphasis was placed on work and less on discipline. We have witnesses testifying before this court that the hours that these prisoners worked became longer, a minimum of 11 hours a day.

But this change that took place in Dachau was not the product of any kindness on the part of Weiss. This change was one dictated by economic needs of the times. These prisoners were forced to work and were given less food. In his methodic and economic Nazi mind he had determined the maximum output of labor with the least input—the least input, the least investment by means of food and maintenance. No regards were had for the fact that by following such procedure total exhaustion and ultimate death were inevitable. No effort was made to avoid such results— this was the more subtle approach and certainly the most economical approach to the ultimate end which was the extermination of those who opposed the Nazis.

---

effort by his defense counsel to avert his death sentence was unsuccessful, and Piorkowski was hanged at Landsberg on October 22, 1948.

46. Martin Weiss (1905–1946) was commandant in several concentration camps: Neuengamme (from April 1940–September 1942), Dachau (September 1942–October 1943), Majdanek (November 1943–May 1944), Mühldorf (where he was likely commandant from November 1944–April 1945; his title is unclear but he held the top rank in the sub camp), and finally Dachau again (end of April 1945). His position as the last commandant of Dachau earned him top-billing in the first (parent) trial of Dachau concentration camp guards. Weiss was convicted of war crimes and hanged at Landsberg in May 1946.

That there was in fact a common design to kill, beat, to torture and to subject these people, these civilians, of nations then at war with the then German Reich, is illustrated by the magnitude of the operations here at Dachau and in the by-camps of Dachau. The record shows that between 1940 and 1945, the 29th of April, 161,939 prisoners were processed through Dachau. In view of such a tremendous figure as 161,939, it is inconceivable that it could be argued that this operation could be conducted without the close cooperation of those whose duties and participation brought about the recorded deaths of over 25,000 in the same period of time. I say recorded deaths, but it appears from the testimony that literally thousands of other prisoners died in Dachau and the by-camps whose deaths were not recorded. Thus it is ridiculous to contend that these deaths were not the product of a common design or scheme, but were isolated cases of misconduct by specific individuals, I wish to point out to the court that we are not trying men for isolated cases of misconduct but we are trying them for participation in this common design or scheme.

The segregation of the Jews into the Kaufering and Landsberg camps[47] and the systematic looting from these prisoners of their valuables and clothing is but another bit of evidence of the existence of this common design.

The invalid transports that contained persons disliked by those in operation of Dachau, and those wretched souls whose bodies were so wasted by sickness and malnutrition, took literally thousands to their deaths. During 1942, 1943, the record discloses at least two such transports, one containing a thousand persons and the other six to eight hundred, I call the court's attention to testimony of Redwitz[48] and Weiss. They

---

47. The reference here is to the complex of Dachau's subsidiary ("sub") camps built near the town of Landsberg am Lech in June 1944. Kaufering was one of two camps (the other was Mühldorf) constructed to house underground facilities for fighter aircraft and V-2 rocket production. Primarily Jewish prisoners from Auschwitz were used as slave laborers to build the camps and toil in them under horrific conditions. Malnutrition, epidemic disease, and the brutality of camp guards led to soaring death rates, as did the death march of camp prisoners evacuated from the camps in late April 1945. The fates of prisoners too ill to leave the camp were yet grimmer: the SS set fire to their barracks and burned them alive.

48. Michael Redwitz (1900–1946) was an SS *Hauptscharführer* and veteran of several concentration camps, among them Mauthausen, Gusen, Ravensbrück, and Dachau. In the Dachau camp he became the "First Preventive Custody Camp Leader" (*Erster*

testified that these transports could not have gone out of camp without their knowledge. Certainly this whole procedure required the cooperation of Redwitz and Weiss. The scale upon which the particular form of extermination was carried out again negates the idea that it was the act of one specific individual. Starting at the bottom of the scale the record shows that the room eldest, block leader, doctor, *Schutzhaftlagerführer*, labor department, political department and camp commandant all played parts in the preparation of these prisoners for the "heaven transport."

The mass killings at the crematory and rifle range on the alleged administrative determinations by the Reich Main Security Office[49] again evidences the existence of a common design, the execution of which was without the power of a single individual, but required the support and participation of many to secure the nefarious end that was achieved.

The evacuation transports that left Dachau and the transports that brought prisoners to this indescribable hell are but other examples of the existence of this scheme for extermination. The cannibalism that resulted on some of these transports describes more adequately than I could the horrible conditions that prevailed before a man was blessed with death. In other words, these people were subjected to conditions that forced them to eat the flesh of each other in order to survive it. It would be useless to point out in detail the many other facts contained in this record which clearly indicates the existence of the common design for subjecting these prisoners to killings, to beatings, to tortures and to starvation. Suffice it to say that the overcrowding, lack of sanitary facilities, starvations, disease, destruction of human dignity, and utter disregard of all human

---

*Schutzhaftlagerführer*), in the capacity of which he was directly subordinate to the camp commandant. Redwitz was responsible for general conditions and daily functioning within the camp, including the roll calls completed in the morning and evening. His duties included supervision of punishment meted out to prisoners for infractions of camp rules. He was later transferred to Buchenwald before assignment to the Waffen-SS on the Western Front, where he ended the war. Prosecuted at the Dachau parent case, Redwitz was convicted of war crimes (he confessed to being present at forty executions of prisoners) and given a death sentence. He was hanged at Landsberg on May 29, 1946.

49. The Reich Security Main Office (*Reichssicherheitshauptamt*, or RSHA) was the most significant division within the SS. Headed by Reinhard Heydrich when the Final Solution was launched, it consisted of two branches, each of them heavily implicated in Holocaust criminality: the Security Police (*Sicherheitspolizei*) and the Security Service (*Sicherheitsdienst*). The Security Police embraced the Secret State Police (*Gemeime Staatspolizei*, or Gestapo) and the Criminal Police (*Kriminalpolizei*, or Kripo).

rights as evidenced by the mistreatment, and, in particular, the series of experiments that were conducted here, all point with unerring accuracy at the presence of this barbaric scheme. The experiments here point to the existence of a common scheme or design.

The administrative set up of Dachau, may it please the court, shows the mechanics by which each one of these individuals participated in the common design, and clearly shows the relationship that each member of the staff had to the scheme and to each other. The statement of Michael Redwitz, a former *schutzhaftlagerfuhrer* [sic], in charge of the discipline, good order and cleanliness of the camp illustrates the interdependence of the individual who worked here at Dachau upon each other. May it please the court, I quote from prosecution's exhibit number 95A, which is the sworn statement of Michael Redwitz. This is the English translation.

"We all worked together, and our respective spheres or work overlapped in such a way that it is impossible to make an exact delimitation of all rights and responsibilities. There is hardly one question arising out of or possibly originating in connection with the leadership or the camp in which not all leaders directly subordinate to Obersturmbannfuehrer Weiss would have been interested. It is likewise difficult to make one of the leaders particularly responsible for a certain condition in the camp as this condition, probably was created by the cooperation of all departments."

This statement demonstrates beyond all peradventure of a doubt that all worked together, that the problems that arose were the problems of all, and that the conditions that existed cannot be ascribed to any one department or individual but to all.

. . .

Now, the record discloses to this court that Russian prisoners of war started arriving here at Dachau in the latter part of 1941 and continued to arrive here in Dachau thereafter up until practically the end of the war. At one time, in 1942 the record shows that one portion of the camp was set apart as a PW[50] cage with a sign on it designating it as a PW camp. The record shows that anywhere between two and eight thousand Russian prisoners of war were liquidated during 1942 and the blocks were no longer designated as a little PW camp. Also we have the execution of a French General Dé Lestraint,[51] and other. So that the record shows

---

50. I.e., POW (prisoner of war).

51. Charles Delestraint (1879–1945), a French lieutenant general and member of the French Resistance, was executed at Dachau by the Gestapo on April 19, 1945.

that prisoners of war were victims of a common design to kill, to beat, to torture and to starve the different prisoners here at Dachau.

It might be urged on the court that some of these accused did not participate, or encourage, or aid this common design because they had no knowledge of it. Such a contention becomes completely absurd on its face. The magnitude of the operation is sufficient to refute any such argument in its entirety. Any man who had a chance to observe the prisoners in Dachau proper or the by-camps could see that starvation literally screamed from faces. They would have to have less than one eye to observe a Russian hanged in public view in front of the Messerschmidt barracks. The law is very plain with respect to charging a man with having knowledge of those matters that may be seen by those who look. To say that these people were not aware of this design to kill, to beat, to torture is utterly contemptable.

. . .

This court should not concern itself with trying to determine how many prisoners [the defendants] Eichberger shot or Mahl hung, or on what date Endres[52] killed a prisoner by inoculation. Again, let me emphasize, that we are not trying these men for their own individual specific acts of murder, but we are trying them for their participation in a common design to subject these prisoners to killings, beatings, tortures, and starvation. As I have stated before this court before, this court could find these men guilty by showing that not a single man in that dock actually killed a man, but it would be sufficient to show what his participation was as Schutzhaftlagerführer or Rapportführer as a doctor it wouldn't be incomplete on the part of the prosecution to show that pregnant Russian women died as a result of Doctor Hintermayer's[53] injections but that he, as camp doctor, participated in this common design. But this evidence

---

52. Anton Endres (1909–1946) worked in the medical service of the Dachau camp. As a part of his duties he participated in lethal medical experiments on camp prisoners. Endres later worked in both Majdanek and Auschwitz; in the latter camp he was involved in gassing Jews. Returning to Bavaria in 1943, he was assigned to a subsidiary camp of Dachau in Augsburg. Endres was convicted of war crimes at the Dachau parent case and hanged at Landsberg in May 1946.

53. Fritz Hintermayer (1911–1946) was the chief doctor of the Dachau concentration camp. He was charged with war crimes at the Dachau parent case—among them, administering lethal injections to two pregnant women and contributing to the murders of seven mentally ill prisoners. He was convicted and sentenced to death. Hintermayer was hanged at Landsberg in May 1946.

was available in order to established the fact that killings did take place, that beatings and tortures and starvation were rampant. The witness who came could testify as to killings that Tempel participated in and the beatings that Endres and the various others participated in.

So that type of testimony was submitted to the court, but I ask the court not to try these men on the basis of the specific act of misconduct but to the fact as to whether or not they had any part to play in the execution of this plan or design to subject these nationals and prisoners of war to killings and tortures and starvation itself.

The question the court ought to ask itself should [have] been, first of all, was there in fact a common scheme to subject these prisoners to killings, to tortures, to beatings, and to starvation. If the answer to that is Yes then you proceed to the next questions. What, if anything, is the participation of each one of these individuals in that particular plan or scheme or design as shown by the record of trial. If the answer to both of the questions is yes, then your job is simple. With respect to the guilt or innocence of these accused, there would only remain then the question of punishment. This court knows that every war crime is punishable by death or lesser punishment. These accused have committed a war crime that has shocked the sensibilities of a civilized world. These acts were committed by individuals who profess to belong to that civilization and it is enough to make one stop and wonder. When we examined the mute evidence on the atrocities that have been committed here as to whether or not they are not beasts and certainly could not lay claim to being human in any respect. There has been no doubt about the fact that the conduct of these accused will have turned back the hands of the clock of civilization at least a thousand years, if this court, in any manner, condones the conduct that has been presented to it. And I am sure that this court will not by its sentences or by the findings in any way condone this conduct but will impose a sentence which the world at large can understand as making the position of this court absolutely clear that such crimes will not be again tolerated on this earth. I believe, and am convinced, that every man in that dock has forfeited his right to mingle in decent society.

. . .

### Defense (Captain May)

. . . As to the common design, these forty defendants are like links in a chain, but you know that a chain is no stronger than its weakest link, and there are some weak links in this chain. Becher, Mahl, Knoll[54]—how could there be a common design between those three and the SS? How could there be common design to murder between master and prisoner? Between the conqueror and the conquered? Yes, there are weak links, and also some missing links in that chain. Hitler is one of the missing links. He started it. Himmler is another missing link. Bongartz and Weiter[55]— you can't bring them in. You picked forty Germans and accuse them— these forty—of common design. What about Doctor Blaha?[56] He was a prisoner here. He was forced to do things that I presume he didn't want to do, just like Kahl was. They were both prisoners. Blaha admits that he performed operations, and took hearts out of people—hearts that were still beating. Do you suppose that he wanted to do that? No more than Mahl wanted to put the noose around the neck of others. What about Siebold, the prosecution witness? He was just like Mahl. He was a capo, a prisoner ordered to do these things. Why don't they bring him in and make him a defendant. Is it because he was willing to turn state's evidence that he went free, and Mahl is sitting here accused? Somebody has to pay for Dachau, so we go out and pick forty people—it doesn't matter who they are. You can go into the courtroom and pick out forty Germans, and get the same thing. Somebody must pay for Dachau. Yes, the prosecution has had the popular side. They had everything on their side. Their witnesses came eagerly, seeking revenge. From the crowned heads of Europe to the arch-criminals of Germany, it as easy for them to get witnesses. Everybody wants to punish somebody. Our witnesses were reluctant, or else afraid. Afraid of the United States Government. Afraid that they were testifying against the United States Government. Afraid that they would be forced to buck the rising tide. . . .

*Defense (Major McKeon)*

Lawyers can talk, sometimes, ad infinitum, say nothing, and bore everybody in doing it. But it is necessary for me, in this particular case, to refer to the prosecution's case, which I must confess, somewhat confuses me,

---

54. Each of these defendants were *Kapos*, or prisoner guards, at Dachau.

55. Eduoard Weiter (1889–1945) was Martin Weiss' successor as commandant of Dachau in September 1943. He fled the camp before its liberation, later dying mysteriously at a castle hideout in Austria.

56. A physician, former camp prisoner, and government witness.

and I do believe, and submit, that it somewhat confuses some of the members of the court. The prosecution, particularly Colonel Denson, yesterday stated in his summation of the prosecution's case, and I quote: "Not one thing is in this record to indicate that a common design did not exist." I submit to this court that there is not one iota of evidence, not one centilla [sic] of statement in the entire record showing that a common design did exist. I submit to the court that from the standpoint of the prosecution, from the standpoint of the plaintiffs in the case, that that is a most novel way of proving beyond a reasonable doubt, by saying that there is nothing to show that it did not exist. That is truly an amazing way to prove a case. To add to my state of confusion, Colonel Denson goes further, and says to the court, "The isolated case, —the isolated case of misconduct by any one of these forty defendants is not on trial before the court." I submit to the court that the alleged shooting, by Boettger,[57] is not to be considered by this court because we are working solely on common design, which the record doesn't indicate by any testimony. To go a little farther in the state of the confusion. Yesterday the court, itself, stated quite properly that we are working under the theories of international law. So counsel for the prosecution in his summation, cites Wharton's Criminal Law, section 256, and then goes on further, and cites section 375, saying, in his citation "this is American criminal law," and then goes further and cites the applicable law in a decision by the Theater Judge Advocate, and then adds further to the state of confusion of the law in this case, by reading a citation from Wheaton's International Law, and then contradicts it with a statement from our own Technical Manual 27-10, which provides that orders are admissible in evidence for the purpose of mitigation, or, even, defense. Again referring to the statement of Justice Jackson, of June 8, 1945, which was cited by Captain Niles, "Orders are admissible in evidence, to be considered by the court as a defense and likewise can be considered by the court as circumstances in mitigation." We are all here on orders. Can we say—can this court say definitely to the American public, which is watching with interest, and to the world at large, which is likewise watching this case, and our conduct of it, that superior orders of an army officer are not

---

57. Franz Böttger (1888–1946) was assigned to the Dachau "protective custody" (*Schutzhaftlager*) camp, where he organized labor battalions and prisoner transports and contributed to executions at the camp crematoria. He was prosecuted for war crimes at the Dachau parent case, convicted, and given the death sentence, carried out in May 1946 at Landsberg prison.

to be followed? For instance, take a little incident that happened here in this court that was told to me as I walked out of the courtroom. The president of the court requested that the windows be opened. The courtroom got cold. A doctor in the audience said that the room was too cold. The guard said, "I can't close the windows, because the general said that they have to be open." That is an example of the orders we follow in the army. That is the reason we are in the army. That is the reason we have generals, colonels, majors, captains, and lieutenants. So that we can have order; so that we can issue an order and have that order followed. If the general says that he wants the windows open, they stay open, that's all. Nobody's going to cross him. And if I say, in my office, that they will stay opened, they'll stay open, or I'll know why. If the court please, I submit to this court, just what does the prosecution expect this court to do in the decision of this case? They say that there is nothing in the record to indicate that common design doesn't exist. Therefore, they say, because nothing is there to show that it doesn't exist, it must exist. Therefore, you shouldn't try any of these men for their isolated acts of misdemeanor or misconduct. So what can we try? What is there, as far as the prosecution is concerned, for the court to consider in its deliberations? I must submit that this expression "common design"—"common design"—is an ethereal expression, from thin air. I don't know if the prosecution picked it up. I don't think so. I think they have been saddled with it, and don't know what to do with it, either. The only thing before the court is the individual acts of these accused. The prosecution says in its defense of common design that it is a plan to exterminate people, to exterminate a race, to exterminate people opposed to the existing Nazi state. I submit that even the proofs in this case are contrary to that conception. Take Commandant Weiss. The prosecution admitted in their summation that he did not, here in Dachau, itself, exterminate anybody. They almost went to the point of ridicule by calling Dachau a rest-camp, because during Weiss' time he was known as humane. Even these unsolicited letters indicate that he was humane. For the principal reason—yes, I'll admit that—that he could get them back to work. As long as a man is able to work, I submit that he is not going to die, and is not being given inhumane treatment, and there is no evidence of a plan to exterminate him as long as he is kept on his feet, able to work. Whether he wanted to work when he came, or not, this court is not concerned with that. It is only concerned with the extermination of a people, of a race, or of those opposed to the Nazi party. Again referring to Weiss, all of one hundred seventy witnesses paraded before the court; he is the only one who spoke of a plan, and it was upon my question to him: "Weiss, did you know of the existence of a plan to exterminate, to abuse, to starve people, that existed when you became commandant of Dachau?" And, with his military training behind him he answers "Nein." He is the only witness who ever spoke of any kind of plan in this court. To go further I ask the court to consider how could such a plan exist. How could these men know of the existence of such a plan, and, in furtherance of it, aid and abet such a plan, when from one minute to the next, like you gentlemen, and like any of us, and like the rest of the officers here, conducting this trial, they didn't know where they were going to be? Here today, and on some other job tomorrow. Weiss came here from some other concentration camp. He came to Dachau. How long was he in Dachau? He was taken out and sent to some other job, supervising the building of other camps. Does that indicate any preconceived knowledge of a plan? None whatsoever. There is no indication that he knew of, or was aiding and abetting in the extermination of a people or a race. Take some of our doctors—Witeler [sic],[58] Eisele,[59] Puhr[60]—they were all combat physicians, all attached to combat units.

---

58. Wilhelm Witteler (1909–date of death unknown) was an SS physician assigned to the Dachau concentration camp. He murdered prisoners deliberately infected with malaria by Dr. Klaus Schilling, a tropical disease expert who ran medical experiments with human test subjects at Dachau. Witteler, moreover, prepared the death certificates, which contained no mention of the decedent being infected with malaria by Schilling. Convicted of war crimes and sentenced to death at the Dachau parent case, Witteler's sentence was later commuted to a twenty-year prison term. He was released from Landsberg prison in March 1954.

59. Hans Eisele (1913–1967) was an SS doctor assigned to the Dachau camp in February 1945, where he served under Fritz Hintermayer. Eisele had the rare distinction of being prosecuted in two US military commissions: the first at the Dachau parent case, where he was convicted and sentenced to death for contributing to three executions in the camp (the sentence was commuted to a life sentence), and the second at the Buchenwald parent case, which likewise ended with his conviction and death sentence for murdering some three hundred prisoners. The reviewing authority commuted the death sentence to a ten-year prison term that ended with Eisele's premature release in February 1952.

60. Fridolin Karl Puhr (1913–date of death unknown) was an SS doctor and troop doctor assigned to the Dachau concentration camp from December 1944 until April 1945. He was prosecuted at the Dachau parent case for war crimes for his participation in executions carried out in the camp. Convicted and sentenced to death, his sentence was commuted to a twenty-year prison sentence. Puhr never served his full sentence; he was released from confinement in Landsburg in 1950. Resuming his practice in Munich, he fled Germany to Egypt in 1958 due to an investigation in which he was incriminated. The remainder of Puhr's life was spent living under a pseudonym in Cairo.

They served on the eastern or the western fronts—I don't recall where it is indicated that they were. I believe that Witeler and Puhr were on the western front, and Hintermayer on the eastern front. They were attached to combat outfits, and suddenly transferred as troop physicians and doctors here at Dachau. Does that indicate that they know, or had knowledge of a preconceived plan of extermination, or were part of a common design to aid and abet killings and atrocities here in Dachau. Colonel Bates said that we are not trying to paint Dachau white. That is not what we are trying to do, but where justice is justice, it must be served. A great hue and cry has been sent up by the prosecution that the doctors attended executions; that doctors were ordered down to executions, and attended them, and saw people shot, saw people hung. I submit—"How atrocious"; we do the same thing in the United States. There is no execution in any of the thirty-six states that recognize capital punishment, in the United States, that is performed without the presence of a doctor to certify as to death.…

As for Weiss, we have the unfortunate situation that he is the only commandant present for trial. It is unfortunate that this court does not have before it, as a defendant, Commandant Piorkowsky, or Commandant Weiter, as well as Weiss. Can we say, as some people have indicated to me, personally, in this courtroom, that we Americans are putting on a show? That this is only a theatre. That is what we have been accused of. That is the reason that I take pleasure in my role as assistant defense council, because it hasn't been theatrical. Can this court say that Weiss is not guilty of any inhuman treatment, or, in the converse, can it say that the evidence indicates that Martin Weiss was a cruel commander, and, because somebody under him in this camp kicked the ears off of somebody, or the teeth out of the head of somebody, or shot and killed somebody on the outside, during a transport, that Martin Weiss, a commanding officer of Dachau, was guilty? I submit that, if the court please, there is not evidence in this case to indicate that definite guilt of Martin Weiss, for anything other than being in the unfortunate position of commandant of Dachau. Now Suttrop[61]—a military orderly—an adjutant who had no command functions whatsoever in Dachau. There is no evi-

---

61. Rudolf Suttrop (1911–1946) was adjutant to the camp commandants at both the Groß Rosen and Dachau camps. At Dachau he served under Alexander Piorkowski, Martin Weiss, and Eduard Weiter. Although no specific criminal act could be proven against him at the main Dachau trial, Suttrop was convicted on a theory of complicity in a common design to commit war crimes and sentenced to death. He was hanged at Landsberg in May 1946.

dence whatsoever that he had command functions. There is testimony by the prosecution's witnesses that he, too, attended executions. I submit, again, our bug-a-boo: orders. He was ordered down there. . . .

Prosecution (Lieutenant Colonel Denson): May it please the court, counsel for the defendants has stated that they do not understand this "common design." That the prosecution does not understand this design, that the prosecution was saddled with it, and has had to stick with it. Yes, the prosecution was saddled with the truth, the prosecution has shown to this court, by the evidence presented, the existence of common design. Counsel for the defendants has seen fit to choose one sentence out of the opening statement of the prosecution to the effect that there is no evidence that common [design] did not, in fact, exist. Yes, that statement was made, but that statement was made in conjunction with, and after, evidence had been described and pointed out to the court, of the existence of a common design, and not to this minute has a single counsel from the defense sought to explain away the existence of invalid transports as being evidence of the common design. Not to this time has a single counsel for the defendants raised voice to explain away the inference that can be drawn from the magnitude of this operation as being evidence of a common design. Those are but two of the main factors that have been pointed out to this court as being evidence of the existence of that common design, and the reason is fairly obvious as to why they have chosen to ignore that phase of the case. They have no answer because it is apparent on its face that there was a common design to bring about the murder, the tortures, the beating, and the starvation of these prisoners here at Dachau. They ask this court to administer American justice, to try each man on the facts of his own case. Yes, we ask the court to administer American justice. The only difference between the request made by the defense and the request we make is as to the type of conduct we ask the court to examine to determine the culpability of each one of these accused. As was pointed out in the opening statement, they wished that this court would determine the culpability of Eichelsdorfer [sic][62] by the

---

62. Johann Baptist Eichelsdörfer (1890–1946) was a German army captain and last commandant of the Dachau subsidiary camp of Kaufering IV. At trial during the Dachau parent case, American prosecutors alleged that some four thousand prisoners died or were killed at Kaufering IV under his supervision; at the time of the camp's liberation in April 1945, only twelve survivors remained. Eichelsdörfer was convicted of war crimes and hanged at Landsberg prison in May 1946.

number of prisoners he shot, of Tempel and of Jarolin[63] by the number of prisoners they beat or killed. We do not ask the court to apply that test at all. We ask that the court first determine whether or not there was, in fact, a common design to kill, beat and torture and starve these prisoners. If there was no such common design, then every man in that dock should walk free because that is the essential allegation in the particulars that the court is trying. As to examination of the specific conduct of each one of these accused, the test to be applied is, not did he kill or beat or torture, or starve, but whether or not he encouraged this common design. Did he, by his conduct, aid or abet the execution of this common design, and, finally, did he participate in this common design? It is unfortunate that the defense counsel are unable to understand English, because the particulars state very clearly that these individuals, acting in pursuance of a common design, did subject prisoners to killings, beating, tortures, and to starvation. That, may it please the court, is the test we ask this court to apply in determining the culpability of each one of these accused. Counsel does not feel it necessary to go into the statements made by the defense counsels with respect to each one of the accused that they discussed. They would, as was anticipated, take each man and attempt to point out any deficiencies, or possible conflict that exists. As to whether or not Endres injected a particular man at a particular time. It is not felt necessary at this time to answer such argument. They did not deny in any way that Endres participated in this design. They could not deny it. The testimony that has appeared before this court is much more convincing than any argument that I could make, as to his participation in aiding, abetting, encouraging that common design, or as to the aiding, abetting, and encouragement that each one of these forty men did with respect to this common design. That is the test that we ask you to apply. There has been some argument made to the effect that there are missing links in this chain. True enough, but it is certainly a novel proposition that these forty men should be acquitted because they are not forty other men sitting here for trial for their misconduct. This court has a duty to try these men, even though there may be forty equally, or more, culpable than they. The

---

63. Josef Jarolin (1904–1946) was an SS guard in the protective custody camp at Dachau and commandant of the Dachau satellite camp of Allach. He was accused at the Dachau parent case of kicking and beating prisoners during interrogations and of shooting three of them. Convicted of war crimes, he was hanged at Landsberg in May 1946.

problem of this court is to determine their relationship to the charge laid against them. Now, counsel has stated that it was very confused; that the prosecution made a statement, in substance that it wasn't necessary to show that any men over there did a particular act. Again, that statement was taken out of context, which had this point: "that it was not necessary to show that Eichelsdorfer killed a man before he can be found guilty." But it was necessary to show that he did aid, abet, encourage, or participate in the common design. That is not confined to acts of participation or acts of actual killing. That participation, aiding, abetting, or encouraging, can be shown in a thousand different ways, and has been shown in a multitude of different ways by witnesses before this court. . . .

*Defense (Lieutenant Colonel Bates)*

. . . This court is sitting by authority of our country, and under its flag. It has two heavy responsibilities: first, to protect forty individuals—defendants in this case—from unrelenting bitterness and hate[,] a result of centuries of conflict and a decade of subjugation. From all directions, from places high and low, is heard a primitive cry, "Blood for the atonement of Dachau." It matters not whose blood, so long as it is German blood, preferably SS. I submit that the court will not countenance and further the application of a discredited doctrine—"An eye for an eye, and a tooth for a tooth." The most talked-of phrase has been common design. Let us be honest and admit that common design found its way into the judgment for the simple expedient of trying forty defendants in one mass trial instead of having to try one defendant each, in forty trials. The very working of the charge itself does not undertake to bracket all defendants under one common design. On the contrary, it charges all defendants with acting in pursuance to a common design with doing certain specific things. Not participating in a common design to do certain things, but each defendant acting in pursuance to a common design, his acts of aiding, abetting, or encouraging the commission of certain specific offenses. Where is the common design? About the middle of the second week of this process, the common design was still very conspicuous by its absence, and then it became apparent to the prosecution that the common design must be established for the purpose of trapping some of the defendants against whom there was an outstanding shortage of proof. By showing that if

Schoepp[64] was guard at a camp, he thereby was responsible for everything that went on within the camp. I submit for your consideration a parallel to that. At this American post today there are guards on each gate, and isn't it far-fetched to say that each guard on the gate is responsible for any and every crime that may be committed within the confines of this large area? So prosecution left the local common design and began to branch out. He went to Oranienberg [sic],[65] headquarters of the concentration camp, I think—it's not too clear. Now they're at Berlin, and probably went back years ago to Munich and Nurnberg [sic]. I'm surprised that *Mein Kampf* is not in it as yet. I submit that there may perhaps be common design—the common design to wage aggressive warfare. The adjudication of this common design, which was born in the minds of the policy formers of the Third Reich, is now in process at Nurnberg, and if every one of these defendants is guilty of participation in that large common design, born in Berlin, or wherever the policy formers gathered, then it becomes necessary to hold responsible, primarily, every member of the party, since the inception of that party, every citizen of Germany who contributed to the waging of total war, and I submit that that can't be done. I would like to read an editorial that I read today in *Life* magazine: "And yet justice cannot be measured quantitatively. If the whole of Germany is guilty of murder, no doubt it would be just to exterminate the German people. Burke did not say you should not indict a whole people, he merely said he didn't know how to do it. The real problem is to know who is guilty of what."

---

64. Johann Schöpp (1911–date of death unknown) was a Romanian SS member and guard in the Dachau satellite camp of Feldafing. He was prosecuted in the Dachau parent trial and convicted of war crimes. Although no specific act committed by Schöpp in violation of the law of war could be proven, the US military commission found him guilty based on his participation in the common plan to perpetrate war crimes at Dachau. Sentenced to a ten-year prison term, his sentence was subsequently reduced to five years, and in February 1950 he was released from Landsberg prison. The example of Schöpp demonstrates how thoroughly the military commission members endorsed the common design construct of collective liability advanced by the prosecution.

65. The Oranienburg camp was among the first Nazi concentration camps, established on March 21, 1933, by SA Regiment 208 in the town of Oranienburg, located twenty kilometers north of Berlin. There the Nazis confined their alleged political enemies from Berlin and its environs: Communists, Social Democrats, and gay men, among others. After the bloodletting of the "night of the long knives," the SS assumed control of Oranienburg. It was officially closed in 1936 and effectively replaced by the Sachsenhausen concentration camp.

Perhaps the prosecution has arrived at the solution as to how an entire people can be indicted as an acting part of a mythical common design. Was Schoepp [Schöpp], a Corporal, drafted from the Romanian Army into the German Army, into the Waffen-SS, acting as a reserve guard on an evacuation transport, which was fleeing the battle, along toward the latter part of April—was that Corporal in junction [sic] with the common design with the inhuman Luftwaffe experiments conducted here by Doctor Rascher?[66] Did Eichelsdorfer, a soldier in two wars who should have been retired, almost in his dotage, did Eichelsdorfer discuss with Himmler the method of conducting malaria experiments? Is that the common design that this court must recognize, and, by words of counsel for the prosecution, if you will not recognize it, you will be justified in turning everyone loose? That is a quote from counsel for the prosecution—not from me. I don't agree. . . .

## Military Commission Verdict

President: It is the desire of this court to announce sentences in open court. We will do that only if the audience demonstrates ability to maintain complete silence, with no exclamations of approval, or disapproval.

This court desires to make certain comments before announcing sentence. The evidence present [sic] to this court convinced it beyond any doubt that the Dachau Concentration Camp and the by-camps of Dachau subjected its inmates to killings, beatings, tortures, indignities and starvation to an extent and to a degree that necessitates the indictment of everyone, high and low, who had anything to do with the conduct and the operation of the camp. This court reiterates that although appointed by a conquering nations [sic] as a military government court in a conquered land, it sits in judgment under international law and under such laws of humanity of and customs of human behaviour that is recognized commonly by civilized people. Many of the acts committed at Camp Dachau had clearly the sanction of the high officials of the then

---

66. Sigmund Rascher (1909–1945) was an SS doctor involved in high altitude, freezing, and blood coagulation experiments with coerced prisoners at Dachau. Expressly approved by SS head Heinrich Himmler, the experiments led to the killing, maiming, and torture of numerous prisoners. Rascher fell into a bad odor with Himmler due to charges of financial and other irregularities, for which he was himself imprisoned—first in Buchenwald, then in Dachau. He was executed (some accounts claim he was murdered) on April 26, 1945.

government of the German Reich and of the de facto laws and customs of the then German government itself. It is the view of this court that when a sovereign state sets itself up above reasonably recognized and constituted international law or is will [sic] to transcend readily recognizable civilized customs of human and decent treatment of persons the individuals offending such policies of their state must be held responsible for their part in the violation of international law and the customs and laws of humanity. . . .

# Section 4
# Trials by Polish Courts

## 4.1

## Trial of Amon Göth by the Supreme National Tribunal, August 27–September 5, 1946[67]

*Outside of notorious war criminals like Adolf Eichmann and Hermann Göring, Amon Göth might today be the best known Nazi war criminal prosecuted after the war. His posthumous fame is due in no small degree to the film* Schindler's List, *in which Göth was played by English actor Ralph Fiennes. Fiennes' Göth is a coarse, selfish, and sadistic man able to refresh his ample cruelty from a seemingly bottomless well of malice. The cinematic Göth does not stray too far from its historical model. Göth's 1946 trial before the Polish NTN revealed him as a dangerous criminal psychopath, belying the "ordinary men" thesis of average people ensnared in the spider's web of a ruthless, genocidal government. There is nothing ordinary or banal about Göth's wickedness: it is as shocking to the human conscience today as it was in 1946. Differing from the numerous "desk killers" among the mid-level bureaucrats of the Nazi state, Göth was a direct perpetrator responsible for the murders of thousands of people with his own hands.*

. . . [T]he Court proceeded to read the full document of the indictment.

### The Prosecution of the Highest National Tribunal

Amon Leopold Goeth [Göth]—Born on the 11th of December 1908, in Vienna, citizen of Austria, divorced, author by profession, at present detained in prison, is accused as follows. . . .

---

67. Source: http://www.holocaustresearchproject.org/trials/goeth1.html (accessed July 30, 2019).

As member of the N.S.D.A.P. in Austria and Germany, from the year 1932, also as a member of *"Waffen-SS"* from the 5th March 1940 to the 13th September 1944 within the territories of the Republic of Poland took part in a criminal organisation, being a member of that party, which under the command of Hitler has taken the path to rape, waging wars of terror against civilians, and with the assistance of other crimes, one of which has been the mass murder of Poles and Jews, aimed at the subjugation of the world and establishment of a Nazi order, in this Amon Goeth personally ordered the deprivation of freedom, torture, extermination of small groups, as well as whole communities of people, as well as personally killing, maiming and torturing an unknown number of people, Jews and Poles, in addition a great number of other nationalities.

+ The accused Goeth as commander of a forced labour camp in Kraków Płaszów[68] from 11th February 1943 to the 13th September 1944 caused the death of approximately 8,000 persons who were interned. In addition to, on many occasions ordering the killing of various groups of prisoners, probably considerably greater in numbers than the original 8,000, personally with his hands killing, or ordering for prisoners to be savaged by dogs, he beat, tortured, subjected prisoners to various carefully thought out methods of torture, resulting with the prisoners dying or becoming crippled.

+ As *SS-Sturmfuhrer* he conducted on directives of *SS-Sturmbannfuhrer* Willi Haase,[69] the final liquidation of the Ghetto in Kraków, which commenced on the 13th March 1943.

+ As *SS-Hauptsturmfuhrer* conducted on the 3rd of September 1943 the liquidation of the Ghetto in Tarnow, ordering for

---

68. Płaszów, or Kraków-Płaszów, was built by the SS on the site of two Jewish cemeteries near Kraków as a labor camp for Jews. By 1944 it had become a fully fledged concentration camp containing up to twenty thousand Polish Jews, Roma, and non-Jewish Polish prisoners. Before its liberation by the Red Army in January 1945, the camp's prisoners were sent on a death march to Auschwitz, where many were murdered upon arrival. Amon Göth was assigned to oversee construction of the camp, serving as commandant from its opening until his removal in September 1944 on suspicion of stealing Jewish property.

69. Willi Haase (1906–1952) was an *SS-Sturmbannführer* and chief of staff for the SS police leader in Kraków, Julian Scherner. The Poles hanged Haase in 1952 at Montelupich Prison/Kraków for his contributions to the liquidation of the Kraków ghetto on March 13–14, 1943, in which two thousand Jewish residents of the ghetto were killed.

inhabitants to be deprived of their freedom, life or health of approximately 8,000 persons, against whom this action was directed, during these operations, an additional unknown number of people were killed on the spot in the Ghetto, others suffocated during the journeys in the transports, and yet others died on arrival in the concentration camps especially Auschwitz as result of the extermination policy. At all times during this action, Goeth personally participated in the killing, beating, tormenting many inhabitants, and instructing his assistants to kill likewise.

+ During the period of September 1943 to the 3rd of February 1944, Goeth conducted the progressive liquidation of the forced labour camp in Szebnia near Jaslo giving orders to kill great many Ghetto, others suffocated during the journeys in the transports, and yet others died on arrival in the concentration camps especially Auschwitz as result of the extermination policy. At all times during this action, Goeth personally participated in the killing, beating, tormenting many inhabitants, and instructing his assistants to kill likewise.

+ During the period of September 1943 to the 3rd of February 1944, Goeth conducted the progressive liquidation of the forced labour camp in Szebnia near Jaslo giving orders to kill great many inmates on the spot, transporting the remnants to other camps, as a result of these actions several thousands persons lost their lives, the exact number of these, it is impossible to establish.

+ In the course of abovementioned operations, Goeth confiscated and in many instances kept for himself, the valuables of the victims, gold, money, and even clothing or furniture, as also any other item of value, which the inhabitants of the various locations had to abandon prior to being forcefully taken away.

+ Sending many of these valuables on to Germany, the value of these items is estimated to have reached millions as estimated in terms of the exchange rates prevailing at the time. For irregularities in these matters Goeth has been arrested by the German SS police investigation authorities, on the 13th of September 1944, but due to the collapsing fortunes of Germany, the investigation could not proceed.

. . .

**Chairman:** How was this *"health appell"* [i.e., selection of camp prisoners for transportation to a death camp] conducted?

*Witness Pemper:* The men were assembled, on the parade ground, the women were likewise assembled, but in the women's camp, which was separated from the men. All prisoners were assembled in groups representing the blocks they were living in, they were ordered to undress, Goeth hastened this, by ordering that the undressing is to be done according to blocks being dealt with.

There was a table, on which was placed the file belonging to the particular block, there were four such files. The prisoners were lined up in alphabetical order, according to each block, and paraded in front of Dr. Blanke.[70] Blanke would point at certain prisoners these would receive a certain mark in the files against their names. These marks were written I believe by Lansdorfer [sic].[71]

In this transport of the 14th of May, 1,400 persons were sent to Auschwitz, among these were 286 children, if I remember correctly. I would point out that I did not handle the correspondence connected with this matter, as it was strictly confidential, and as the accused was very anxious this was maintained, a German shorthand typist of Goeth was used.

I did however manage to study these papers, when due to the negligence of someone dealing with these documents, the copies were left unattended. And so on that day Goeth sent a telegram to Auschwitz, advising that in accordance with the permission of Maurer, on such and such a day a transport is being sent off to Auschwitz containing so and so many prisoners from Kraków-Płaszów, indicating the various categories, with separate figures for children, elderly, unfit for work and ailing prisoners.

---

70. Dr. Max Blanke (1909–1945) was an SS doctor assigned to the Buchenwald and Dachau camps before reassignment to Natzweiler-Struthof, Majdanek, Lublin (where he was the head doctor for Odilo Globocnik, the SS police leader/Lublin), and in March 1944 to Płaszów. At Majdanek and Płaszów he participated in "selections" of ill prisoners for gassing. He was at the Dachau satellite camp of Kaufering IV at the end of the war. Here Blanke issued the order prior to the camp's liberation to set fire to the prisoners' barracks, which resulted in the deaths of 360 forced laborers. Blanke committed suicide along with his wife at their home on April 27, 1945.

71. Lorenz Landstorfer (1914–1948) was an SS *Hauptscharführer* and commandant of the Polish camp at Płaszów. In 1948 a Polish court convicted him and sentenced him to death. He was hanged in the same year.

Also drawing attention to the fact that persons with infectious diseases, were mixed on the train together with healthy prisoners, to anyone conversant with the behaviour of the SS, we had no doubt whatsoever, that these people were being sent to their death. I would also point out, that the expression *"Sonderbehandlung"*[72] was a synonym used, and well understood among the SS for gassing.

The project Goeth was following was to cleanse the camp, according to him, of unproductive elements, and thereby produce the necessary space for new victims. Irrespective of this, the day following the departure of this transport, Goeth prepared a second telegram to the commander of Auschwitz.

Advising that on the 5th of May an escape of a prisoner, the first since the camp had been accorded the status of a "KL" has taken place. In connection with this escape, all the prisoners of Płaszów, with the exception of those permanently based within the camp, must wear striped suits, so that escape should be made more difficult or impossible.

The allocation of these suits was no simple matter, they were difficult to obtain. And so, because the transport of the 14th of May contained many dressed in the striped suits, Goeth in his telegram to Auschwitz, asked politely the commander there that in view of the shortages of these striped suits, would they be returned to him, from these prisoners.

For me, from the end of April, when discussions regarding this transport started, the destination of this transport left little to the imagination, the additional telegram removed all doubts, and was a clear sign that everyone on that transport went to his death.

As far as I know the people on that transport did not figure any more on the camp records of Płaszów or Auschwitz. They were admitted into Auschwitz in a similar manner, as the transports arriving in Płaszów from the prison in Montelupich, sentenced to death. These transports of people were arriving in closed trucks, for these prisoners Płaszów was the place where their lives were to be lost.

And thus the action of the 14th May is in my opinion quite clear, in light of the documents that were before me, all these people were despatched to their death. In addition we had reports from people, who were sent to Auschwitz later, and who survived the War, that there were frequent transports of people arriving, who were not entered into the register of prisoners in Auschwitz, they were not allocated any numbers but

---

72. "Special treatment," a Nazi code word for killing.

sent directly into the gas chambers. This was also the fate of all in the action of the 14th of May 1944.

I have pointed out in my testimony, that all requests for penalties within the camp were submitted to the camp commander's office. This rule was so strict and specific, that even application for flogging of a prisoner had to be typed, and countersigned in triplicate, before any action was to be taken. In practice however, this has worked in a completely different way in Płaszów, as follows:

When any prisoner was caught for any number of reasons, and flogging was suggested to be administered, this was carried out almost immediately, as during the period when the camp was simply a labour camp, and irrespective of this an application for flogging was despatched to be confirmed by higher SS authorities. After approximately two months a reply would be received, confirming the request of the camp commander, and the prisoner or prisoners would be beaten for the second time.

The accused, at all times, and that without exception, applied for the application of the highest penalty applicable and possible to each case. Among these penal sentences prisoners were transferred to penal work companies, and also solitary confinement for prolonged periods, in a cell, where sitting was impossible and the prisoners in question were kept in a standing position.

Such a cell was a cavity in a wall, approximately 60 cm wide, the prisoner entered, the door was shut behind him, and after this he could not move in any way, irrespective if he was slim or heavily built, as rods were inserted to ensure that movement was impossible. This type of penalty was administered for periods of more or less 12 hours, to periods of 48 hours. I know of one case, where a prisoner was kept in one of those cells for a full week, and on release was taken straight to be hanged, this was for attempted escape.

. . .

The second type of penalty was flogging and third was transfer to a penal company. As regards flogging, it is interesting to note that the accused Goeth always proposed and requested the highest possible degree of sentence, i.e. 50 strikes with a stick, very often we had however cases when this was exceeded and the beating continued beyond 100 strikes as well.

What I have found most intriguing and curious, was to receive decisions from the SS in Berlin, authorising the beatings or sentences in principle but correcting them (reducing) in favour of the prisoners. This would mostly be ignored, but sometimes the sentence would be reduced from 25 to 15 or 10 strikes.

The penal company presented a different type of danger it involved transfer of all such designated prisoners to work in a stone quarry. These quarries were in most cases a sentence of death to a prisoner.

In Płaszów, the quarries were under the command of an SS man called Lehmer,[73] who was specially selected for this function by Goeth, as he was excelling himself in brutality, with many victims on his conscience in Płaszów alone. This company also included women; [sic] the work was in two shifts around the clock. The women were subjected to work well beyond their physical ability, pushing narrow gauge rail wagons, loaded with rocks uphill leading towards the villa occupied by the accused Goeth.

As the Eastern front, with the approach of the Red Army became nearer, the liquidation of the camp began in the following manner. The accused would send a message that such and such number of prisoners were ready for transfer. The reply from Berlin was in the form of a directive, instructing where they are to be sent to, for example, from Wieliczka[74] a transport of approximately 2,000 persons was sent to Flossenburg at that time.

Following that, larger transports of prisoners from Płaszów were sent out, in September several transports of women were sent to Auschwitz, great many of these were lost, later to Stutthof, and to Mauthausen, most of these people died there, also in stone quarries. And later, but this after the arrest of the accused Goeth by the SS, the transports were sent to Gross Rosen.

. . .

[Pemper next testified to Goeth's arrest by the SS in September 1944 on suspicion of embezzlement of camp valuables. The investigation of these charges was conducted by an SS Police Court in Kraków.]

The interrogations also dealt with the matter of the "penal companies" which apparently were also part of the charges against Goeth. The interrogating SS judge was fully aware that this company was a synonym for death, that inclusion in this company meant very harsh conditions at work, linked with beatings, and very often even death.

Thereafter, the questioning touched upon the matter of Chilowicz, who had been shot by Goeth on the 13th of August 1944, and who, as

---

73. In charge of two stone quarries in which Płaszów forced laborers worked.

74. The reference here is likely to the Wieliczka salt mine located near Kraków.

the SS judge was by then fully aware, was removed off the scene, as he knew too much of Goeth's shady deals.

The camp at that time of August 1944 was in a state of evacuation, many thousands of prisoners had already left and due to the rapidly advancing proximity of the front, following transports were being prepared all the time.

And thus, there was this fear that Chilowicz might somehow be included in one of those transports, find himself somewhere in Germany's many camps, and there start divulging incriminating information, on the very shady deals he and Goeth conducted, and of course, all the many matters that Chilowicz settled for Goeth, all of which were quite illegal. Very significant are the dates in this matter, 6th and 7th of August several transports left Kraków and on the 13th, just prior to further departures, Chilowicz and his family were shot.

The accusations laid against Goeth, paradoxically included the fact that he treated the prisoners brutally, well beyond the SS regulations as laid down by the SS high command. They have of course not given any allowance to the fact, that in the situation then prevailing, autumn 1944, the SS officers in the camp laughed at the thought of according the prisoners any mercy.

. . .

*Witness—Helena Horowitz (age 30, seamstress)*

Witness: I arrived in the camp on the 13th of February. I managed to obtain work in the camp kitchen, where I worked as a potato peeler. Right at the beginning I received 10 strokes on my back for allegedly not working hard enough. A short while after, I have been selected by the kitchen Kapo to work in the kitchen for the Germans.

I enjoyed the work there, and I have been promised that if I continue to work as at present, I will be retained there permanently. At that moment I was there in place of a maid who was taken ill with Typhus, at a later stage I have been retained to work there permanently.

At the beginning I believed this to be tremendously lucky, but at that time I have not been aware of the terrible behavior of the accused. My first encounter with him, was as follows:

After a dinner I threw out the bones remaining on a plate, in the evening the accused appears in the kitchen and demands to know where are the bones, I replied I threw them out. He struck me in the face, with such a force, that I fell over and he tells me that if I will not obey his orders, he will shoot me. Once in the "Red House" entering a room I noticed a rifle, or another type of weapon.

Chairman: You must clarify what was this "Red House?"

Witness: This was the private residence of the accused. That is where I noticed how he held a rifle, and congratulating himself on his ability, or his expertise, in front of other Germans also present in the room, he was firing at a group of people working at a distance of maybe 200 metres from the apartment window. . . .

# 4.2

# Verdict of the Circuit Court of Lublin in the case of Wilhelm Reinartz, May 14, 1948

*Like the Nuremberg tribunals, the Supreme National Tribunal was an ad hoc court created for the express purpose of trying the crimes of high-ranking Nazis. However, other courts in Poland prosecuted offenses alleged against Nazi perpetrators, including permanent bodies like the circuit courts of Lublin. The 1948 re-trial of Wilhelm Reinartz, a German medic accused of atrocities in Majdanek and sentenced to death in his first trial, reveals the willingness of Polish courts to acquit accused war criminals when the testimony of victim-survivors supported their defense.*

## Verdict[75]

*IN THE NAME OF THE REPUBLIC OF POLAND*

The Circuit Court in Lublin, 1st Penal Division, . . . prosecuted on May 14, 1948, the case of August Wilhelm Reinartz, . . . born on March 17, 1910 in the Rhineland (Germany), who is accused of

---

75. Source: Winfried R. Garscha, Claudia Kuretsidis-Haider, Siegfried Sanwald et al., *Das KZ Lublin-Majdanek und die Justiz: Strafverfolgung und verweigerte Gerechtigkeit. Polen, Deutschland und Österreich im Vergleich* (Graz, Austria: Clio, 2011), 138–40.

I.    in the period from August 1942 to February 1944 in Lublin, assisting the authorities of the German state in the concentration camp Majdanek and participating there in the killings of prisoners by making so-called "selections" of prisoners to be killed in gas chambers as a member of the SS organization and as a medic and supervising the process of the gassing;

II.   in the period from September 1939 to February 1945 in Lublin and in the territory of the German Reich, belonging to the criminal SS organization (Schutzstaffel) created by the authorities of the German state;

## Decision

With respect to the charges against him in paragraph II, August Wilhelm Reinartz is guilty provided that he acted on orders. In accordance with Art. 4, sec. 1 and Art. 5 of the Decree of 8/31/44 (conforming with the text of 12/11/1946 . . .) the defendant is sentenced to a prison term of two years with credit for time served in the period from 5/9/1945 to 5/14/1948. For the duration of two years the defendant's public rights and civil rights are suspended . . .; his property is forfeited. . . .

## Rationale

. . .

The defendant . . . admits that he was drafted into the German military in 1939 and was assigned as a medic to a front-line unit of the Waffen-SS. In this capacity he participated in the campaigns in France and Holland. Due to injuring his hand twice he was unfit for service on the front and in January 1943 he was assigned as a medic in Lublin and later as a physician for Polish prisoners. Moreover the defendant was responsible for complete oversight of the security force and care of the patients as well as their nourishment with food. He did not participate in selections. This was entrusted to the camp doctor Dr. Blancke. He did not harm anyone, but on the contrary contributed significantly to the well-being of the Polish prisoners. The capo Otto Reider, a German career criminal, was an acquaintance of the defendant. In Moscow the defendant admitted his participation in selections and in the work of the gas chambers.

That however he never did because a prisoner told him his arms and legs would be broken if he did not sign such a statement. On account of subversion of defense power he was punished by the German authorities and stood therefore under constant surveillance. The defendant was extradited to Poland on May 9, 1945.

And what today do the witnesses who came into contact with him as prisoners in Majdanek, or talked with him outside the camp, say about the defendant:

Stefania Sawicka testified that the defendant during her stay in Majdanek had helped numerous patients, particularly at the end, and that she would not have been able to do more had she been in his position. Dr. Blancke had performed the selections, who always arrived with a large group. At the end the defendant was a part of the group and did not speak with Dr. Blancke. He arranged a meeting between a female prisoner and her mother, who brought her food.

The witness Bolesław Burski stated that thanks to the help the defendant gave him he was able to inform his family after three years that he was in Majdanek. He was with the defendant for five weeks and heard nothing bad about him. Dr. Blancke had carried out the selections. One time he was present when a prisoner was caught in the kitchen. The defendant did not beat him because of this infraction, but rather told him that he had to be careful in the future. When the defendant one time asked him, Burski, why he had been imprisoned, he had answered "because I'm a Pole and I fight for Poland." He had not suffered the slightest unpleasantry for this answer and further had no fear of the defendant because everyone trusted him.

The witness Baran stated that after his illness from typhus he had received wine from the city. The defendant caught him in the act but did not seize the contraband; he only explained to him that he needed to be careful. During his typhus illness he had received injections thanks to the defendant. The prisoner Dr. Hanusz accompanied the defendant to the city and brought medicine and secret messages for the prisoners.

Dr. Blancke had performed selections, during which he had been accompanied by many Germans; at the end, however, the defendant was not among them. Upon questioning of the defendant the witness stated that the Polish doctors in the camp had celebrated Polish national holidays and that the defendant had known that and that they had not experienced any repercussions.

In this manner the witnesses spoke about the defendant. And what do the other witnesses say about him, who spontaneously came forward in response to news about the proceeding against the defendant Reinartz:

· · ·

Dr. Tadeusz Lipecki stated that in 1942 together with other persons he organized a secret relief effort for prisoners in Majdanek. At the beginning there was contact between the prisoners and the civilian workers in Majdanek. In 1943 he got in touch with the defendant, who accompanied the physicians of the Polish Red Cross. Because they had conceived a type of blind faith in the defendant, the defendant had simply been admitted into the organization. The defendant received nothing for his service. Through the defendant the witness Lipecki was able to send secret messages, money, and medicine for the prisoners in Majdanek. The defendant was in constant contact with the organization, he registered every prisoner transport from the camp and every execution. One time he even proposed to free prisoners he was accompanying on the street with force. At the time he declared that for this act he would receive a six month prison term. The witness Lipecki even ventured to say that without the defendant the aid provided by the organization for the prisoners would not have succeeded. In view of these statements the court will disregard further factfinding by means of the examinations of the witnesses Christians and the envoy Dabek, to which the defense particularly refers.

The court under these circumstances finds the statements of the witness credible that he was involuntarily drafted into the Waffen-SS, that he performed his service under duress, and where he was able he had helped the Poles and thereby endangered himself, that he did not participate in selections, which all of the witnesses have corroborated. The court rejects the testimony of the witness Otto Rejder because it contradicts the statements of all the other witnesses.

For these reasons the court acquits the defendant Reinartz of the first charge in the indictment and finds him guilty of the second charge with the provision that he acted on orders. With respect to his person, his good behavior, and the proven aid he gave Polish prisoners the court believes it appropriate to impose an extraordinarily lenient punishment and sentences him to two years in prison with credit for all time served preliminary to his trial.

# Section 5
# Trials by Soviet Courts: The Kharkov Trial, December 15–18, 1943

*The earliest Holocaust-related trials were conducted by the Soviets in 1943. The first of these proceedings were "show trials" targeting collaboration with the Einsatzgruppen, carried out in Krasnodar, Krasnodon, and Mariupol. The first public Soviet trial of German war criminals, however, was the Kharkov trial of December 15–18, 1943. The third-largest city in the USSR, Kharkov (Kharkiv in Ukrainian) was conquered, lost, recaptured, and lost again by the Germans during the war. Trapped in the boiling crucible of near constant war, the city suffered immensely at the hands of the Germans and their Ukrainian accomplices. Although historians have disparaged the trial as yet another Soviet kangaroo court, the crimes of the Nazis in the Kharkov region were real enough: they included the December 1941 massacre of 15,000 Jews in the ravine of Drobytsky Yar by elements of Einsatzgruppe C and the Order Police, as well as one of the first uses of gas vans on Soviet territory. The gassings in Kharkov contributed to the murder of 97,000 Ukrainian Jews by means of three gas vans between December 1941 and June 1942.*

## Verdict
### of the Military Tribunal in the Case
### of Atrocities Committed by German-Fascist Invaders
### in the City of Kharkov and Kharkov Region During
### Their Temporary Occupation[76]

December 15–18, 1943

In the Name of the Union of Soviet Socialist Republics.

On 15-18 December 1943, the Military Tribunal of the 4th Ukrainian Front . . . in an open trial in the city of Kharkov examined the case of atrocities committed by German-fascist invaders in the city of Kharkov and Kharkov Region at which the following were tried:

---

76. Source: https://forum.axishistory.com/viewtopic.php?t=43263 (accessed July 16, 2019).

1.  Wilhelm Langheld, born 1891 in the city of Frankfurt on the Main (Germany), German, member of the Nazi Party since 1933, officer in the German Army's military counterespionage, captain.

2.  Hans Ritz, born 1919 in the city of Marienwerder (Germany), German, higher education, member of the Nazi Party since 1937, deputy commander of an SS company, SS Untersturmfuehrer.

3.  Reinhard Retzlaw, born 1907 in the city of Berlin, German, secondary education, official of the German secret field police in the city oi Kharkov, Senior Lance-Corporal.

4.  Mikhail Petrovich Bulanov, born 1917 in the station of Dzhanibek, Kazakh SSR, Russian, non-Party man.

All four had committed crimes specified in Part 1 of the Decree of the Presidium of the Supreme Soviet of the Union of Soviet Socialist Republics dated 19 April 1943.

The material of the preliminary and court investigation of the Front's Military Tribunal established:

Having perfidiously attacked the Soviet Union and temporarily occupied part of her territory, German-fascist troops, on direct orders from Hilter's government, despite the fact that Germany had signed and ratified international conventions on the rules of war conduct brutally exterminated peaceful population, deported to German slavery hundreds of thousands of citizens, robbed, burned and destroyed material and cultural valuables of the Soviet people.

On the territory of the city of Kharkov and Kharkov Region acts of atrocity and violence were committed against Soviet peaceful inhabitants by officers and men of:

✦    the SS "Adolph [sic] Hitler" Division commanded by SS Obergruppenfuehrer Sepp Dietrich;[77]

---

77. Josef "Sepp" Dietrich (1892–1966) was an SS *Oberstgruppenführer* (a rank equivalent to a four-star general) and commander of the 1st SS Panzer Division "Leibstandarte SS Adolf Hitler," an elite division of the *Waffen* (armed) SS involved in the Malmedy massacre in December 1944. For his role in the massacre, Dietrich was tried by a US military tribunal in 1946, convicted of war crimes, and given a life sentence, subsequently reduced to twenty-five years. He was released on parole from Landsberg prison in 1955 but subsequently indicted by a Munich court for participating in Hitler's murderous purge of the SA in June 1934, for which he was sentenced to a nineteen-month prison term, again served in Landsberg. He was released in February 1958.

+ the SS Death's Head Division commanded by SS Gruppenfuehrer Simon;[78]

+ German punitive bodies;

+ the Kharkov "SD Sonderkommando" led by Sturmbannfuehrer Hanebitter;

+ the German secret field police group in the city of Kharkov beaded by Police Commissioner Karkhan;

+ and the defendants in this case Wilhelm Langheld, Hans Ritz, Reinhard Retzlaw, as well as their accomplice Mikhail Bulanov, traitor to the homeland.

During the temporary occupation of the city of Kharkov and Kharkov Region, the German-fascist invaders had shot, hung, burned alive and poisoned by carbon monoxide gas more than 30,000 peaceful completely innocent citizens, including women, old people and children.

Thus, in November 1941 in the city of Kharkov, some 20,000 peaceful Soviet citizens on orders or the Gestapo, were moved from their city apartments to barracks located on the territory or the Kharkov Tractor Plant. Subsequently, in groups of 200–300 persons, they were sent to the nearest ravine and shot.

The German Command, carrying out the direct orders of the piratical Hitlerite government on the extermination of the Soviet people, did not hesitate also in killing patients and wounded Soviet citizens, including children, who had been hospitalized.

Thus, in December 1941, the Gestapo shot 435 patients being treated at the Kharkov Regional Hospital, and among them were many elderly people and children.

In March 1913, 800 wounded officers and men of the Red Army, who were being treated at the 1st Army Marshalling Hospital of the 69th Army located in Kharkov on Trinkler Street, were shot and burned alive.

Numerous arrested innocent Soviet citizens were subjugated [sic] to brutal torture and all types of humiliation, in the Fascist torture-chambers

---

78. Max Simon (1899–1961) was an SS *Gruppenführer* (a rank equivalent to a general) who fought in the Russian campaign as the commander first of the SS Death's Head Infantry Regiment 1, then of the SS Panzergrenadier Division "Death's Head." For his involvement in atrocities on thousands of civilians while affiliated with the latter, Simon was indicted at the Kharkov trial in absentia, convicted, and sentenced to death.

of the Gestapo and other punitive organs. It was often the case that such "interrogations" were fatal.

Regardless of generally accepted laws and customs of war conduct, the German Command forcibly put peaceful Soviet citizens, who had been seized on the temporary occupied territory of the Soviet Union, into prisoner of war camps and considered them as being war prisoners.

At these camps there took place, through torture, shootings, starvation and inhuman conditions, the mass annihilation of prisoners of war and the civil population kept in these camps.

The German-fascist invaders used the so-called "gazenwagens" [sic]—large enclosed trucks—for the mass killings of Soviet citizens. (The Russians called them "dushegubki," i.e., murdergas vans.) The German-fascist invaders forced Soviet citizens into these gas vans and suffocated them by filling the vehicles with a special deadly gas—carbon monoxide.

With the purport of covering up the traces of their monstrous crimes and mass extermination of Soviet people by way of poisoning them with carbon monoxide in the "gazenwagens," the German-fascist criminals burned the bodies of their victims.

During the successful Red Army offensive in the summer of 1943 and the liberation of the city of Kharkov and Kharkov Region from the German occupants, the monstrous crimes committed by the German-fascist criminals were discovered by Soviet bodies and corroborated at preliminary and court investigations.

Having listened to the explanations of the defendants, testimonies of witnesses, conclusions of forensic medical experts, as well as the speeches of the state prosecutor and the defence, the Military Tribunal established the guilt of each of the defendants in the following:

1.  Wilhelm Langheld, as an officer of the German military counter intelligence, participated actively in the shootings and atrocities committed against prisoners of war and the civil population, in the interrogations of war prisoners and by means of torture and provocations tried to obtain false evidence.

    He personally was involved in the fabrication of a number of cases on the basis of which one hundred completely innocent prisoners of war and civilians were shot.

2.  Hans Ritz, as Deputy Commander of an SS company attached to the Kharkov SD Sonderkommando, personally took part in the torture and shootings of peaceful Soviet citizens in the vicinity of

the village of Podvorki near Kharkov, organized the shootings carried out by the SD Sonderkommando in the city of Taganrog, and interrogated prisoners beating them with rods and rubber hoses, trying to obtain fictitious evidence.

3.   Reinhard Retzlaw, as an official of the German secret field police in the city of Kharkov, conducted investigations of cases pertaining to arrested Soviet citizens, tried to wring out of them through torture—pulling out the hair of prisoners and sticking pins into them—false evidence, compiled fictitious conclusions in relation to 28 Soviet citizens allegedly guilty of anti-German activities, as a result of which some of them were shot and the rest killed in gas vans.

He personally forced Soviet citizens into a bus assigned for extermination of people, accompanied the gas vans to the place of unloading, and took part in the cremation of the bodies of his victims.

4.   Mikhail Petrovich Bulanov, traitor of the Socialist homeland, voluntarily went over to the enemy's side, worked for the Germans as a chauffeur of the Kharkov branch of the Gestapo, participated personally in the extermination of Soviet citizens by means of the gas vans, took Soviet citizens out to be shot and participated in the shooting of 60 children.

In this way, the guilt of all the above-listed defendants in the crimes specified in Part 1 of the Decree of the Presidium of the Supreme Soviet of the USSR dated April 19, 1943 was proven both in the preliminary investigation and in court proceedings.

Governed by Article 296 of the Criminal Code of the Ukrainian SSR and Decree of the Presidium of the Supreme Soviet of the USSR dated April 19, 1942, the Military Tribunal of the Front.

*SENTENCES*

Wilhelm Langheld, Hans Ritz, Reinhard Retzlaw and Mikhail Petrovich Bulanov to death by hanging.

. . .

# Section 6
# Trials by German Courts

## 6.1

## Euthanasia trials: The trial of Hilde Wernicke and Helene Wieczorek

*The first German euthanasia trial unfolded in a Berlin courtroom less than a year after the end of the war. The defendants were a physician at the Meseritz-Obrawalde mental hospital in Pomerania, Hilde Wernicke, and her nurse, Helene Wieczorek. The case demonstrates the German judges' willingness to convict both a doctor and her subordinate nurse as perpetrators of murder.*

### Indictment of February 5, 1946

The Oberaerztin [chief physician] of the Institution, Dr. Hilda Wernicke of Wernigerode, arrested in this matter on 10 August 1945; since 27 November 1945 held for investigation in the women's prison in Berlin No. 18, Bernimstrasse 10; born 11 November 1899 in Sleswick; single; Evangelical

the nurse of the institution Helene WIECZOREK of Wemigerode, arrested in this matter on 10 August 1945; since 27 November 1945 held for investigation in the women's prison in Berlin No. 18, Bernimstrasse 10; born 14 September 1904 in Hindenburg O./S.; single; Catholic,

are accused

of having during the years 1943 and 1944, through several independent actions, treacherously and from base motives, together with other physicians and nurses of the Mental Institution Gorswaldt, put to death several hundred people, in the case of the first accused, and at least one hundred, in the case of the second accused.

—Crimes according to paragraphs 211, 47,74 of the Penal Code—

*Essential result of preliminary investigation.*

The defendant WERNICKE passed the state medical examination in 1924, in spring 1925 she received the title of doctor, and on 15 August 1925 her medical appointment after having served half of her medical internship at the Polyclinic in Warburg and the other half at the Mental Institution in Regensburg. She worked in this last mentioned institute until the end of 1926. Then she worked with the physician Dr. ICOCK in Osterwicck [sic] and became *Assistenzärztin* [assistant physician] at the Mental Institution Messeritz-Obrawalde on 1 October 1927. In 1929 she was appointed Oberaerztin[79] at this Institution and thereby permanently employed as official physician. She remained in this position until 29 January 1945, the day on which the evacuation of this institution was ordered.

In 1933 she joined the NSDAP.

The defendant WIECZOREK attended public school in Hindenburg 0/S until she was 14 years old, and after that kept house for her widowed father. On 1 August 1925 she entered the Mental Institution in Obrawalde, was there trained and then employed as a nurse. She too remained in Obrawalde until the evacuation was ordered.

After the evacuation of Obrawalde, at the end of January 1945, the accused, who became friends in the course of their activity, went to Wernigerode where the father and brothers and sisters of the defendant Wernicke live. On 10 August 1945 they were provisionally arrested and then transferred to Berlin, as they were suspected of having participated in the killings of mentally ill patients in the Institution [of] Obrawalde. Both defendants admit this latter.

The defendant WERNICKE stated the following: When she started her work in Obrawalde in 1927, the institution had besides the wings for the insane, numerous relief institutions for mentally healthy people, such as a T.B.[80] Sanatorium[,] a maternity ward[,] a baby nursery, a

---

79. Chief doctor.

80. Tuberculosis.

home for the aged. All that changed [when] the institution was assigned to the province of Pomerania. From then on only mental cases were confined there; in 1939 about 900 persons, in the following years the number of patients mounted up to about 2000. She had mainly to treat the women's section. The inmates of the institution had changed often. Often large groups of patients were brought there from areas destroyed by air raids from the Berlin institutions Wittenau, Wuhlgarten and Buch, and other patients were transferred further on to the east. Many patients supposedly died because of the overcrowding in the institution in Obrawalde and because of the shortage of medicines and water, among those a particularly large number of patients who had been transferred from other institutions as they were very much exhausted from the trip.

In spring 1943, the Director (Leiter) of the institution, GRABOWSKI,[81] who wasn't a physician but in the beginning only the administrative director ... is alleged to have demanded that she take part in the killing of incurable mental patients. At first she claims to have refused. GRABOWSKI allegedly made her understand that he knew of a remark she had once made to an administrative official of the institution named MARTH. This remark had indicated that she was dissatisfied with HIMMLER and the SS, for she had said: "They are all crazy, all of them should be committed to an institution." On account of this remark he had threatened her with the death penalty. She was thereby intimidated to such an extent that she supposed it would cost her head if she were reported. Under this duress she had followed GRABOWSKI's directions.

The mentally ill were handled as follows:

Accompanying the patients transferred to Obrawalde from other institutions was a list indicating which persons were to be killed. It had been her duty to examine these patients in order to determine whether they were really incurable. In those cases where she refuted this the persons were to remain as working patients in the institution; the others after a while were given the lethal injections. For this purpose morphine or morphine scopolamine was used. These drugs had had a narcotic

---

81. Walter Grabowski (1896–date of death unknown) was the administrative director of the Obrawalde mental hospital, in which as many as eighteen thousand patients were murdered in connection with the T-4 program. He served in this role from November 1941 until January 1945. Thereafter, he disappeared from history.

effect and depending on the strength of heart activity of the particular patient induced sooner or later the death of the persons so treated. She had never given an injection herself but this had been done in the ward under her direction by the head nurse RATAJCZAK; performing the killing herself, because she as a doctor needed the confidence of the patient: in the years 1943 and 1944 according to her calculation 1200 inmates of the institution Obrawalde met their death, but about 40% of these had died a natural death. This had especially been the case with most of the children had been brought to Obrawalde with the instruction that they were to be killed; those had mostly been so undernourished and exhausted by the trip that they had died soon after arrival. Until the institution was dissolved patients could be found in it whose names were on the death list.

She could not have supposed that she was not contrary to the law by participating in actions that served to kill incurable, mentally ill persons. She had been ordered to do so by her superiors. She had knowledge at the beginning of her activities that for three years already incurable, mentally ill persons had been killed, and she was told that the law ordering the killing was in existence but would not be published during the war, so that the [German] people would not be worried. She could not imagine that a Reich Office would commit illegal actions for three years. It had not been possible for her to make other investigations, since Director GRABOWSKI had prohibited her under threat of imprisonment or death from speaking about her conversation with him.

The defendant WIECZOREK stated:

In the ward of the institution of Obrawalde in which she worked there were only people who were mentally ill. They changed frequently. Lists accompanied the newly arrived patients. These were handed to the head nurse GESCHKE. She then divided up the patients among the several wards. The defendant WERNICKE and the physician Dr. WOOTZ then selected the patients who were still able to work and designated them as not to be put to death. The other patients were gradually killed off with morphium-scopolamine injections. At first only the head nurses RATAJCZAK and ERDMANN gave the injections. But then Director GRABOWSKI had called her and other nurses to him and had told them that a law had been passed according to which the sufferings of the mentally ill were to be reduced, and that they had to assist the head nurses, who could no longer manage the injections themselves. When she refused, GRABOWSKI told her that it was of no use, that being a civil servant she had to do her duty especially during war-time. If she did not do what he asked he would have to denounce her to the Gestapo. After that she helped in giving injections. She was unable to state how many persons she had given injections.

She was not conscious of having incurred any guilt as she had only executed the orders of her superior.

According to those statements both defendants took part in putting to death the mentally ill.

The defendant WERNICKE cannot protest that she did not herself give injections and that she selected only those patients who were not to be put to death. For by this selection she delivered those persons not designated by her as fit for work to death; whereas without her activity they never would have fallen victim to the injections.

Neither defendant is freed from the responsibility for her actions by the fact that she acted upon the orders of her superiors.

For these deeds violate all moral laws and offend against humanity and cannot, even upon the order of a superior, become lawful. The defendants were aware of this. For they at first refused to comply with the instructions of Director GRABOWSKI. But then, against their better judgment they took part in the destruction of numerous human lives in order to save their own, thus acting from base motives. They adopted the ideas of the National Socialists, whom the defendant WERNICKE joined readily in 1933 and presumed to decide whether a human being was worthy of continuing his life. They considered unworthy all those who needed food and care, who could not help them in striving for their abominable war aims, and who represented in their eyes only a burden for the people in their pursuit of these aims. Their liquidation was, therefore, helping the war effort.

In addition the actions of the defendants were treacherous, for, by making the injections which brought about their death, they abused the confidence the patients had in their doctors and nurses that they would cure them or at least alleviate their suffering.

...

It is requested:

that the main trial be opened before the court of assizes (*Schwurgericht*) and that the continuation of the pre-trial imprisonment be ordered.

...

## Verdict of the Assize Court in Berlin, March 25, 1946[82]

The Assize Court in Berlin in the session of 25 March 1946 holds as follows:

Both defendants [Wernicke and Wieczorek] are guilty of murder and sentenced to death. The defendants are deprived of their civil rights for the remainder of their lives. . . .

*Rationale*

[The evidence at trial showed that Wernicke had freely participated in the murder of patients. In her defense, Wernicke portrayed herself as a sincere proponent of euthanasia with the insinuation that she had acted from lofty rather than base motives.]

. . . A right to euthanasia has hitherto not been legally recognized. However, even if the permissibility of euthanasia for reasons of humanity in individual cases is not to be ruled out, . . . such as one involving an unbearably painful and prolonged illness that is ended by a painless cause of death, this is certainly not the situation here. The defendant Wernicke, according to her own testimony, made her selections not because of humane empathy, pity, or other noble motives. Rather, the persons whose names were placed on the list through her decision were considered from the first as lunatics who should be exterminated. The defendant Wernicke alone had the right and duty, based on her medical knowledge and experience, to select from the lists those persons who in her view were still capable of productive work. [The court pointed out that Wernicke merely skimmed most of the patient records, and on this cursory basis she made her final judgment.] . . . If empathy or pity had been the impelling force of her action, then she would have been able to designate for killing only those patients who also suffered from corporal, unbearably painful illnesses. . . . On these grounds the assize court considers it proven that the defendant Wernicke as well as the defendant Wieczorek, who had immediately and without hesitation declared herself ready to cooperate, and who herself assisted in killing numerous institutionalized patients, acted from base motives. Both defendants participated significantly in the work of extermination.

Moreover, Wernicke and Wieczorek's conduct may be characterized as treacherous [*heimtückisch*] within the meaning of §211 of the German

---

82. Source: C. F. Rüter and D.W. DeMildt, eds., *Justiz und NS-Verbrechen: Sammlung deutscher Strafurteile wegen nationalsozialistischer Tötungsverbrechen 1945–1999* (Amsterdam: Amsterdam University Press, 1999), Case No. 003 (translated by the author).

Penal Code. The killing is treacherous if it is marked by falsehood or deviousness. The perpetrator acts treacherously if he abuses another's reasonable trust, such as when he himself elicits the trust of another. The institution at Obrawalde had the correct designation of "mental hospital." Persons who were admitted as patients into this institution considered it self-evident that patients in the institution would experience either a cure or an improvement of their suffering, or that—in the event that neither a cure nor an improvement were possible—they would receive at least appropriate medical care and treatment. In their role as chief doctor and nurse, the defendants betrayed this trust in a manner grossly repugnant to all human feeling; through their actions they caused immeasurable suffering to many hundreds of people. The death penalty is the only just punishment [for such actions]. . . .

# 6.2

# Euthanasia trials: The Hadamar Trial

*The 1947 prosecution of staff members from the Hadamar mental hospital followed the trend line drawn in the Wernicke/ Wieczorek case. Like their counterparts in Berlin, the judges in Frankfurt presiding over the Hadamar trial convicted staff doctors Adolf Wahlmann and Hans-Bodo Gorgass as perpetrators of murder under German law. The Frankfurt court, however, broke new ground by convicting Hadamar nurses of murder as accomplices rather than perpetrators—meaning that a more lenient punishment was virtually assured them. In German courtrooms by the late 1940s, this "subjective" approach to the accused's state of mind became a dominant mode of analyzing degrees of participation in Nazi crimes. It nearly always worked to the advantage of the defendant.*

### Verdict of the Frankfurt Circuit Court, March 21, 1947[83]

[At trial, Gorgass had argued that he could only be prosecuted under the older version of the German homicide law, which was substantially

---

83. Source: Rüter and DeMildt, *Justiz*, Lfd. Nr. 017 (translated by the author).

revised in 1941. The old version had defined murder as an illegal killing carried out with premeditation. In its assessment of Gorgass' guilt, the Frankfurt judges found that his actions violated both the old and new versions of the law.]

. . . Premeditation was not lacking here [as was evident from] the defendant's statement to the court that he had been distraught and had considered suicide. It is clear from his words how much the defendant had to wrestle with himself repeatedly and how again and again he had brought himself to perform the killings; the "for" had prevailed over the "against." Herein lies the defendant's premeditation in his actions. Therefore, he carried out the killings intentionally and with premeditation and, in so acting, committed murder in the sense of the old version of §211, which provides exclusively for the death penalty.

According to §211 of the German Penal Code, new version, a person is guilty of murder who has killed another person from base motives or treacherously—only these two conditions are relevant here.

[The court found that Gorgass had not acted from base motives; rather, his involvement in euthanasia was due to a "certain human weakness that does not bear the stamp of moral reprehensibility." Next, the court turned to consider whether Gorgass had acted treacherously.]

By contrast the defendant in the view of the court acted treacherously because he committed his crimes secretly, deceitfully, and duplicitously. The patients were first separated from their relatives by means of a visitation ban; most were then transferred to other institutions without notification to their families of the destinations' names. Severe threats, compulsory pledges of secrecy, and false statements ensured that the killings would not come to public light. The patients themselves were pacified by these measures, then deceived to the worst degree. While it was pretended they would be cured or given care, they were with guile and every means of diversion led into gas chambers that appeared to be showering facilities. Hypocritical expressions of sympathy were sent to their relatives concerning the sudden deaths of the patients. Thus, much as the entire "operation" was built on dishonesty, deviousness, and disingenuousness, it was executed in the same fashion. Every detail [of this scheme] was known to the defendant Gorgass; therefore, he performed his crimes treacherously. Consequently, murder under both the old and the new versions of §211 has been committed.

· · ·

[The court ultimately convicted the Hadamar doctors of murder as perpetrators. The nursing staff, however, were only found guilty of aiding and abetting murder (*Beihilfe zum Mord*).]

As far as the defendants among the nursing staff are concerned, the court is of the view that, contrary to our assessment of the doctors, a certain mildness in judging their actions is called for. All the defendants have lived an irreproachable life [until their involvement in euthanasia at Hadamar] and have always fully and completely fulfilled their difficult responsibility. All of the defendants of the nursing staff are simple people, who as nurses were accustomed to obey the doctor as subordinates of the state leadership. They were all inwardly too dependent and possessed by a strong inertia of the will to cope adequately with situations of such gravity. Added to that was their exposure to the confusing propaganda of a state authority that was able to cloud their clear perception and their personal feeling. Above all, however, they saw their medical models, who they were accustomed to regard with respect and reverence, behaving weakly and submissively and found in them neither support nor a role model. Not a criminal mindset but rather human weakness induced the defendants to ignore the voice of nature or of conscience and meekly follow the path on which the persons they were accustomed to obeying were already walking.

All of these circumstances have caused the court to view the conduct of the defendants—aside from the fact that they just committed aiding and abetting—in an entirely different light from the accused doctors. . . . [In the case of the defendant Irmgard Huber] the court has considered it in her favor that she experienced extreme psychological suffering as a result of her actions and tried repeatedly to be reassigned from Hadamar. It should be added that she did whatever she could for the patients. She secretly provided food to them and in spite of considerable hostilities and dangers she furnished secret religious care to the patients. She also stood under the influence of the chief administrator at the time, Alfons Klein, a man with a decidedly reprehensible character, who repeatedly succeeded in exerting a baneful influence on the defendant. . . .

Since the court was not able to ascertain the precise details in the individual killings, it judges the actions of the defendant Huber in their severity uniformly and views it as appropriate to impose a prison term of three years for each action, for a total prison term of eight years.

# 6.3

# Euthanasia trials: The trial of
# Drs. Karl Todt and Adolf Thiel

*German law did not recognize the defense of necessity until
1927, when the German Supreme Court for the first time allowed
it as a defense against homicide. One spin-off of necessity was
the doctrine of "collision of duties" (Pflichtenkollision), which
held a killer blameless for his or her actions if committed to avoid
a "greater harm." This defense would emerge in 1948 as the first
successful ground for acquittal in a euthanasia case. The benefi-
ciaries were the former director of the Scheuern mental hospital
in Hessen-Nassau, Karl Todt, and a physician employed in the
same hospital, Adolf Thiel. Both men were charged with crimes
against humanity for involvement in the murder of their patients.*

## Verdict of the 3rd Penal Chamber of the
## Koblenz district court, October 4, 1948[84]

[Mentally ill patients were not murdered at Scheuern; rather, in March
1941 the institution was converted into a T-4 transit station, to which
patients designated for killing in other facilities were sent en route to
their final destination of Hadamar. Scheuern, like other transit stations,
had the function of both concealing the fates of patients consigned by T-4
officials to extermination, as well as affording more opportunity to spare
patients falling outside T-4 guidelines, such as war veterans or patients
capable of productive work. Todt and Thiel were accused of receiving the
arriving transports and transferring them to Hadamar with the knowledge that they would be killed there. Even when they had exempted some
patients from the transports, they did so at the cost of ensuring the deaths
of other patients. Further, Todt was charged with completing registration
forms on his patients with the knowledge that the forms would be used
as a rationale for killing them while Thiel was accused of providing lists
of patients unable to work to T-4 officials.]

---

84. Source: Rüter and DeMildt [spelled de Mildt], *Justiz*, Lfd. Nr. 088 (translated by
the author).

... From the vantage point of the law, the external legal element of the offense of actual accessory to murder ... has been fulfilled. The defendants through their actions committed aiding and abetting ... in approximately 1,000 cases, [in which patients] were killed from base motives, treacherously, and cruelly. Of course, they did not inwardly identify with the death of the patients yet they were aware that they assisted the crimes of the murderers through their actions. ...

However, before the court delivers its verdict ... it has to inquire thoroughly whether in the assessment of their behavior reasons may exist that exclude their guilt or at least their liability to punishment, or operate to mitigate it. The following justifying or exculpatory grounds should be considered:

1) Acting on orders,

2) Necessity, especially necessity arising from intimidation ...

3) Extrastatutory necessity, and finally,

4) Sabotage committed by the defendants from the standpoint of the collision of duties.

[The judges discounted the first three of these defenses before turning to the fourth, the collision of duties.]

... The Reichsgericht [pre-1945 German Supreme Court] has held that the higher duty may be followed at the cost of the lower. What are we to make, however, of a situation in which two equal duties are in conflict? Is it allowable to save the life of a single person, or even several people, by collaborating in the delivery of other persons to their death? We are confronted with at least a tragic conflict of duties in which the accomplice ... shoulders the blame in order to prevent greater harm. ...

[The court went on to frame the issue as follows: "Whether and under what conditions may an act of sabotage serve to justify or at least excuse collaboration of the accomplice in acts of killing from the standpoint of a collision of duties?"]

The court is ... convinced that the defendants after careful and conscientious examination of the entire factual situation acted with the intention of avoiding greater harm by remaining in their positions [instead of resigning]. The witnesses ... have reported how both defendants repeatedly declared that the only thing that kept them from resigning was their feeling of duty and their efforts to avoid greater harm. That their words were serious is proven ... by their numerous acts of sabotage. ...

[The judges then listed the defendants' actions that were indicative of sabotage. On several occasions, the defendants permitted patients unfit for discharge to be prematurely sent home or accommodated in jobs outside the institution. In sixteen cases the court considered proven, Todt hired patients as employees of the hospital in a sham operation that saved most of their lives. Some of these "employees" were on the lists of patients to be transported. The judges retailed these and other examples of the defendants' efforts to work at cross-purposes with the T-4 program. Their sabotage was performed at significant risk to their own lives. The court estimated that their actions saved every fifth patient (20%) from transfer to Hadamar and death.]

In view of these findings, the court holds ... that it appears justified to treat the defendants' actions in the case at bar as excused. ... The defendants consciously incurred objective and subjective guilt but with only the will through their overall conduct to avoid greater harm. Whether the defendants can inwardly feel free from all reproach is a matter of their personal conscience. ...

# 6.4

## Reich Night of Broken Glass trials: Verdict of the Regional Court of Freiburg i.B. in the Case of Reinhard Boos et al., July 29, 1947

*Along with T-4 crimes, German courts prosecuted a series of cases in the immediate postwar era relating to the Reich Night of Broken Glass* (Reichskristallnacht) *pogrom of November 9–10, 1938. Despite grave misgivings about retroactivity, German courts in the French and British zones often charged pogrom defendants under both German law and the crimes against humanity provision of Control Council Law No. 10. In the case excerpts that follow, the former mayor of the southwest German city Lörrach, Reinhard Boos, and eleven others were charged with a crime against humanity, aggravated trespass, breach of the peace, revilement of religion, damaging property, and destroying a building, i.e., violations of both domestic*

*German and international law. Seven of the twelve defendants were convicted; Boos was among the five accused to be found not guilty. The prosecution appealed Boos' acquittal, which was reversed. (Unlike Anglo-American law, acquittals in German criminal trials may be abrogated on appeal.) In a second trial, Boos was again found not guilty, and for much the same reason as in his first trial, namely, lack of evidence that he knew of the plans for the pogrom beforehand or contributed to its occurrence.*

# In the Name of the People!
## Judgment
### In the criminal case against Reinhard Boos from Lörrach and 11 others for breach of the peace and other offenses.[85]

. . .

It is determined that:

On account of crimes against humanity, in coincidence with aggravated trespass, revilement of religion, and damage of property injurious to the public and destruction of buildings,

1.  the defendant Karl Glünkin is sentenced to a prison term of two years and 6 months, with one month credited for time served,

2.  the defendant Fritz Böhringer from Basel is sentenced to a prison term of nine months . . .

3.  the defendant Friedrich Schneider from Mannheim is sentenced to a jail term of six months,

. . .

The defendants Reinhard Boos from Lörrach
Rudolf Greiner from Lörrach
Leo Köpfer from Lörrach
And Edhuard Kähny from Lörrach
are acquitted.

. . .

---

85. Source: 4 Js 689/46, II AK 25/47, Staatsarchiv Freiburg, F 176/22, Nr. 3/2 (translated by the author).

*Rationale*

[After German diplomat Ernst vom Rath died from his wounds on November 9, Nazi propaganda minister Joseph Goebbels met with Hitler, then later exhorted Nazi leaders to take "retaliatory" action against the Jews. Party activists phoned their subordinates throughout Germany to instigate attacks against German Jews. In Lörrach, orders to attack the city's Jews arrived from party offices in Stuttgart on November 10. Heeding these orders, a group of security service men broke into the city's synagogue and confiscated its religious objects. At 9:00 a.m. another group of twenty to thirty SA men under the command of Karl Glünkin destroyed the synagogue interior. In March 1939 the city of Lörrach acquired the synagogue, now a dilapidated shell, from the Jewish community. It was leveled sometime in the spring of 1939. After reciting these and other facts, the Second Penal Chamber of the Freiburg Regional Court turned to assessing the actions of the defendants. Here we focus on the judges' assessment of Karl Glünkin and Mayor Reinhard Boos.]

## Karl Glünkin

. . . In May 1931 [Glünkin] joined the Nazi party and immediately became a *Kreispropaganda-leiter* [district propaganda director]. When this position became full-time in 1937, Glünkin opted to continue operating his business and resigned his office. In December 1937 he took over the position of the Ortsgruppe [chapter] Lörrach-North, which he held until March 1945. During the war he was active as the deputy district propaganda director. . . .

Concerning his participation in the events of 11/10/38, the defendant provides the following representation.

He was called on the morning of the 10th to the district committee and met there with [defendants] Oldenboerhuis and Hofer, who told him "it's getting started against the Jews" and that he needed to come along. To his objection that he had to first contact the district director they replied the district director had already agreed that he, Glünkin, should come along. He understood this statement to mean that his participation had been ordered by the district director.

When he went with Oldenboerhuis and Hofer to the synagogue, they had already forced an opening into the building and a larger number of persons were present there than they had said. Demolition had not yet been undertaken. Shortly after their arrival 20–30 SA people appeared. They began to tear down the railing of the gallery, hurling the benches onto the floor and breaking out the windows. With the aid of other persons he, Glünkin, smashed the candelabrum with a long brass rod. Further, he chipped away the inscriptions above the altar with a hammer.

He participated in the destruction of the synagogue chiefly therefore because something had to be done against the Jews and because he wanted to avoid worse [outcomes], especially abuses. He therefore also extinguished the fire, delivered a calming speech, and warned against further excesses. He had not participated in subsequent efforts to tear down the synagogue.

· · ·

From the depiction, so far as it is credible, of the defendant Glünkin it is proven that he played a leading role in the crowd's destruction of the interior of the synagogue. Glünkin thereby committed a crime against humanity. (Control Council Law 10, Art. II, 1c.) The pogrom of November 1938 deprived the Jews of their religious rallying point, injured them in their most sacred feelings, filled them with terror, and tore from them the foundation of their human existence. No further demonstration is needed to show that this pogrom should be regarded in its very nature as an inhumane persecution based on racial grounds. Glünkin here participated as a co-perpetrator [*Mittäter*] through his contribution to the destruction of the Lörrach synagogue.

[Due to his central role in the synagogue's destruction as proven by the commencement of the vandalism upon his arrival and his ability to end it with his "calming speech," the court branded Glünkin as the ringleader. The court rejected his defense of necessity and duress because there was no evidence that he acted reluctantly; on the contrary, the evidence indicated that he had "willed the crime as his own" (*als eigene gewollt hat*). The judges later turned to assess Mayor Reinhard Boos' responsibility for the pogrom.]

. . . The defendant Boos . . . joined the [Nazi] Party on August 8, 1930 and immediately took over the chapter consisting at the time of twelve men. In March 1931 he became a district director, [and] in 1933 the mayor of Lörrach. He held this office until Germany's defeat. From 1936 until September 30, 1939 he was also again honorary district director of Lörrach.

· · ·

The indictment considers Boos the spiritual initiator and instigator of the destruction of the Lörrach synagogue. [Relying on Glünkin's testimony, the prosecution had accused Boos of receiving the order to initiate the pogrom by telephone and relaying it to other Nazi Party offices. According to Boos, he did nothing more than receive an order from the district director instructing him to keep the telephone open for future calls. The court noted that Glünkin, whom the judges deemed an unreliable witness, had recanted his previous testimony and now agreed with Boos' defense that he had only kept the phone lines open for calls from higher Gau offices.]

. . .

It is scarcely believable that a pogrom the execution of which lay in the hands of the SS and SA should have been initiated by a local party office. Boos's account sounds much more probable—namely, that Oldenboerhuis and Hofer as SS- and SA-majors received their orders directly from their superior offices, much as the SD [Security Service] from Stuttgart was ordered to collect the religious objects from the synagogue. His account is supported by the fact that Oldenboerhuis already early that morning had come from Haltingen to Lörrach, that he therefore had clearly already received his orders by that time. . . .

[In the view of the judges, the local Nazi party office in Lörrach most likely knew of the planned pogrom; however, it was not proven that Boos was aware of it. It was significant for the court that Boos had already by that date resigned his offices of district director and deputy. The court held that Boos nonetheless remained a "leading Nazi personality" in Lörrach even after resigning his posts; his ability to retain his job as mayor was due to Boos' political reliability.] It is therefore less likely that he knew nothing of the planned pogrom and learned of it only after the synagogue had been destroyed. However, neither is this by any means impossible. At any rate a more certain proof that he knew has not been presented, and above all it has in no way been substantiated that he collaborated somehow as initiator, organizer, advisor, or otherwise or participated through his acquiescence. [The fact that Boos was one of the oldest and most prominent Nazis in Lörrach] is circumstantial evidence suggesting suspicion of connivance and also some kind of participation of Boos in the pogrom staged by the highest Party offices. . . . In spite of this suspicion, Boos has to be acquitted for lack of proof.

# 6.5

# Trials of Political Murders: Verdict of the Regional Court of Karlsruhe regarding the Murder of Ludwig Marum, June 4, 1948

*We conclude this short introduction to Nazi crimes and their punishment with the trial of four men accused of murdering the Social Democratic leader Ludwig Marum in 1934. Marum was one of thousands of political opponents of the Nazis taken into "preventive custody" and imprisoned in concentration camps after Hitler's seizure of power. By the outbreak of World War II such camps held some twenty-five thousand persons, most of them political prisoners. During the Weimar Republic the German-Jewish Marum had been a city councilor and a Socialist Party (SPD) member of the Baden state parliament before his election to the Reichstag. In 1933 he was a highly visible— and vocal—critic of Hitler and the Nazis, with whom he was entangled in litigation. His opposition to Hitler led to his arrest and detention in a Karlsruhe prison in March 1933, followed by his transfer in May 1933 to the labor/concentration camp Kislau near Bruchsal, a city twenty kilometers northeast of Karlsruhe. It was here that four men acting on the orders of the Gauleiter of Baden, Robert Wagner, garroted Marum as he lay asleep in his cell in the early morning hours of March 29, 1934. Staged to look like a suicide, Marum's death was treated as a homicide after the war, and the four men involved in the killing were prosecuted in a Karlsruhe regional court from June 2 to 4, 1948.*

## Judgment[86]

...

The [following] defendants are sentenced
Karl Sauer from Karlsruhe to life in prison for murder,
Heinrich Stix from Aue to a three-year prison term
for aiding and abetting murder,

---

86. Source: 1 KLs 4/48, General State Archives/Baden-Württemberg (GLA) 309/4809 (translated by the author).

Paul Heupel from Brachbach to a twelve-year prison term
for manslaughter and
Otto Weschenfelder from Karlsruhe to a one year and three month
prison term for aiding and abetting manslaughter. . . .

*Rationale*

. . .

II

On 16 May 1933 Dr. Ludwig Marum, at the time a 50-year-old state
councilor and attorney from Baden, was transferred along with other
opponents of National Socialism by the authorities to the protective custody camp Kislau and assigned tasks as a political prisoner within the
camp. . . . From the beginning of March until the beginning of April 1934
[the camp director Mohr] was on vacation. He designated as his replacement for the period of his vacation the defendant Sauer. Around March
27, 1934 Sauer, in his position as head of the camp, . . . reported that
Marum illegally smoked during his work and had allowed food sent him
by his relatives and stored in his cupboard to spoil. Sauer called his superior, the councilor Berckmüller, in Karlsruhe and reported the incident.
Berckmüller recommended that Sauer assign Marum to an outdoor job
and in the event he refused to punish him with arrest and impose on him
a package embargo. Sauer had Marum brought to him and told him he
was being assigned to outdoor work. When Marum refused to perform
such work, Sauer punished him with three days detention and a multiple
week package embargo. Marum was sequestered from the other preventive custody prisoners and locked in a cell for solitary confinement situ-
ated in the administrative building of the camp. On the same floor were
four rooms . . . that could be entered through a narrow hallway. The office
of the camp commandant was in the first of these rooms. Two of the
adjoining rooms were used at the time for solitary confinement, while the
fourth room served as the orderly room and office of the defendants Stix
and Weschenfelder. Marum was in the cell located next to the commandant's office. The hallway led past the orderly room into the first wing, in
which the prisoners' common rooms were located.

On the morning of 3/28/1934 the personal adjutant to
Gauleiter and Reich Governor [Robert] Wagner,[87] *SS-Standartenführer*

---

87. Robert Heinrich Wagner, born Robert Heinrich Backfisch (1895–1946), was gauleiter of Baden and Alsace as well as chief of the civil government of Alsace during the

Bock,[88] came to the Kislau camp and asked Sauer what had happened with Marum. He demanded to speak with Marum. Sauer led him into the cell where Bock castigated [Marum] violently. Afterward Bock asked Sauer to drive with him to Karlsruhe to the Reich Governor Wagner, who wished to speak with him. Sauer drove together with Bock to Karlsruhe, where Bock led him into the Reich Governor's offices to Wagner. The Reich Governor told him in Bock's presence according to his testimony that he [Wagner] was conveying to him [Sauer] an order from the highest office in Berlin and from the *Führer* that Marum was to be shot; he, Wagner, bore for this act full responsibility. As Sauer objected that he could not carry out such an assignment, Wagner asked him where Marum was being kept. When Sauer told him that he was in solitary confinement, Wagner ordered that he should be hanged. Sauer claims to have answered that he could personally not do it, whereupon Wagner is supposed to have said he did not have to do it himself, he could [have it done] by two other people. After Wagner swore Sauer to secrecy about the matter, he left him and Sauer returned to Kislau.

On the afternoon of 28 March 1934 the defendant Heupel received an order from his boss at the time, the Police President and SA-Standartenführer Wagenbauer, to drive to Kislau and report to the camp director Sauer. He would learn of the purpose of the trip from Sauer. In accordance with the order Heupel drove to Kislau in his boss's car, possibly together with SS-Oberscharführer Eugen Müller, who was killed in the war. Müller was the facility manager of the Reich Governor's offices, a good friend and compliant dupe of Wagner's, to whose personal protection he was assigned. In any case Sauer and Müller, meeting in the office of the camp director, recruited Heupel to join in the plan to get rid of Marum. Marum was to be attacked the following night while asleep in his cell, strangled, and then hanged from the mullion and transom of the cross-window of the cell in order to create the misimpression of suicide. Heupel would himself draw the noose over Marum's head and strangle him while Sauer and Müller held him down. A string would be used to strangle him, one that had bound a parcel that had arrived on the same

---

German occupation of France. After the war, Wagner was tried by a French military tribunal in Strasbourg, which charged him with a miscellany of offenses, including complicity to premeditated murder. He was convicted and executed by firing squad in August 1946.

88. Karl Bock (1899–1943) was adjutant to gauleiter and Reich governor Robert Wagner at the time of Marum's murder.

day for Marum and the contents of which Sauer had handed over to Marum. The parcel envelope as well as the string still lay in the office on the table.

Sauer then called the defendant Stix, the leader of the camp police force, into the office and told him that the State- and Interior Ministry had decided to get rid of Marum. . . . Sauer ordered Stix to fetch the defendant Weschenfelder, the camp clerk. . . . Weschenfelder came together with Stix to Sauer in his office, where Sauer told him, after he was sworn to the strictest secrecy, that Marum was to be hanged that night. Sauer dismissed Weschenfelder's objections with the assertion that the matter was backed by Wagner. Sauer now gave Weschenfelder the order to wait in readiness in his orderly room and at the moment that had been prearranged, to go to the guardhouse and to linger there for a while as the crime was carried out so that no guards left the guardroom. Thereafter he was to leave the guardhouse and return to his room.

. . . [Over dinner that night Sauer, Heupel, Stix, and Müller] again discussed the murder plan. . . . Between 12 and 1:00 a.m. [they] returned to the camp and went to Sauer's office. Here the entire plan was again thoroughly discussed and the roles [of each man] defined. Sauer and Müller would hold Marum down, Heupel would slip the noose around [Marum's] throat, one of them was to help with the act of strangling, together they would then hang Marum so as to fake his suicide. Stix meanwhile would watch the hallway to ensure that the guard responsible for Marum's cell was not there. Müller and Sauer repeatedly assured the hesitant Heupel that there was no turning back. Sauer gave Heupel the string from Marum's package with which the killing was to be carried out.

Shortly after the on-duty guard Benz had checked Marum's cell on his inspection round, Sauer informed Weschenfelder, who held himself ready in his orderly room, that it was beginning. Weschenfelder now in accordance with his orders walked down the hall . . . to the guardhouse. Sauer, Müller, and Heupel went to the entrance of Marum's cell while Stix went to the rear portion of the hallway in order to ensure that the patrolling guard did not surprise the perpetrators. Sauer unlocked the cell door, which opened inwardly to the right; he was the first to enter the cell. He was followed by Müller and finally Heupel. The light in the cell was on throughout the night. Marum slept on his wood pallet, which stood on the left side at the front near the door. The [end of the pallet where Marum's head lay] was on the door side. Other than the pallet secured to the floor there was a stool in the cell. According to Heupel's account Marum raised his head slightly. At the same moment Heupel slipped the string around his throat and drew it tight, with which Müller assisted him. At the same time Sauer held down Marum's feet while Müller held his arms.

After Marum was dead Sauer, Heupel, and Müller together hanged the corpse from the string they had used to strangle Marum, which was attached to the mullion and transom of the cell window, and overturned the stool in order to fake Marum's suicide. . . . Weschenfelder during this time had followed his orders to remain in the guardhouse and chat with the guards in order to keep them from leaving the guardhouse and patrolling the administrative building. After he had fulfilled his task, he returned to his room that he shared with Stix and where shortly thereafter Stix arrived after carrying out his order. . . .

[The court eventually turned to assess the legal guilt of each defendant for Marum's murder. The judges examined the accused men's actions in light of the pre-1941 version of the German homicide statute, in which premeditation rather than base motives was the essential attribute of murder.]

The defendant Sauer through his actions committed a murder. He carried out the crime with premeditation in the meaning of §211 of the Penal Code (old version). He planned its implementation carefully, discussed it at length with Heupel, Müller, and Stix, divided up the roles and by means of the deployment of both watchdogs Stix and Weschenfelder guaranteed its undisturbed execution. Shortly before the crime he again went over [the plan] in minute detail with Heupel, Stix, and Müller and once more defined the roles [of each]. He got down to work methodically, and in the firm belief of the court he was capable . . . of weighing the factors urging him to act against those restraining him with sufficient clarity and prudence. . . . Sauer killed Marum treacherously because he attacked his victim, who slept unsuspectingly in his cell and was thus completely helpless, in the night together with both of his confederates and strangled [him] before he became fully conscious or was even able to somehow defend himself. Moreover Sauer intentionally killed Marum because he knew that he killed him and he also willed his death. He was also aware of the circumstance that the manner in which the crime was executed was treacherous and he absorbed it into his will.

. . .

The crime of the defendant Heupel legally fulfills the element of manslaughter in accordance with §212 of the Penal Code. §212 of the Penal Code as it existed in its old version is properly applied here because it allows in this version only a punishment of five to fifteen years in prison while in the new version a life-long prison term is provided for; hence the old version is the more lenient law. It is the court's conviction that Heupel did not carry out the crime with premeditation as defined in §211 of the German Penal Code. He was initiated into the murder plan in all of its details by Sauer and Müller, and he also carried out the role he had been assigned. However, [the witnesses have credibly testified that] Heupel is a primitive person easily influenced and devoid of his own capacity for judgment, soldier-like in the sense of the mercenary, [a person] who does whatever he is told to do [and] does not consider his own responsibility for carrying out an order if he believes he is acting under orders. The court has also formed this impression of him in the main proceeding, and it believes his claim that he was convinced there was no other option and that he thought he could no longer avoid collaborating in the crime after he had been initiated into the murder plan and both Müller and Sauer told him repeatedly—including shortly before commission of the crime—that there was no turning back. Heupel himself never made a single intellectual contribution at any point in the crime; the whole plan was developed by Sauer and Müller and given to him with his role in all its particulars laid out and the string serving as a tool for execution placed in his hands shortly before the crime by Sauer. Heupel was simply swept up into the crime by Sauer and Müller. He was in its commission no longer capable of weighing the factors pro and con of his action but rather acted emotionally.

Because the element of premeditation cannot be determined, Heupel can only be convicted of manslaughter. He committed the crime with the intent to kill because he knew that Marum was supposed to be killed and he desired his death.

Heupel of course was under a certain pressure from the moment he was initiated into the murder plan, and Sauer and Müller convinced him to believe the elimination of Marum was ordered by higher authority. This pressure, however, was not so powerful as to negate his guilt. . . . Because he himself does not at all assert that he had been threatened by Sauer or Müller or anyone else; in the assurance of his accomplices that there was no turning back there can be glimpsed no threat in the sense of

§52;[89] it solely represents the attempt to strengthen Heupel's guilty will [to commit] the crime.

. . .

The contribution to the crime of the defendant Stix legally constitutes aiding and abetting murder in accordance with §§211, 49 of the Penal Code. He was in any case present after his return from Mingolsheim until commission of the crime in Sauer's office and his role was assigned to him. By proceeding to the hallway on the basis of his orders in the vicinity of the scene of the crime, Marum's cell, and ensuring that the perpetrators would not be surprised by a guard on patrol, he furthered and facilitated Marum's murder. Through his service as a watchdog he assured the perpetrators while they carried out their crime, and through this act he inwardly fortified the perpetrators, who trusted that they would be protected by Stix from potential surprises in the commission of their crime. Stix thereby knew that at least Sauer and Müller committed the killing with premeditation because shortly beforehand he had heard how Sauer and Müller developed the murder plan once more in all its particulars and assigned to every accomplice his role for carrying it out. However, he had absorbed those circumstances of the crime into his awareness that characterized the manner in which the crime was committed as treacherous because he had heard that the unwitting Marum was to be attacked while sleeping and strangled before he could fully gain consciousness. Therefore Stix knew of the will of the perpetrators to commit the murder and consciously contributed through his aid to carrying out the crime desired by the perpetrators. Furthermore he desired Marum's death, . . . and he accepted Marum's death in the event. . . .

The defendant Weschenfelder legally fulfilled through his actions the elements of the offense of aiding and abetting manslaughter in accordance with §§212, 49[90] Penal Code. Just as much as Stix he furthered and facilitated Marum's killing by stopping by the guardhouse on Sauer's instruction before the crime was committed and chatting with the guards so as to prevent them from leaving the guardhouse and surprising the perpetrators in the commission of their crime. Sauer, Müller, and Heupel knew that during the commission of the crime they were protected from unwanted surprises by Weschenfelder's service as a watchdog, and this

---

89. At the time of the trial, the duress paragraph of the German Criminal Code.

90. At the time, the paragraph on accomplice liability in the German Criminal Code.

reinforced them in their criminal will. Weschenfelder knew that Sauer, Heupel, and Müller wanted to kill Marum because this was revealed to him that afternoon in Sauer's office. He also performed his contribution to the crime in the knowledge that he was aiding its commission; at the very least he acted with conditional intent because he wanted to perform his watchdog service even though the possibility was known to him that Marum would be killed, and he approved of this possible outcome.

Weschenfelder was not present when the perpetrators discussed the plan in all its particulars in Mingolsheim shortly before they committed the crime. He was only called that afternoon into Sauer's office, where it was revealed to him that Marum was to be hanged and that he was to go to the guardhouse at a sign from the others. The particulars of execution were not shared with him, and he was unaware that Sauer, Neupel, and Müller killed Marum treacherously. . . . Weschenfelder could therefore not be convicted of aiding and abetting murder but only of aiding and abetting manslaughter.

· · ·

[Neither Stix nor Weschenfelder, according to the court, could invoke a defense of justification or excuse because the illegality of Marum's killing was clear to each of them. Neither man could plead duress insofar as neither had acted in the face of "a present danger for life and limb." The court then announced its findings on the guilt of the four men.]

With that said, the defendants

Sauer intentionally and treacherously killed a human being and carried out the killing with premeditation and in concert with others;

Heupel intentionally and treacherously killed a human being and carried out the killing with premeditation and in concert with others;

Stix knowingly rendered assistance to the perpetrators in the commission of a murder through his action and

Weschenfelder knowingly rendered assistance to the perpetrators in the commission of manslaughter through his action. . . .

# SELECT BIBLIOGRAPHY

Annas, George J., and Michael A. Grodin. *The Nazi Doctors and the Nuremberg Code: Human Rights in Human Experimentation.* New York: Oxford University Press, 1992.

Bass, Gary J. *Stay the Hand of Vengeance: The Politics of War Crimes Tribunals.* Princeton, NJ: Princeton University Press, 2000.

Bazyler, Michael J. *Holocaust, Genocide, and the Law: A Quest for Justice in a Post-Holocaust World.* New York: Oxford University Press, 2016.

————. "The Role of the Soviet Union in the International Military Tribunal at Nuremberg." In *The Nuremberg Trials: International Criminal Law Since 1945,* edited by Herbert R. Reginbogin and Christoph Safferling, 45–52. Berlin: De Gruyter, 2006.

Bazyler, Michael J., and Frank M. Tuerkheimer. *Forgotten Trials of the Holocaust.* New York: New York University Press, 2014.

Betts, Paul. "Germany, International Justice and the 20th Century." *History and Memory* 17 1/2 (2005): 45–86

Biddle, Francis. *In Brief Authority.* Garden City, NY: Doubleday, 1962.

Bloxham, Donald. *Genocide on Trial: War Crimes Trials and the Formation of Holocaust History and Memory.* New York: Oxford University Press, 2001.

Borodziej, Włodzimierz. "'Hitleristische Verbrechen': Die Ahndung deutscher Kriegs- und Besatzungsverbrechen in Polen." In *Transnationale Vergangeheitspolitik: Der Umgang mit deutschen Kriegsverbrechern in Europa nach dem Zweiten Weltkrieg,* edited by Norbert Frei, 399–437. Göttingen: Wallstein, 2006.

Broszat, Martin. "Hitler und die Genesis der 'Endlösung.' Aus Anlaß der Thesen von David Irving." *Vierteljahrshefte für Zeitgeschichte* 25 (1977): 737–75.

————. "Siegerjustiz oder Strafrechtliche 'Selbstreinigung'? Aspekte der Vergangenheitsbewältigung der deutschen Justiz während der Besatzungszeit 1945–1949." *Vierteljahrhefte Für Zeitgeschichte* 29 (1981): 477–544.

Browning, Christopher R., and Jürgen Matthäus. *Fateful Months: Essays on the Emergence of the Final Solution.* New York: Holmes & Meier, 1991.

————. *The Origins of the Final Solution: The Evolution of Nazi Jewish Policy, September 1939–March 1942*. Lincoln, NE/Yad Vashem, Jerusalem: University of Nebraska Press, 2004.

Bryant, Michael S. *Confronting the "Good Death": Nazi Euthanasia on Trial, 1945–1953*. Boulder: University Press of Colorado, 2005.

————. "Dachau Trials-Die rechtlichen und historischen Grundlagen der US-amerikanischen Kriegsverbrecherprozesse, 1942–1947." In *Historische Dimensionen von Kriegsverbrecherprozessen nach dem Zweiten Weltkrieg*, edited by H. Radtke, D. Rössner, T. Schiller, and W. Form, 111–22. Baden-Baden, Germany: Nomos, 2007.

————. "Ein Verbrechen oder viele? Die deutsche Konkurrenzlehre in der Rechtsprechung des Obersten Gerichtshofs für die Britische Zone am Beispiel der 'Reichskristallnachts'—Prozess in Nordrhein-Westfalen." In *Verbrechen gegen die Menschlichkeit—Der Oberste Gerichtshof der Britischen Zone*, Justizministerium des Landes Nordrhein-Westfalen, ed., 114–23. Cologne, Germany: Justizministerium des Landes Nordrhein Westfalen, 2012.

————. *Eyewitness to Genocide: The Operation Reinhard Death Camp Trials, 1955–1966*. Knoxville: University of Tennessee Press, 2014.

————. "Punishing the Excess: Sadism, Bureaucratized Atrocity, and the U.S. Army Concentration Camp Trials, 1945–47." In *Nazi Crimes and the Law*, edited by Nathan Stoltzfus and Henry Friedlander, 63–85. New York: Cambridge University Press, 2008.

————. *A World History of War Crimes: From Antiquity to the Present*. London: Bloomsbury, 2016.

Buscher, Frank M. "Bestrafen und erziehen: 'Nürnberg' und das Kriegsverbrecherprogramm der USA." In *Transnationale Vergangenheitspolitik. Der Umgang mit deutschen Kriegsverbrechern in Europa nach dem Zweiten Weltkrieg*, edited by Norbert Frei, 94–139. Göttingen, Germany: Wallstein , 2006.

————. *The US War Crimes Trial Program 1946–1955*. Westport, CT: Praeger, 1989.

Cooper, John. *Raphael Lemkin and the Struggle for the Genocide Convention*. New York: Palgrave Macmillan, 2008.

Cooper, R. W. *The Nuremberg Trial*. Harmondsworth, UK: Penguin, 1947.

Crowe, David M. *The Holocaust: Roots, History, and Aftermath*. Philadelphia: Westview Press, 2008.

————. *War Crimes, Genocide, and Justice: A Global History*. New York: Palgrave Macmillan, 2014.

Dawidowicz, Lucy S. *The War against the Jews, 1933–1945.* New York: Holt-Rinehart-Winston, 1975.

de Mildt, Dick. "Die Unschuld der Strafjustiz: Über due Ahndung von Kriegs- und Holocaustverbrechen in den Niederlanden 1945–1953." In *Kriegsverbrechen, NS-Gewaltverbrechen und die europäische Strafjustiz von Nürnberg bis Den Haag,* edited by Heimo Halbrainer and Claudia Kuretsidis-Haider, 158–70. Graz, Austria: Clio, 2007.

———. *In the Name of the People: Perpetrators of Genocide in the Reflection of Their Post-War Prosecution in West Germany.* Amsterdam: Martinus Nijhoff, 1996.

de Mildt, Dick, and Joggli Meihuizen. "'Unser Land muss tief gesunken sein . . .' Die Aburteilung deutscher Kriegsverbrecher in den Niederlanden." In *Transnationale Vergangenheitspolitik: Der Umgang mit deutschen Kriegsverbrechern in Europa nach dem Zweiten Weltkrieg,* edited by Norbert Frei, 283–325. Göttingen, Germany: Wallstein, 2006.

Douglas, Lawrence. *The Memory of Judgment: Making Law and History in the Trials of the Holocaust.* New Haven, CT: Yale University Press, 2001.

Earl, Hilary. *The Nuremberg SS-Einsatzgruppen Trial, 1945–1958: Atrocity, Law, and History.* New York: Cambridge University Press, 2009.

Eiber, Ludwig and Robert Sigel, eds. *Dachauer Prozesse: NS-Verbrechen vor amerikanischen Militärgerichten in Dachau 1945–48: Verfahren, Ergebnisse, Nachwirkungen.* Göttingen, Germany: Wallstein, 2007.

Elster, Jon. *Closing the Books: Transitional Justice in Historical Perspective.* Cambridge: Cambridge University Press, 2004.

Fest, Joachim C. *The Face of the Third Reich: Portraits of the Nazi Leadership.* New York: Da Capo Press, 1999.

Finder, Gabriel N., and Alexander V. Prusin. *Justice behind the Iron Curtain: Nazis on Trial in Communist Poland.* Toronto, Canada: University of Toronto Press, 2018.

Fleming, Gerald. *Hitler and the Final Solution.* Berkeley: University of California Press, 1987.

Fratcher, William F. "American Organization for Prosecution of German War Criminals." *Missouri Law Review* 13/1 (1948): 45–70.

Friedlander, Henry. "After Nuernberg: German Law and Nazi Crimes." Lecture presented at the American Historical Association Annual Meeting, Los Angeles, CA, December 1981.

———. "The Judiciary and Nazi Crimes in Postwar Germany." *Simon Wiesenthal Center Annual* 34/1 (1984): 27–44.

Friedrich, Jörg. *Das Gesetz des Krieges: Das deutsche Heer in Russland, 1941 bis 1945: der Prozess gegen das Oberkommando der Wehrmacht.* Munich, Germany: Piper, 1993.

———. *Die kalte Amnestie: NS-Täter in der Bundesrepublik.* Frankfurt a.M., Germany: Fischer, 1984.

———. *Freispruch für die Nazi Justiz: Die Urteile gegen NS-Richter seit 1948. Eine Dokumentation.* Reinbek/Hamburg/Berlin: Rowohlt, 1983.

Fulbrook, Mary. *Reckonings: Legacies of Nazi Persecution and the Quest for Justice.* New York: Oxford University Press, 2018.

Garscha, Winfried. "The Trials of Nazi War Criminals in Austria." In *Nazi Crimes and the Law,* edited by Henry Friedlander and Nathan Stoltzfuss, 139–50. Cambridge: Cambridge University Press, 2008.

Gilbert, G. M. *Nuremberg Diary.* New York: Farrar, Straus, 1947.

Ginsburgs, George. *Moscow's Road to Nuremberg: The Soviet Background to the Trial.* Leiden, Netherlands: Brill, 1995.

———. "The Nuremberg Trial: Background." In *The Nuremberg Trial and International Law,* edited by George Ginsburgs and Vladimir Nikolaevich Kudriavtsev, 9–37. Amsterdam: Martinus Nijhoff/Kluwer, 1990.

Haberer, Erich. "History and Justice: Paradigms of the Prosecution of Nazi Crimes." *Holocaust and Genocide Studies* 19/3 (2005): 487–519.

Haffner, Sebastian. *Anmerkungen zu Hitler.* Frankfurt a.M., Germany: Fischer Taschenbuch, 1981.

Harris, Whitney. *Tyranny on Trial: The Evidence at Nuremberg.* Dallas, TX: Southern Methodist University Press, 1954.

Hartmann, Christian, Thomas Vordermayer, Othmar Plöckinger, and Roman Töppel, eds. *Hitler, Mein Kampf: Eine Kritische Edition.* Munich-Berlin, Germany: Institut Für Zeitsgeschichte, 2016.

Hayes, Peter. *Why?: Explaining the Holocaust.* New York: W. W. Norton, 2017.

Hebert, Valerie. *Hitler's Generals on Trial: The Last War Crimes Tribunal at Nuremberg.* Lawrence: University Press of Kansas, 2010.

Hilger, Andreas. "'Die Gerechtigkeit nehme ihren Lauf?' Die Bestrafung deutscher Kriegs- und Gewaltverbrecher in der Sowjetunion und der SBZ/DDR." In *Transnationale Vergangenheitspolitik. Der Umgang mit deutschen Kriegsverbrechern in Europa nach dem Zweiten Weltkrieg,* edited by Norbert Frei, 180–246. Göttingen, Germany: Wallstein, 2006.

Hilger, Andreas, Ute Schmidt, and Günther Wagenlehner, eds. *Sowjetische Militärtribunale*, 2 vols. Cologne, Germany: Böhlau, 2001–2003.

Hirsch, Francine. "The Soviets at Nuremberg: International Law, Propaganda, and the Making of the Postwar Order." *The American Historical Review* 113/3 (2008): 701–30.

Irvin-Erickson, Douglas. *Raphaël Lemkin and the Concept of Genocide*. Philadelphia: University of Pennsylvania Press, 2017.

Jardim, Tomaz. *The Mauthausen Trial American Military Justice in Germany*. Cambridge, MA: Harvard University Press, 2012.

Kershaw, Ian. *Hitler 1889–1936: Hubris*. New York/London: W. W. Norton, 1998.

Klee, Ernst. *Was sie taten, was sie wurden: Ärzte, Juristen und andere Beteiligte am Kranken- oder Judenmord*. Frankfurt a.M., Germany: Fischer, 1986.

Knight, Robert. "Denazification and Integration in the Austrian Province of Carinthia." *Journal of Modern History* 79/3 (2007): 572–612.

Kochavi, Arieh J. "The Moscow Declaration, the Kharkov Trial, and the Question of a Policy on Major War Criminals in the Second World War." *History* 76/248 (1991): 401–17.

———. *Prelude to Nuremberg: Allied War Crimes Policy and the Question of Punishment*. Chapel Hill: University of North Carolina Press, 1998.

Kranzbühler, Otto von. *Rückblick auf Nürnberg*. Hamburg, Germany: Zeit- E. Schmidt, 1949.

Kulesza, Witold. "Der Beitrag der polnischen Nachkriegsjustiz zum europäischen Rechtskulturerbe am Beispiel zweier Prozesse wege der Massenmorde in Warthegau (Posen, Kulmhof)." In *Gerechtigkeit nach Diktatur und Krieg: Transitional Justice 1945 bis Heute*, ed. Claudia Kuretsidis-Haider and Winfried R. Garscha, 115–29. Graz, Austria: Clio, 2010.

———. "Völkermord vor Gericht in Polen: NS-Verbrechen im Reichsgau Danzig-Westpreußen im Lichte des Strafprozesses gegen Richard Hildebrandt." In *Kriegsverbrechen, NS-Gewaltverbrechen und die europäische Strafjustiz von Nürnberg bis Den Haag*, edited by H. Halbrainer and C. Kuretsidis-Haider, 201–11. Graz, Austria: Clio, 2007.

Kuretsidis-Haider, Claudia, Winfried Garscha, Siegfried Sanwald et al., eds. *Das KZ Lublin-Majdanek und die Justiz: Strafverfolgung und verweigerte Gerechtigkeit. Polen, Deutschland und Österreich im Vergleich*. Graz, Austria: Clio, 2011.

————. "Die Volksgerichtsbarkeit als Form der politischen Säube-rung in Österreich." In *Keine "Abrechnung": NS-Verbrechen, Justiz und Gesellschaft in Europa nach 1945*, edited by Claudia Kuretsidis-Haider and W. R. Garscha, 17–24. Leipzig/Vienna: Akademische sanstalt, 1998.

Lebedeva, N. S. *Podgotovka Niurnbergskogo protsessa*. Moscow: Nauka, 1975.

Lessing, Holger. *Der erste Dachau Prozess (1945/46)*. Baden-Baden, Germany: Nomos, 1993.

Liivoja, Rain. "Competing Histories: Soviet War Crimes in the Baltic States." In *The Hidden Histories of War Crimes Trials*, edited by Kevin Heller and Gerry Simpson, 248–66. New York: Oxford University Press, 2013.

Lingen, Kerstin von. *Kesselring's Last Battle: War Crimes Trials and Cold War Politics, 1945–1960*. Lawrence: University Press of Kansas, 2009.

Marrus, Michael R. *The Nuremberg War Crimes Trial, 1945–46: A Documentary History*. Boston: Bedford, 1997.

Meihuizen, Joggli. *Noodzakelijk kwaad: De bestraffing van economische collaboratie in Nederland na de Tweede Wereldoorlog*. Amsterdam: Boom, 2003.

Merritt, Anna J., and Richard L. eds. *Public Opinion in Germany: The HICOG Surveys, 1949–1955*. Urbana: University of Illinois Press, 1980.

Moisel, Claudia. "Résistance und Repressalien: Die Kriegsverbrecherprozesse in der französischen Zone und in Frankreich." In *Transnationale Vergangenheitspolitik: Der Umgang mit deutschen Kriegsverbrechern in Europa nach dem Zweiten Weltkrieg*, edited by Norbert Frei, 247–82: Göttingen, Germany: Wallstein 2006.

Mommsen, Hans. "Die Realisierung des Utopischen: Die 'Endlösung der Judenfrage' im Dritten Reich." *Geschichte und Gesellschaft* 9 (1983): 381–420.

————. "Hitlers Stellung im nationalsozialistischen Herrschafts-system." In *Der Führerstaat. Mythos und Realität*, edited by Gerhard Hirschfeld and Lothar Kettenacker, 43–72. Stuttgart, Germany: Klett-Cotta, 1981.

Neave, Airey. *Nuremberg: A Personal Record of the Trial of the Major Nazi War Criminals in 1945–6*. London: Hodder & Stoughton, 1978.

Neumann, Franz. *Behemoth: The Structure and Practice of National Socialism, 1933–1944*. London: Victor Gollancz, 1942.

Niethammer, Lutz. *Die Mitläuferfabrik: Die Entnazifizierung am Beispiel Bayerns.* Berlin: Dietz, 1994.

Overy, Richard. *Interrogations: The Nazi Elite in Allied Hands, 1945.* New York: Viking, 2001.

Pauli, Gerhard. "Ein hohes Gericht—Der Oberste Gerichtshof für die Britische Zone und seine Rechtsprechung zu Straftaten im Dritten Reich." In *50 Jahre Justiz in Nordrhein-Westfalen.* Vol. 5, *Juristische Zeitgeschichte,* edited by Justizministerium des Landes NRW, 95–120. Duesseldorf, Germany: Justizministerium des Landes Nordrhein-Westfalen, 1996.

Pelt, Robert J. Van and Deborah Dwork. *Auschwitz 1270 to the Present.* New York: W. W. Norton, 1996.

Pendaries, Yveline. *Les Procés de Rastatt: Le jugement des crimes de guerre en zone française d'occupation en Allemagne.* Frankfurt a.M., Germany: Peter Lang, 1995.

Pendas, D. O. "Retroactive Law and Proactive Justice: Crimes against Humanity in Germany, 1945–1950." *Central European History* 43/3 (2010): 428–63.

Persico, Joseph E. *Nuremberg: Infamy on Trial.* New York: Viking, 1994.

Plesch, Dan. *America, Hitler, and the UN: How the Allies Won World War II and Forged a Peace.* London/New York: I. B. Tauris, 2010.

———. *Human Rights after Hitler: The Lost History of Prosecuting Axis War Crimes.* Washington, DC: Georgetown University Press, 2017.

Polunina, Valentyna. "From Tokyo to Khabarovsk: Soviet War Crimes Trials in Asia as Cold War Battlegrounds." In *War Crimes Trials in the Wake of Decolonization and Cold War in Asia, 1945–1956,* edited by Kerstin von Lingen, 239–60. New York: Palgrave, 2016.

Priemel, Kim C. and Alexa Stiller. *Reassessing the Nuremberg Military Tribunals: Transitional Justice, Trial Narratives, and Historiography.* New York: Berghahn, 2012.

Prusin, Alexander V. "'Fascist Criminals to the Gallows!' The Holocaust and Soviet War Crimes Trials, December 1945–February 1946." *Holocaust and Genocide Studies* 17/1 (2003): 1–30.

———. "Poland's Nuremberg: The Seven Court Cases of the Supreme National Tribunal, 1946–1948." *Holocaust and Genocide Studies* 24/1 (2010): 1–25.

Raim, Edith. *Justiz zwischen Diktatur und Demokratie: Wiederaufbau und Ahndung von NS-Verbrechen in Westdeutschland 1945–1949.* Berlin: De Gruyter, 2013.

————. *Nazi Crimes against Jews and German Post-War Justice: The West German Judicial System During Allied Occupation (1945–1949).* Munich, Germany: De Gruyter Oldenbourg, 2014.

Robertson, Geoffrey. *Crimes against Humanity.* New York: The New Press, 2013.

Römer, Felix. *Der Kommissarbefehl Wehrmacht Und NS-Verbrechen an Der Ostfront 1941/42.* Paderborn, Germany: Ferdinand Schöningh, 2008.

Rosenbaum, Ron. *Explaining Hitler: The Search for the Origins of His Evil.* New York: MacMillan, 1998.

Rousso, Henry. "Did the Purge Achieve Its Goals?" In *Memory, the Holocaust and French Justice: The Bousquet and Touvier Affairs,* edited by Richard J. Golsan, 100–104. Hanover, Germany: University Press of New England, 1996.

Rückerl, Adalbert. *The Investigation of Nazi Crimes 1945–1978: A Documentation.* Hamden, CT: Archon, 1980.

Rüter, C. F. "Die Ahndung von NS-Tötungsverbrechen: West Deutschland, Holland und die DDR in Vergleich—eine These." In *Keine "Abrechnung": NS-Verbrechen, Justiz und Gesellschaft in Europa nach 1945,* edited by Claudia Kuretsidis-Haider and W. R. Garscha, 180–84. Leipzig/Vienna: Akademische sanstalt, 1998.

Selerowicz, Andrzej and Winfried Garscha. "Die strafrechtliche Ahndung in Polen." In *Das KZ Lublin-Majdanek und die Justiz: Strafverfolgung und verweigerte Gerechtigkeit: Polen, Deutschland und Österreich im Vergleich,* edited by Claudia Kuretsidis-Haider, Irmgard Nöbauer, Winfried R. Garscha, Siegfried Sanwald, and Andrzej Serlerowicz, 53–115. Graz, Austria: Clio, 2011.

Siebert, Detlef. "Die Durchführung des Kommissarbefehls in den Frontverbänden des Heeres: Eine Quantifizierende Auswertung der Forschung." Unpublished manuscript, 2000.

Sigel, Robert. *Im Interesse der Gerechtigkeit: Die Dachauer Kriegsverbrecherprozesse 1945–1948.* Frankfurt a.M., Germany: Campus, 2008.

Smith, Bradley F., ed. *The American Road to Nuremberg: The Documentary Record, 1944–45.* Palo Alto, CA: Hoover Institution Press, 1982.

————. *Reaching Judgment at Nuremberg: The Untold Story of How the Nazi War Criminals Were Judged.* New York: Basic Books, 1977.

Sorokina, Marina. "People and Procedures: Toward a History of the Investigation of Nazi Crimes in the USSR." *Kritika: Explorations in Russian and Eurasian History* 6/4 (2005): 797–831.

Streit, Christian. *Keine Kameraden: Die Wehrmacht Und die Sowjetischen Kriegsgefangenen 1941–1945.* Stuttgart, Germany: J. H. Dietz, 1991.

Taylor, Telford. *The Anatomy of the Nuremberg Trials.* New York: Knopf, 1992.

————. "The Nuremberg War Crimes Trials." *International Conciliation* 450 (April 1949): 243–371.

Toland, John. *Adolf Hitler: The Definitive Biography.* New York: Doubleday, 1976.

Tusa, Ann, and John Tusa. *The Nuremberg Trial.* London: MacMillan, 1983.

Ueberschär, Gerd. *Der Nationalsozialismus vor Gericht: Die alliierten Prozesse gegen Kriegsverbrecher und Soldaten 1943–1952.* Frankfurt a.M., Germany: Fischer, 1999.

UN War Crimes Commission. "Case No. 37: Trial of Haupsturmführer Amon Leopold Goeth." Vol. 7: *Law Reports of Trials of War Criminals,* edited by the UN War Crimes Commission, 1–10. London: His Majesty's Stationery Office, 1948.

————. "Case No. 38: Trial of Obersturmbannführer Rudolf Franz Ferdinand Hoess." Vol. 7: *Law Reports of Trials of War Criminals,* edited by the UN War Crimes Commission, 11–26. London: His Majesty's Stationery Office, 1948.

————. *History of the United Nations War Crimes Commission and the Development of the Laws of War.* London: His Majesty's Stationery Office, 1948.

Vogt, Timothy. *Denazification in Soviet-Occupied Germany: Brandenburg, 1945–1948.* Cambridge, MA: Harvard University Press, 2001.

Weindling, Paul. *Nazi Medicine and the Nuremberg Trials: From Medical War Crimes to Informed Consent.* Basingstoke, UK: Palgrave MacMillan, 2004.

Wieland, Günther. "Die Ahndung von NS-Verbrechen in Ostdeutschland, 1945–1990." In *DDR-Justiz und NS-Verbrechen. Sammlung ostdeutscher Strafurteile wegen nationalsozialistischen Tötungsverbrechen,* edited by C. F. Rüter, 13–94. Amsterdam: Amsterdam University Press, 2002.

Wieviorka, Annette. *La France et le procés de Nuremberg: Inventer le droit international.* Paris: Les Prairies Ordinaires, 2014.

Wistrich, Robert S. *Who's Who in Nazi Germany.* New York: Routledge, 1995.

Zorya, Yuri and Natalia Lebedeva. "The Year 1939 in the Nuremberg Files." *International Affairs* 10 (Moscow, October 1989): 117–29.

# INDEX

accomplice liability (German law), 72–73, 201, 213, 213n90

aggression, crime of (crimes against peace), 23, 27n46, 31–33, 51, 52, 95, 100, 105, 111–13

Alderman, Sydney, 111

Altstoetter, Josef, xvii, 47, 132

Ankenbrand, Otto, 140

*Archbold Criminal Pleading, Evidence and Practice*, 151, 151n31

Ardeatine massacre, xv, 58

Auschwitz death camp, xiii, 11–16, 57, 65, 66–67, 76, 78, 79, 128, 147, 149, 152–53, 153n32, 155n37, 155n39, 156n44, 158n47, 161n52, 175n68, 176–78, 180

aus der Fünten, Ferdinand, 79

Babi Yar, massacre of Jews at, 62, 63

Bass, Gary J., 88

Baur, Armin, 140–41, 144

Bautzen concentration camp, 74

Bazyler, Michael, 88

Becker-Freyseng, Hermann, 126–27

*Behemoth*, book by Franz Neumann, 85

Belsen concentration camp, xvi, 7, 55, 57, 78, 147–54

Belsen trial (*Trial of Josef Kramer and others*), xvi, 57, 78, 147–54. *See also* British trials

Belzec death camp, xiv, 13, 66. *See also* Operation Reinhard

Betts, Paul, 80–81

Biddle, Francis, xv, 23–24, 87

Biebow, Hans, xvii, 79

Blancke, Max, 177, 183–84

Bloxham, Donald, 88

Bock, Karl, 209

Boepple, Ernst, xviii, 79

Böhringer, Fritz, 203

Bongartz, Theodor, 155–56, 163

Boos, Reinhard, 202–6

Bormann, Martin, 36, 40, 45, 119–20

Böttger, Franz, 164

Bousquet, René, xvi, 59

Brandt, Karl, xvii, 47, 123, 126–27

Brandt, Rudolf, 126–27

British trials, xvi, xvii, xviii, 55, 56–58, 76, 89–94, 147–54

Broszat, Martin, 51, 70, 72, 74, 77, 86

Browning, Christopher, 10, 87

Buchenwald concentration camp, 7, 56, 74, 128, 129, 154n36, 159n48, 166n59, 172n66, 177n70

Bühler, Josef, xviii, 68, 79

Bulanov, Mikhail Petrovich, 187–88, 190

Burski, Bolesław, 184

Camp Ashcan, 39

Camp Dustbin, 39

Chanler, William, xv, 26–28

Chelmno death camp, xiv, 11, 14, 66

Chilowicz, Wileth, 180–81

Churchill, Winston, xiv, xv, 1–2, 16–19, 21–22, 28–29, 34–35, 83

Clay, Lucius, 78

Cold War, 56, 83n136, 84

collaboration, xiv, xvi, 59, 60, 61, 62, 63, 69, 76, 78, 79, 186

collision of duties, defense of, 200, 201. *See also* necessity, defense of

commando order, 58

commissar order, the, xiii, 8–9, 8n10

common plan/design, 34, 42, 55, 76, 100, 101, 105, 111, 113, 117, 171n64

concentration camps. *See* individual camps by name

conspiracy: as basis of Allied case at Nuremberg, 31, 34, 40, 76, 80, 85, 111; Bernays' endorsement of, 23; as charge in the Doctors Trial, 124–25; as charge in the London Charter, 100, 101; compared with common plan/design, 55, 147; conflict among the Allies over, 32–34; and Control Council Law No. 10, 46, 105; as doctrine, 24; IMT analysis of, 111–17; major war criminals convicted of, 44; Pentagon's approval of, 23; and prosecution of the High Command for, 51; and prosecution of IG Farben for, 48; Trainin's advocacy of, 22, 25; use of to prosecute corporate wrongdoers and Socialists, 25; use of to prosecute membership in Nazi criminal organizations, 25; West German refusal to charge, 81

Control Council Law No. 10, xvi, xvii, 46, 51, 60, 70–71, 95, 104–7, 124–25

Cooper, R. W., 43

crimes against humanity, xviii, 6, 42, 44, 46, 60, 69–71, 80, 81, 81n135, 98, 101, 104–5, 111, 117–18, 122–23, 125, 126n20, 129, 133, 202–3

crimes against peace. *See* aggression, crime of

criminal organizations, 24–25, 31–32, 37, 40, 108, 118–23

Crowe, David, 31, 60, 63n96, 69, 76

Dachau concentration camp, xiii, xvi, xviii, 6–7, 37, 53–56, 57, 78, 125, 126, 126n20, 127, 128, 147, 154–73, 177n70

Darnand, Joseph, 59

Dawidowicz, Lucy, 85

death camps. *See* individual death camps by name

Decree against Public Enemies, 136n23, 139, 140, 141, 143–44

Decree of August 31, 1944, xv, 64, 67, 107–9

de Gaulle, Charles, 59

Delestraint, Charles, 160

Denson, William, 154, 164, 168

Dietrich, Josef, 187

Doctors Trial, The (*U.S. v Karl Brandt et al.*), xvii, 47, 123–32, 126n20

Doebig, Friedrich, 134

Doenitz, Karl, 20, 39–40, 44

Dora-Nordhausen concentration camp, 56

Douglas, Lawrence, 88

Drobytsky Yar, massacre of, 186

Drösihn, Joachim, xvi, 40, 57

duress, defense of, 130, 185, 205, 213n89, 214

Eichberger, Leonhard, 155, 161

Eichelsdörfer, Johann Baptist, 168, 170, 172

Eichmann, Adolf, 174

*Einsatzgruppen* (special action
squads), xiii, xiv, 7, 9–10, 48, 49,
51, 61, 71, 76, 186
Eisele, Hans, 166
Eisenhower, Dwight, 53
Enabling Act, the, xiii, 3
Endres, Anton, 161–62, 169
Engert, Georg, 140
euthanasia program (T-4), trials
based on, xvii, 47, 71–73,
77n122, 81, 124, 191–202
ex post facto, criticism of, 32, 33, 70,
77, 82, 133
Extraordinary State Commission for
the Investigation of German War
Crimes, 22

Fest, Joachim, 3, 85
Final Solution, 4, 15, 79, 85–87,
122n17, 159n49
Fischer, Ludwig, xvii, 66, 79
Fleming, Gerald, 85
Flick, Friedrich, xvii, 48
Flossenbürg concentration camp, 56,
154n36, 146n43, 180
Forster, Albert, xvii, 68
Frank, Hans, 35, 36, 38, 40, 44
Franzioh, Karl, 148
French trials, xvi, 58–60, 209n87
Frick, Wilhelm, 36, 38, 40, 44
Friedlander, Henry, 71
Fritzsche, Hans, 40, 44
Fulbrook, Mary, 77
functionalism, 86–87, 86n144
Funk, Walther, 38, 40, 44

gas vans, 11, 61, 186, 189, 190
Gebhardt, Karl, 126–27
General Government, 11, 66, 79
Geneva Conventions, 42, 55, 78, 118
genocide, 4, 6, 11, 15, 41–44, 66, 68,
71, 73, 76, 81, 86–87, 145

German trials: East Germany, 74–76,
77; West Germany, 69–73,
77, 77n120, 81–82, 120n11.
*See also* euthanasia program
(T-4), trials based on; political
murders, German trials of;
*Reichskristallnacht* (Night of
Broken Glass pogrom): German
trials based on
Gestapo (Secret State Police), 3, 23,
70, 79, 122n17, 135, 159n49,
160n51, 188, 189, 190, 195; as
criminal organization, 25, 37, 40,
109, 119, 121–22
Gestapo Summary Court, 11–12, 14
Gilbert, G. M., 87
Ginsburgs, George, 23, 33, 34, 62, 88
Globocnik, Odilo, 11, 177
Glünkin, Karl, 203–6
Goebbels, Joseph, xv, 20, 29, 36, 40,
86, 204
Gorgass, Hans-Bodo, 197–98
Göring, Hermann, xvi, 3–4, 20, 26,
29, 36, 38, 40, 45, 86, 133, 174,
115–16
Göth, Amon, 66, 79, 174–81
Grabner, Maximilian, xviii, 79
Grabowski, Walter, 193–95
Greiner, Rudolf, 203
Greiser, Arthur, xvi, 66
Grese, Irma, 57
Groben, Hans, 140–41
Gross, Ernest, 42–43

Haase, Willi, 175
Hadamar mental hospital: and
euthanasia program, 200, 202;
trials centered on, xvi, 54, 72–73,
197–99
Hague Convention, 42, 55, 118
Handloser, Siegfried, 126–27
Hayes, Peter, 78–80

Hess, Rudolf, 36, 38, 40, 44, 72, 119
Heupel, Paul, 208–14
Heydrich, Reinhard, xiii, 9, 13, 87,
    121, 159
Heydrich-Wagner agreement, xiii, 9
Himmler, Heinrich, xiii, xiv, 10–11,
    14–15, 20, 36, 87, 126, 163, 172,
    193
Hintermayer, Fritz, 161, 166–67
Hirsch, Francine, 18, 19, 23, 25,
    33–34, 83–84, 88
Hitler, Adolf, 1–5, 8, 17, 20, 24,
    27, 29, 36, 40, 58, 82, 85–87,
    112–17, 119, 121, 135, 139, 155,
    163, 175, 187, 204, 207
Hoffmann, Heinz, 140
Hofmann, Franz, 156
Holz, Karl, 134
Hoover, J. Edgar, 84
Horowitz, Helena, 181
Hossbach, Friedrich, 115, 117
Hössler, Franz, 78
Höß, Rudolf, xvii, 11, 14–15, 57,
    66–67, 79
Hughes, Hugh Llewellyn Glyn, 150

IG Farben, xvii, 12–13, 14, 48
intentionalism, 85–86, 87

Jackson, Robert, xv, xvi, 23, 25, 28–33,
    36, 41, 46, 80, 88, 111, 164
Jarolin, Josef, 169
Jodl, Alfred, 37, 39–40, 44
Joint Chiefs of Staff Directive
    1023/10, xv, 52–53, 94–98
Josten, Heinrich, xviii, 79
"justice case," the (*U.S. v. Josef Altstoetter
    et al.*), xvii, 47, 49, 132–46

Kähny, Edhuard, 203
Kaltenbrunner, Ernst, 36, 38, 40, 44,
    121–22

Katyn forest massacre, 82
Katzenberger, Leo, xiv, 139–45
Kaufering, subsidiary camp of
    Dachau, 155n39, 158, 158n47,
    168n62, 177n70
Keitel, Wilhelm, 20, 36, 38, 40, 44
Kellogg-Briand Pact, xii, 23, 27
Kershaw, Ian, 87
Kesselring, Albert, xvii, xviii, 58
Kharkov trial, xv, 61, 76, 186–90
Knoll, Christian, 155
Köpfer, Leo, 203
Kraków, 67, 175, 175nn68–69, 181
Kramer, Josef, 57, 147, 152–53
Krasnodar trial, xiv, 61, 76, 186
Krasnodon trial, 61, 76, 86
Krupp von Bohlen und Halbach,
    Alfried, xvii, 49
Krupp von Bohlen und Halbach,
    Gustav, 40, 49

Lages, Willy, 79
Landsberg prison, xii, 56, 78, 126n20,
    155n37, 157nn45–46, 158,
    158n47, 159n48, 161nn52–53,
    164n57, 166n58, 167n61,
    168n62, 169n63, 171n64,
    187n77
Landstorfer, Lorenz, 177
Langheld, Wilhelm, 187–90
Laval, Pierre, xvi, 59
Law for the Protection of German
    Blood and Honor, 139, 139n25,
    142
Lebensraum (living space), 5
le Druillenec, Harold Osmund, 150
Ley, Robert, 36, 38, 40
Liebehenschel, Arthur, xvii, 67
Lipecki, Tadeusz, 185
London Charter, xvi, 23n39, 46,
    98–104, 108
Lopata, Mosul, 136–37, 139, 145

Lublin, xv, xvii, 11, 64, 65, 68,
    177n70, 182–83

Main Commission for the
    Investigation of German Crimes
    in Poland, xv, 64
Majdanek death camp, xiv, xv, xvii,
    14, 57, 64, 65, 68, 76, 155n39,
    157n46, 161n52, 177n70,
    182–85
Mariupol trial, 61, 76, 186
Markl, Hermann, 135, 140–42
Marrus, Michael, 21, 24–25, 29,
    31–32, 41–42
Marum, Ludwig, xiii, 207–14
Maul, Emil, 156
Maurras, Charles, 59
Mauthausen concentration camp,
    xvii, 7, 56, 57, 78, 154n36,
    158n48, 180
medical experiments, 7, 79, 124–32,
    161n52, 166n58
*Mein Kampf*, xii, 4–5, 24, 113
Mengele, Josef, 79
Meseritz-Obrawalde mental hospital,
    71, 191–94, 193n81, 197
Milch, Erhard, xvii, 47
Moll, Otto, 78, 155
Mommsen, Hans, 86
Morgenthau Plan, xv, 20–22, 24, 41
Moscow Declaration, xiv, 22, 24, 66,
    68, 104, 105
Mrugowsky, Joachim, 126–27
Mühldorf, subsidiary concentration
    camp of Dachau, 56, 157n46,
    158n47
Munich, 1–2, 7, 50 (map),
    156nn43–44, 166n60, 171, 187n77
*Munich Post* (newspaper), 2, 3
murder, definition of (German Penal
    Code, Section 211), 71–73,
    109–10, 198, 212

Mussolini, Benito, xv, 26, 29,
    35–36

Nazi Party (NSDAP), 3, 16, 22, 36,
    74, 165, 187, 204, 205, 206; as a
    criminal organization, 1, 37, 40,
    67, 118–21, 121n14
Neave, Airey, 88
necessity, defense of, 73, 101, 105,
    200–201, 205
Neue Bremm concentration camp,
    60
Neumann, Franz, 85
Nuremberg: American Military
    Tribunals at, xvii, 45–51,
    123–46; International Military
    Tribunal (IMT) at, xvi, 34, 37,
    40, 42, 46, 54, 66–67, 82–84,
    85, 87–88, 108, 119, 120n11,
    121n16; legacy of, 80–84;
    Nuremberg Code, 130–32;
    Palace of Justice in, 17; Soviets at,
    18, 19n29, 23n39, 25, 33, 83. *See
    also* medical experiments
Nuremberg paradigm, 85

Oeschey, Rudolf, 134
Office of Military Government-US
    (OMGUS), 46
Ohlendorff, Otto, xvii, 48–49
Operation Reinhard, 11, 14, 73
Overy, Richard, 17–18, 21, 23–25,
    28–29, 31, 36, 39, 40

"pastoralization" plan, 20
Persico, Joseph E., 88
Pétain, Philippe, xvi, 59
Piorkowski, Alexander, 156–57,
    167
Płaszów concentration camp, 66, 175,
    175n68, 177, 177nn70–71,
    178–80, 180n73

Polish Committee of National Liberation, xv, 64

Polish Military Mission for the Investigation of German War Crimes, 64

Polish trials, 63–69, 174–85

political murders, German trials of, 207–14

Poppendick, Helmut, 126–27

Powers, Francis Gary, 84

Prusin, Alexander V., 66

Puhr, Fridolin Karl, 166–67

Raeder, Erich, 20, 40, 44, 115–16

Rascher, Sigmund, 172

Rauter, Hanns, 79

Ravensbrück concentration camp, xvi, 57, 60

Redwitz, Michael, 158–60

Reich Security Main Office (RSHA), 9, 36, 82, 121nn15–16, 122, 122n17, 159n49

*Reichskristallnacht* (Night of Broken Glass pogrom), xiii, 1, 70, 202–6; German trials based on, 202–6

Reich Supreme Court, 69, 136, 142

Reider, Otto, 183

Reinartz, Wilhelm, xvii, 68, 182–83, 185

Retzlaw, Reinhard, 187–88, 190

Ritz, Hans, 187–90

Robertson, Geoffrey, 81

Roma, 11, 126n20, 175n68

Roosevelt, Franklin Delano (FDR), xiv, xv, 18, 20–23, 34, 39

Rosenberg, Alfred, 36, 38, 40, 44

Rothaug, Oswald, 49 133–35, 137, 139, 141–42, 144–46

Rousso, Henry, 59

Royal Warrant of June 18, 1945, xv, xvi, 56–57, 89–94, 147, 149. *See also* British trials

Rückerl, Adalbert, 60

Rudenko, Roman, 33, 84

Rusk, Dean, 42–43

SA. *See* stormtroopers

Sachsenhausen concentration camp, 4, 127, 128

San Francisco conference, 29–30

Sauckel, Fritz, 40, 44, 120

Sauer, Karl, 207–14

Sawicka, Stefania, 184

Schacht, Hjalmar, 21, 38, 40, 44

Schilling, Klaus, 54, 166

Schmelt, Albrecht, xiv, 14–15

Schmitz, Oskar, 148

Schneider, Friedrich, 203

Schöpp, Johann, 171

Schroeder, Oskar, 126–27, 141

Security Service (SD, or *Sicherheitsdienst*), 37, 40, 109, 121–22, 146, 159n49, 189

Seiler, Reinhard, 140–43

Seyss-Inquart, Arthur, 39–40, 44

show trials, 19, 19n29, 34, 186

Sievers, Wolfram, 126–27

Simon, John (1st Viscount Simon), 16–18, 21, 29, 39

Smolensk trials, xvi, 62

Sobibor death camp, xiv, 13, 73. *See also* Operation Reinhard

Sorokina, Marina, 88

Soviet Military Administration (SMAD), 74

Soviet trials, 60–62. *See also* Kharkov trial; Krasnodar trial; Krasnodon trial; Mariupol trial; Smolensk trials

special courts, 47, 49, 59, 63, 65, 132–33, 135, 135n22, 136, 141

Speer, Albert, 39–40, 44

SS (Schutzstaffel, or "Protective Service"), xiv, 3, 4, 7, 10, 11, 12–16, 23, 25, 46, 48, 49, 51, 55, 57, 59, 61, 85–86, 159n49, 163, 171n65, 172, 175n68, 176, 178–81, 183, 187n77, 193, 206; as a criminal organization, 31, 37, 40, 109, 122–23, 148

Stalin, Joseph, xv, 18–19, 22, 61, 83

State Extraordinary Commission for the Determination and Investigation of Nazi and their Collaborators' Atrocities in the USSR (ChGK), xiv, 61

Stimson, Henry, xv, 21–24, 26–28, 41

Stix, Heinrich, 207–8, 210–11, 213–14

stormtroopers (Sturmabteilung, or SA), xii, xiii, 1, 3, 23, 37, 40, 81, 119, 123, 171n65, 187n77, 204, 205, 206

Streicher, Julius, 36, 38, 40, 44

subjective theory of perpetration, 73

superior orders, defense of, 72, 80, 133, 164

Supreme Headquarters–Allied Expeditionary Forces (SHAEF), 52

Supreme National Tribunal (NTN), xvi, xvii, xviii, 66–68, 79, 174, 182. See also Göth, Amon; Polish trials

Suttrop, Rudolf, 167

Szebnie: ghetto, 66; labor camp, 176

Tarnow ghetto, 66, 175

Taylor, Telford, xvi, 20, 26–27 46, 87–88

Teheran conference, 19–20

Tempel, Wilhelm, 155, 162, 169

Tesch, Bruno, xvi, 57

Thiel, Adolf, 200–201

Todt, Karl, 200–202

Toland, John, 85

Treblinka death camp, xiv, 13, 15, 73. See also Operation Reinhard

Tribunal général, xvi, 60

"triumphalist account" of Nuremberg trials, 18, 34, 88

Truman, Harry S., xv, 29, 32, 36, 84

tu quo que, defense of, 99n5

Tusa, Ann, 88

Tusa, John, 88

Ulbricht, Walter, 74–75

United Nations, 39, 96, 97, 105, 106

United Nations Charter, 16, 29, 39, 40n64, 96, 97, 105, 106

United Nations Declaration of Human Rights, 77, 81, 84

United Nations Genocide Convention, 42–44

United Nations War Crimes Commission (UNWCC), xiv, 39, 40n64, 61, 64

U.S. v. Martin Weiss et al. (the Dachau "parent" case), xvi, 54–56, 154–73

van Pelt, Robert Jan, 15

"victor's justice," criticism of, 77, 77n122

von Blomberg, Werner, 4, 115–16

von Falkenhorst, Nikolaus, xvi, xviii, 57

von Fritsch, Werner, 4, 115–16

von Kranzbühler, Otto, 77

von Leeb, Wilhelm, xvii, 51

von Manstein, Erich, xviii, 58

von Neurath, Constantin, 40, 115

von Papen, Franz, 20, 38, 40, 78, 85

von Ribbentrop, Joachim, 20, 36, 39–40, 44

von Schirach, Baldur, 40, 44
von Weizsäcker, Ernst, xvii, 49

Wagner, Eduard, 9
Wagner, Robert, xiii, 207–10
Wahlmann, Adolf, 197
Waldheim trials. *See* German trials:
   East Germany
Wannsee Conference, xiv, 13, 14
war crimes, xiii, xiv, xv, xviii, 6, 9,
   20, 22, 25, 31, 34, 39, 41–42, 44,
   46, 51–53, 55–58, 61, 63–64,
   63n96, 66, 69, 72, 74–75, 76,
   77, 79, 80, 89–94, 95–98,
   100–101, 104–5, 108, 111,
   117–18, 121, 123, 124–25,
   129; and the Belsen trial, 151;
   and the Dachau trial, 155n37,
   155nn39–40, 156–57nn45–46,
   158n48, 161nn52–53, 164n57,
   166n58, 166–67nn60–61,
   168–69nn62–63, 171n64, 187n77

War Crimes Modification Board,
   xviii, 56
Wartheland, 11, 66, 139n24
Weinbacher, Karl, xvi, 57
Weiss, Martin, xvi, 54, 154, 157–61,
   163, 165–67, 169, 171, 173
Weiter, Eduoard, 163, 167
Weltz, Georg, 126–27
Wernicke, Hilde, xvi, 71, 191–92,
   194–97
Weschenfelder, Otto, 208, 210–11,
   213–14
Wieczorek, Helene, xvi, 71,
   191–92
Wieland, Günther, 74–75, 74n116
Witteler, Wilhelm, 166

Yalta Conference, 28–29

Zill, Egon, 156
Zorya, Yuri, 88
Zyklon B, xiv, xvi, 14, 57